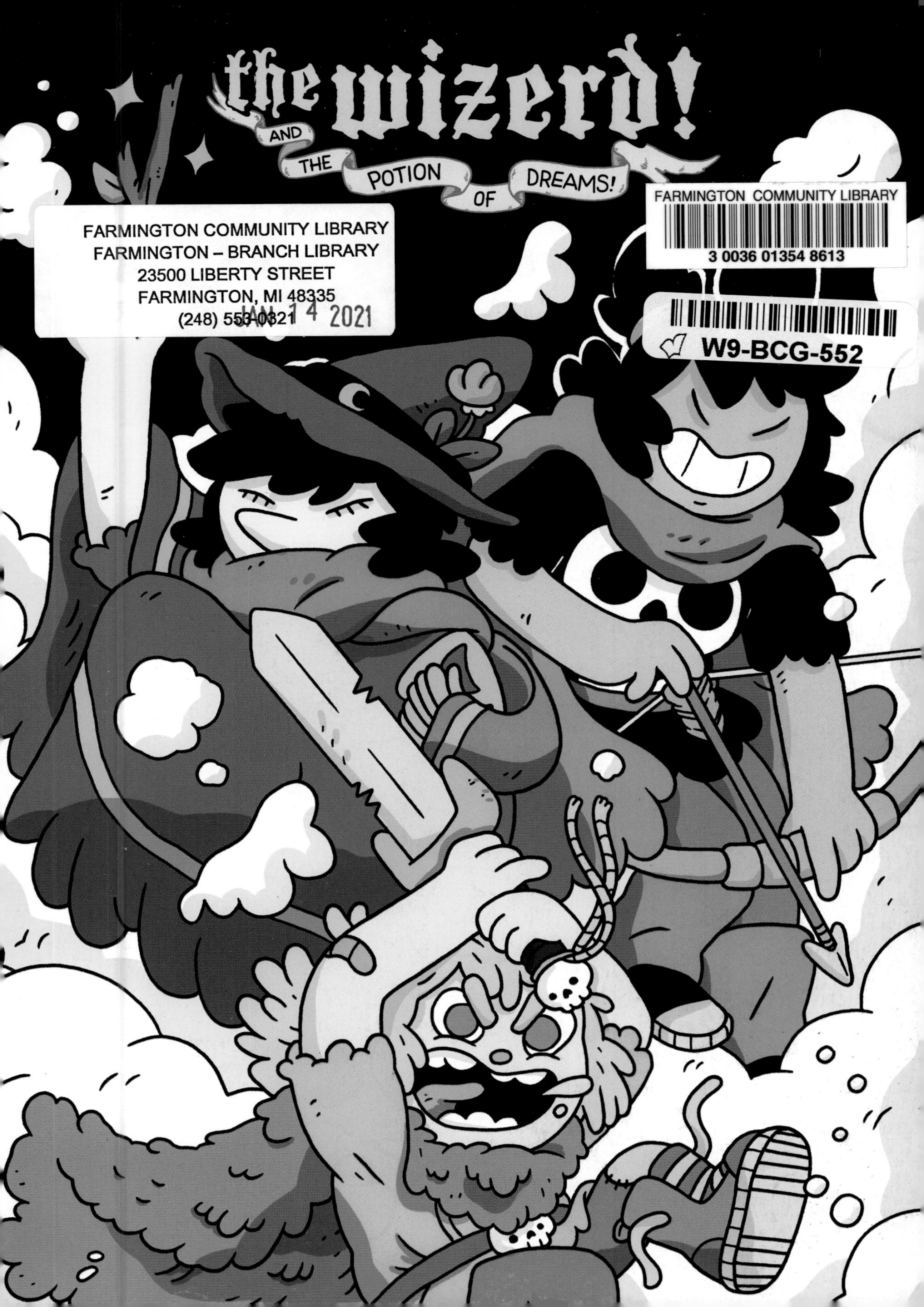
the wizerd!
AND THE POTION OF DREAMS!

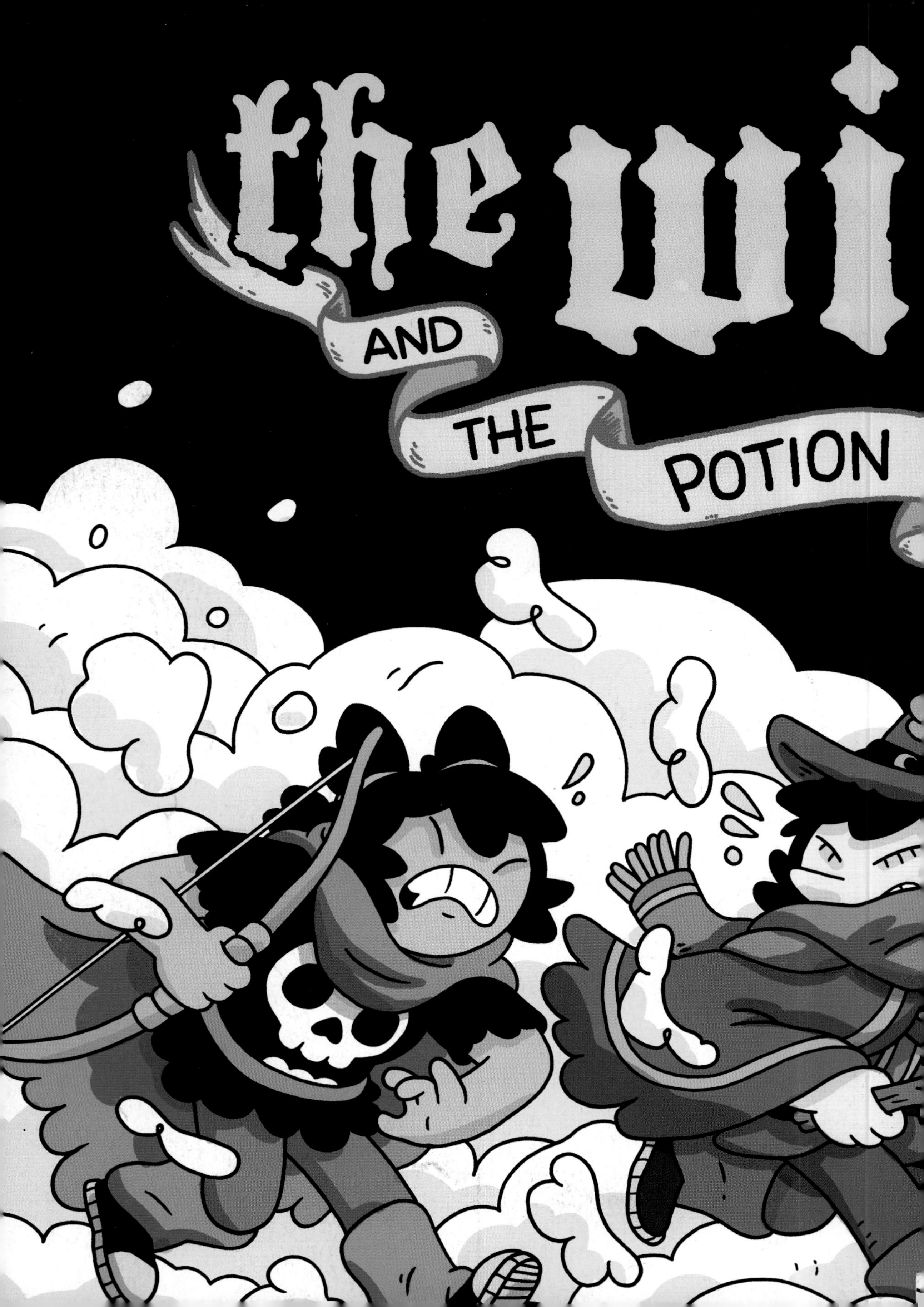
the wi
AND
THE
POTION

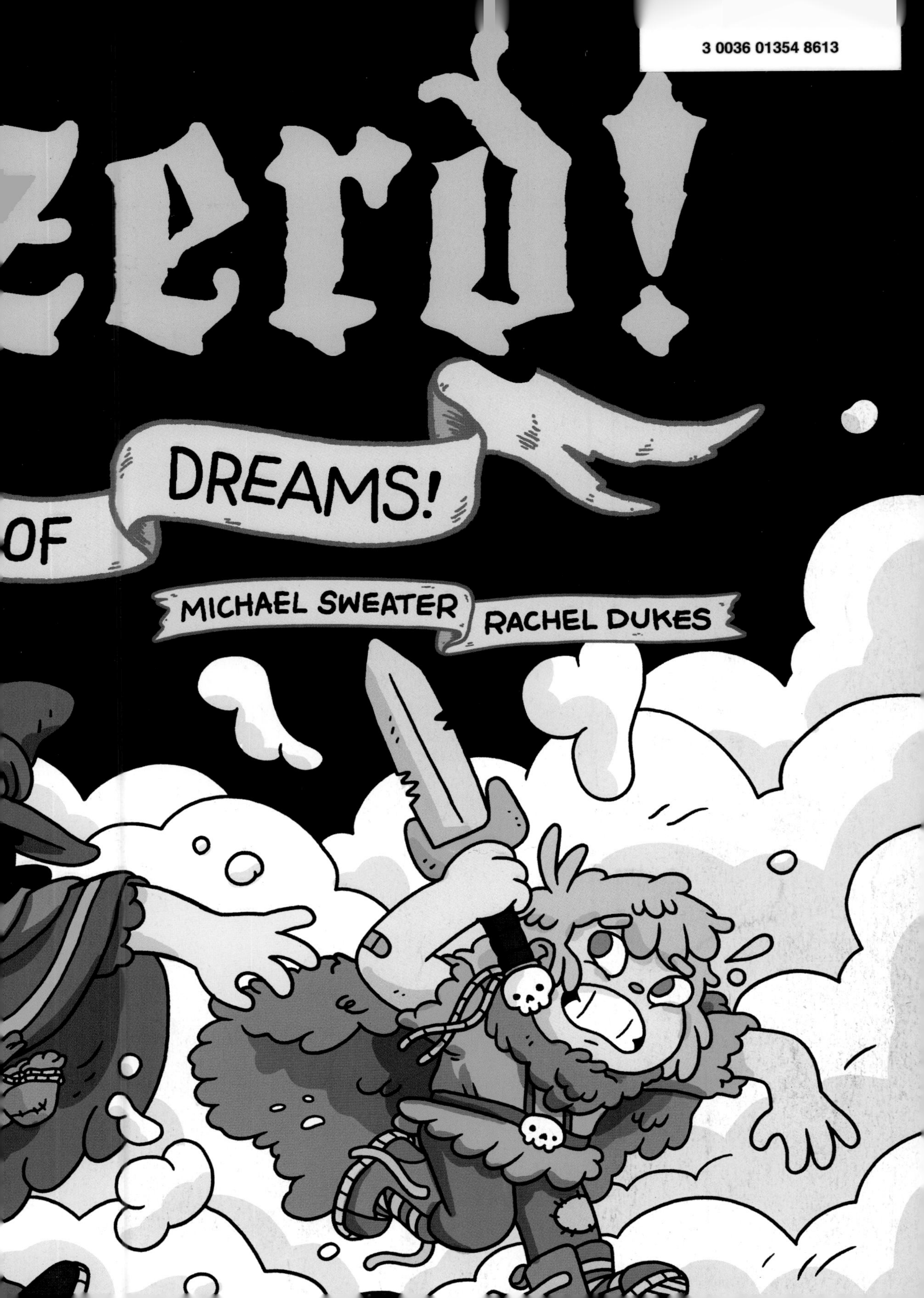
zerd!
OF
DREAMS!
MICHAEL SWEATER
RACHEL DUKES

CREATED BY MICHAEL SWEATER AND RACHEL DUKES
EDITED BY ANDREA COLVIN
ADDITIONAL EDITING ASSISTANCE BY GRACE BORNHOFT
DESIGNED BY CHAD W. BECKERMAN

Published by Oni-Lion Forge Publishing Group, LLC
James Lucas Jones, president & publisher
Sarah Gaydos, editor in chief
Charlie Chu, e.v.p. of creative & business development
Brad Rooks, director of operations
Amber O'Neill, special projects manager
Harris Fish, events manager
Margot Wood, director of marketing & sales
Devin Funches, sales & marketing manager
Katie Sainz, marketing manager
Tara Lehmann, publicist
Troy Look, director of design & production
Kate Z. Stone, senior graphic designer
Sonja Synak, graphic designer
Hilary Thompson, graphic designer
Sarah Rockwell, junior graphic designer
Angie Knowles, digital prepress lead
Vincent Kukua, digital prepress technician
Jasmine Amiri, senior editor
Shawna Gore, senior editor
Amanda Meadows, senior editor
Robert Meyers, senior editor, licensing
Grace Bornhoft, editor
Zack Soto, editor
Chris Cerasi, editorial coordinator
Steve Ellis, vice president of games
Ben Eisner, game developer
Michelle Nguyen, executive assistant
Jung Lee, logistics coordinator

Joe Nozemack, publisher emeritus

onipress.com | lionforge.com
facebook.com/onipress | facebook.com/lionforge
twitter.com/onipress | twitter.com/lionforge
instagram.com/onipress | instagram.com/lionforge

Rachel Dukes | mixtapecomics.com
Michael Sweater | michaelsweater.com

First Edition: September 2020

ISBN 978-1-62010-777-5
eISBN 978-1-62010-798-0

THE WIZERD VOL. 1: AND THE POTION OF DREAMS!, September 2020. Published by Oni-Lion Forge Publishing Group, LLC, 1319 SE Martin Luther King Jr. Blvd., Suite 240, Portland, OR 97214.

Printed in South Korea through Four Colour Print Group, Louisville, KY.

Library of Congress Control Number: 2020934131

1 2 3 4 5 6 7 8 9 10

FOR ASPIRING
CARTOONISTS OF ALL AGES.
YOU DON'T NEED
A WISHING POTION TO
CREATE COMICS.
START TODAY!

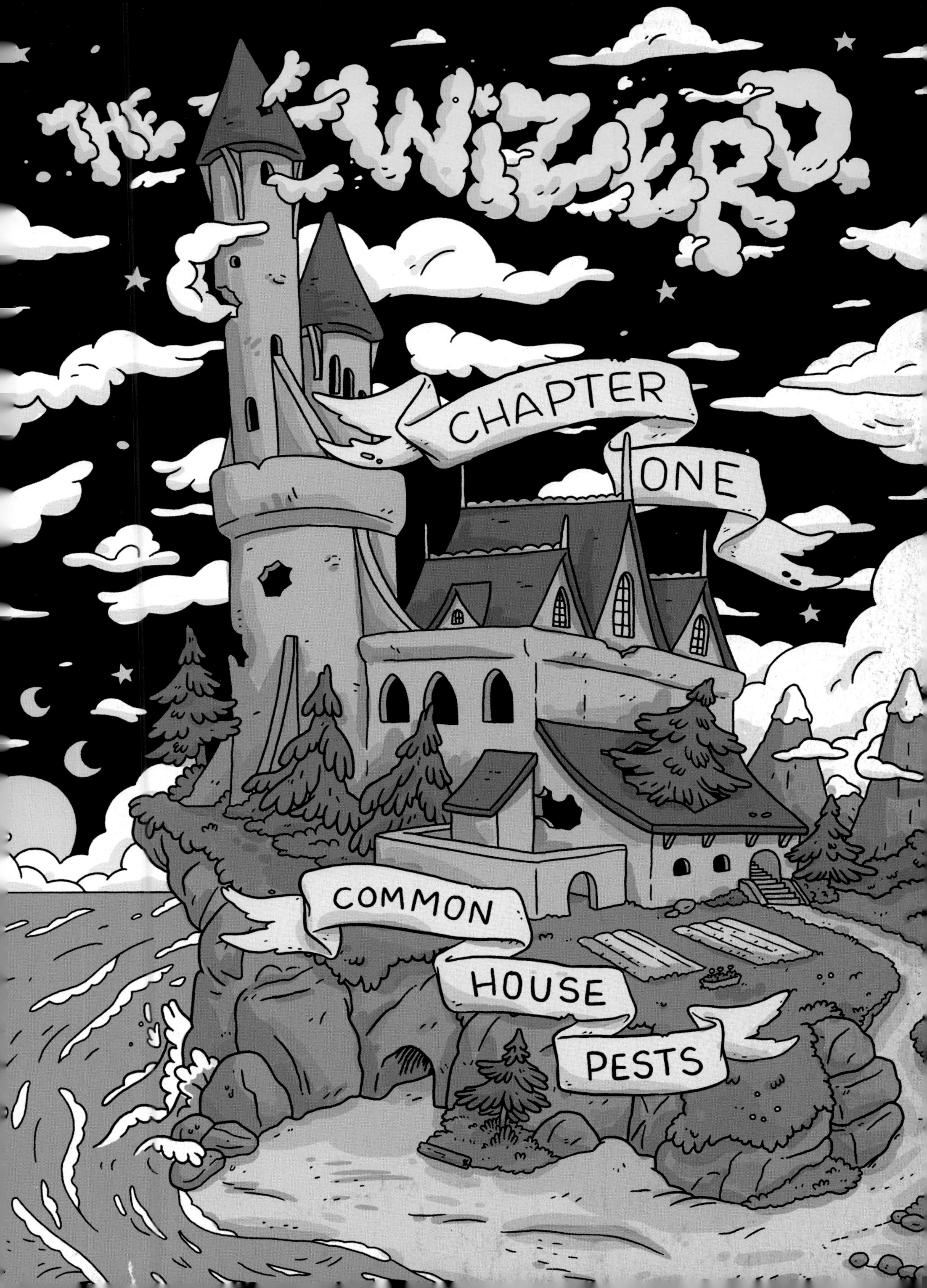
THE WIZZERD.
CHAPTER
ONE
COMMON
HOUSE
PESTS

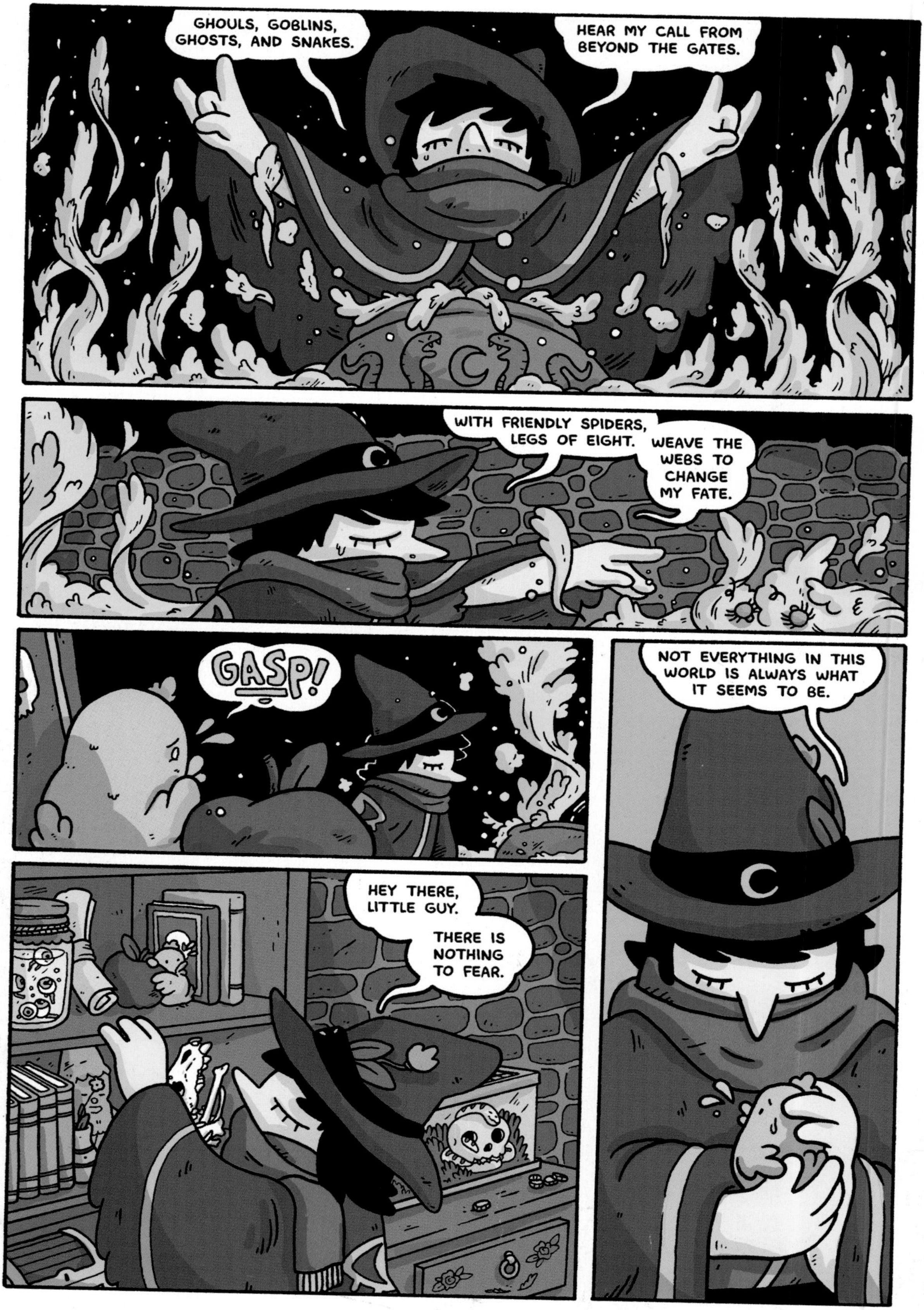

GHOULS, GOBLINS, GHOSTS, AND SNAKES.
HEAR MY CALL FROM BEYOND THE GATES.
WITH FRIENDLY SPIDERS, LEGS OF EIGHT.
WEAVE THE WEBS TO CHANGE MY FATE.
GASP!
NOT EVERYTHING IN THIS WORLD IS ALWAYS WHAT IT SEEMS TO BE.
HEY THERE, LITTLE GUY.
THERE IS NOTHING TO FEAR.

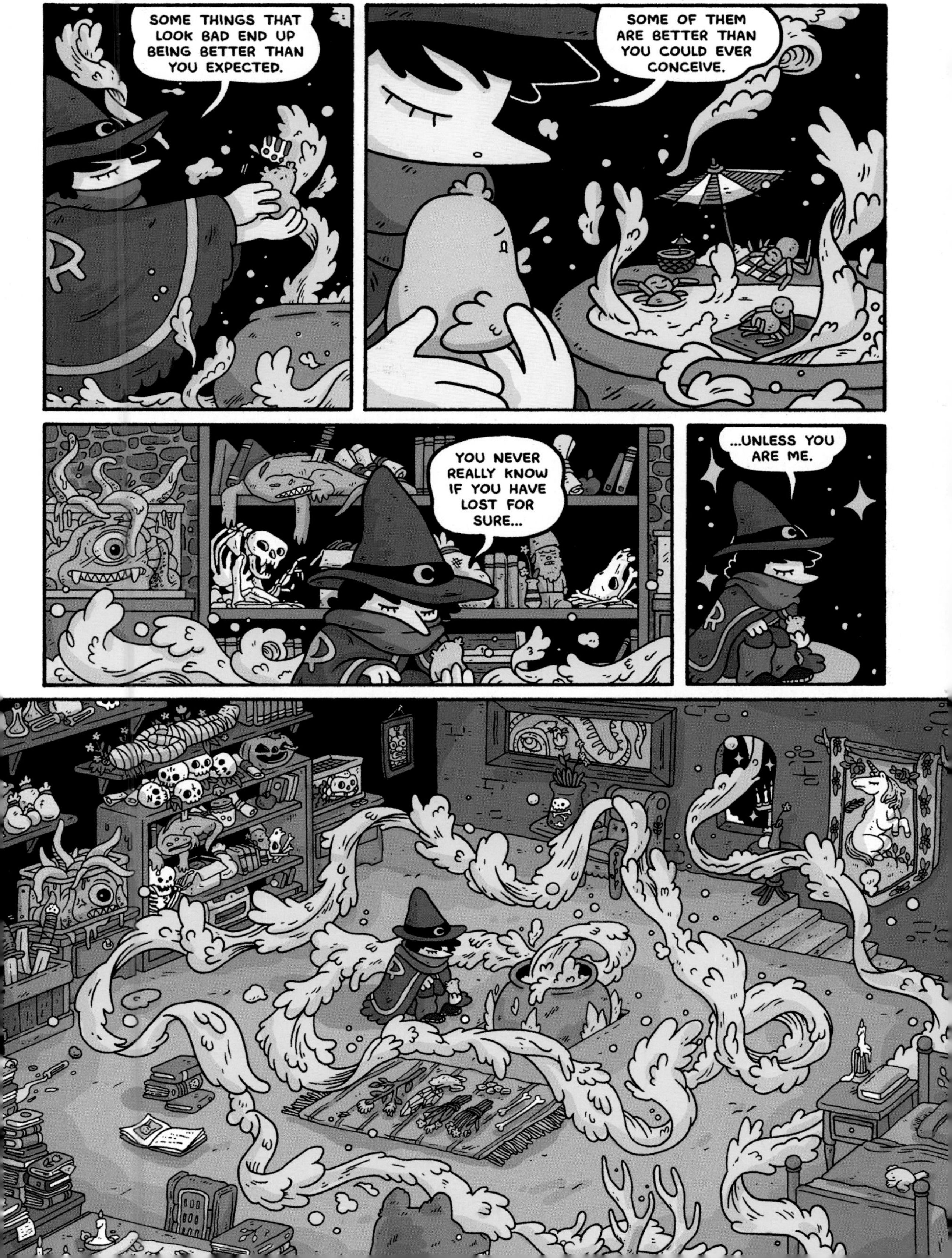
SOME THINGS THAT LOOK BAD END UP BEING BETTER THAN YOU EXPECTED.
SOME OF THEM ARE BETTER THAN YOU COULD EVER CONCEIVE.
YOU NEVER REALLY KNOW IF YOU HAVE LOST FOR SURE...
...UNLESS YOU ARE ME.

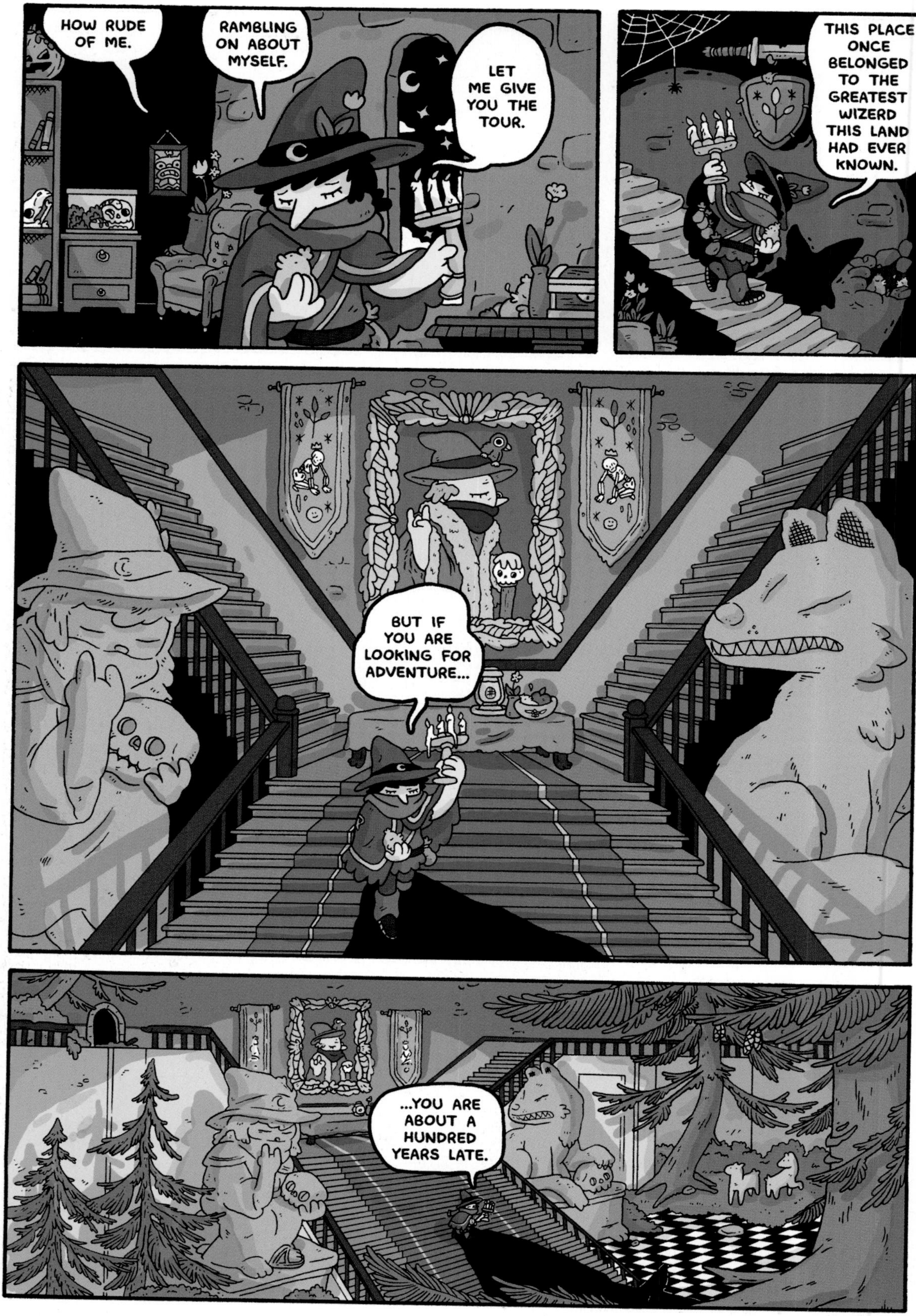

HOW RUDE OF ME.
RAMBLING ON ABOUT MYSELF.
LET ME GIVE YOU THE TOUR.
THIS PLACE ONCE BELONGED TO THE GREATEST WIZERD THIS LAND HAD EVER KNOWN.
BUT IF YOU ARE LOOKING FOR ADVENTURE...
...YOU ARE ABOUT A HUNDRED YEARS LATE.

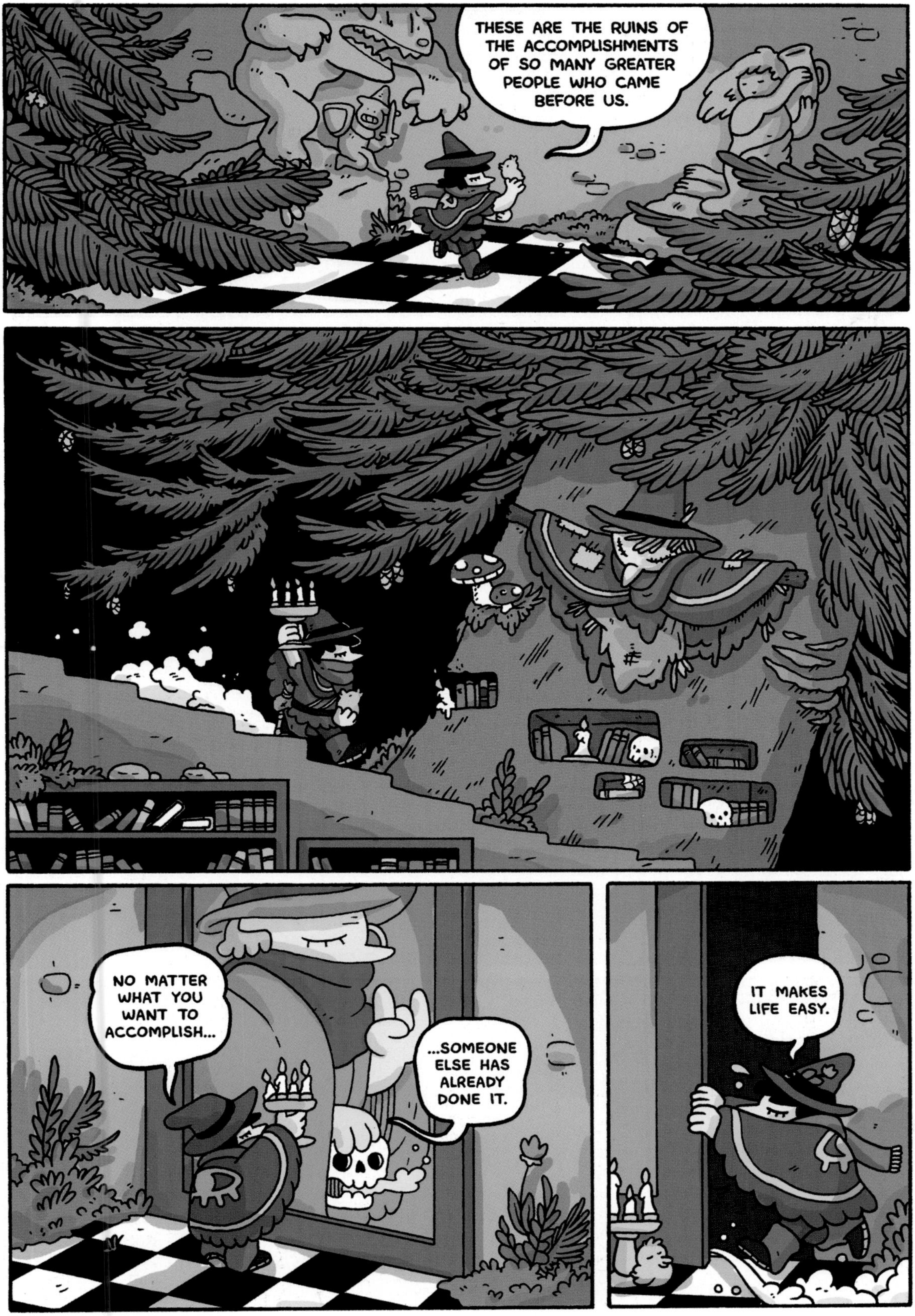
THESE ARE THE RUINS OF THE ACCOMPLISHMENTS OF SO MANY GREATER PEOPLE WHO CAME BEFORE US.
NO MATTER WHAT YOU WANT TO ACCOMPLISH...
...SOMEONE ELSE HAS ALREADY DONE IT.
IT MAKES LIFE EASY.

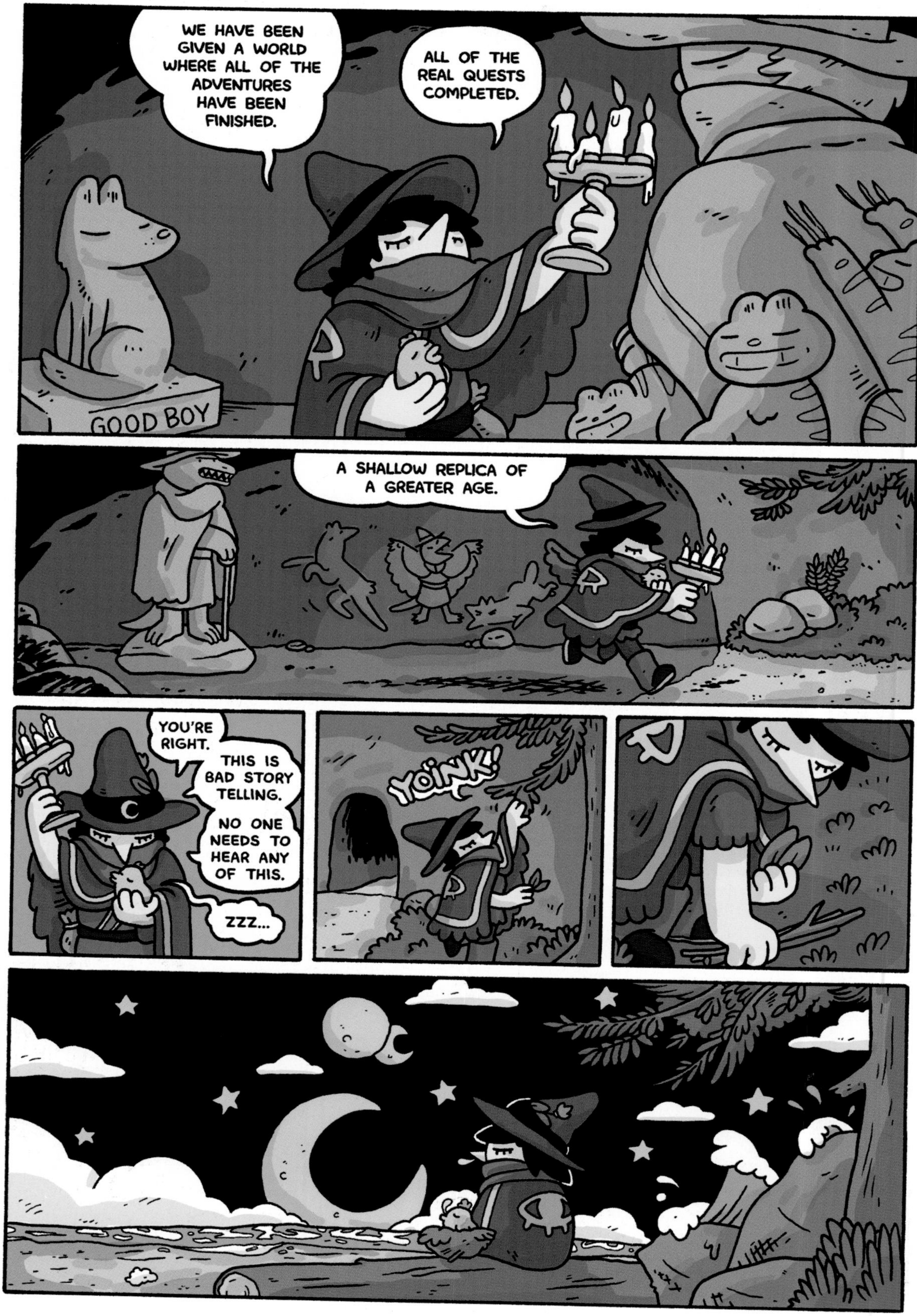
WE HAVE BEEN GIVEN A WORLD WHERE ALL OF THE ADVENTURES HAVE BEEN FINISHED.
ALL OF THE REAL QUESTS COMPLETED.
GOOD BOY
A SHALLOW REPLICA OF A GREATER AGE.
YOU'RE RIGHT.
THIS IS BAD STORY TELLING.
NO ONE NEEDS TO HEAR ANY OF THIS.
ZZZ...
YOINK!

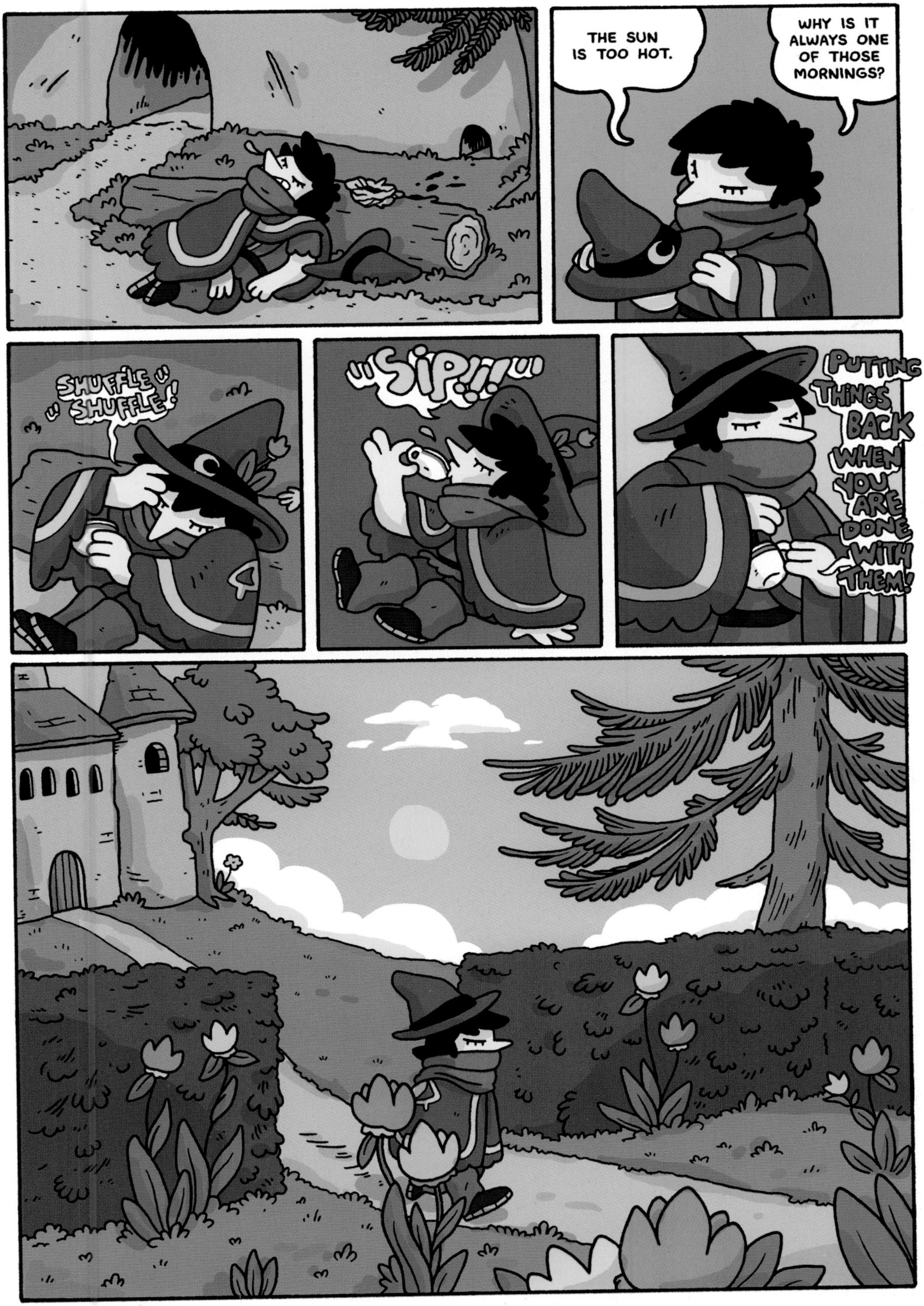
THE SUN IS TOO HOT.
WHY IS IT ALWAYS ONE OF THOSE MORNINGS?
SHUFFLE SHUFFLE!
SIP!!!
PUTTING THINGS BACK WHEN YOU ARE DONE WITH THEM!

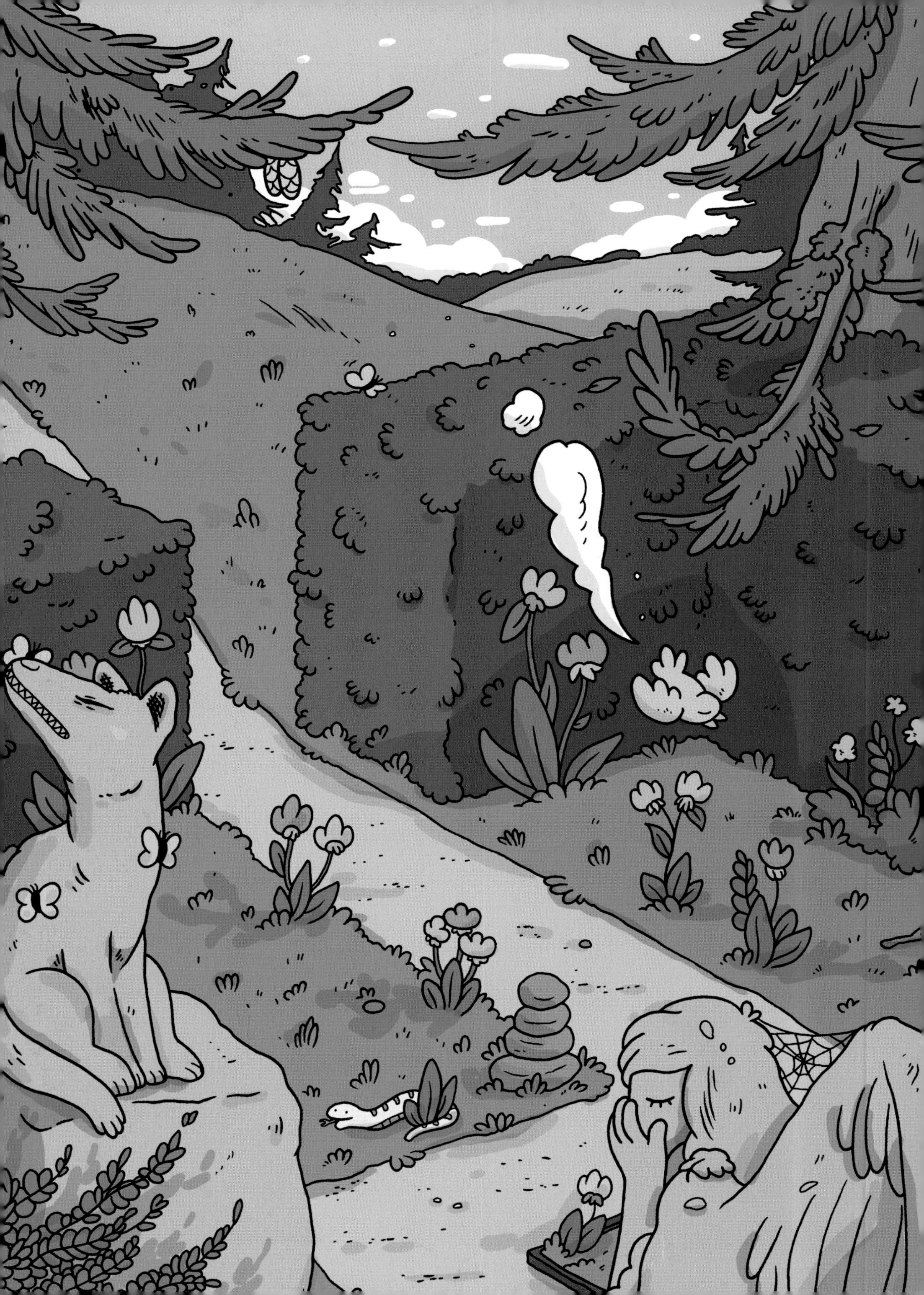

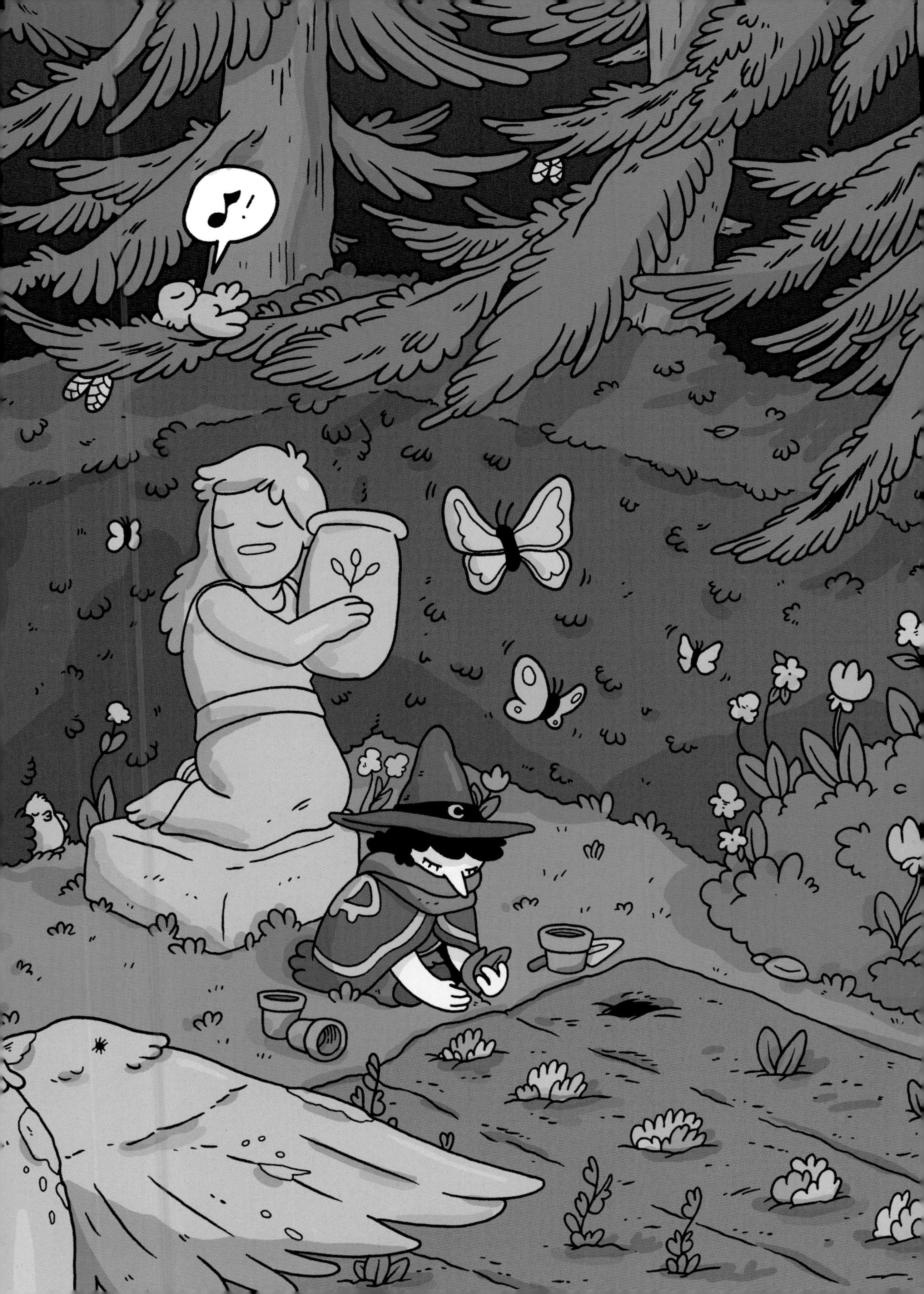

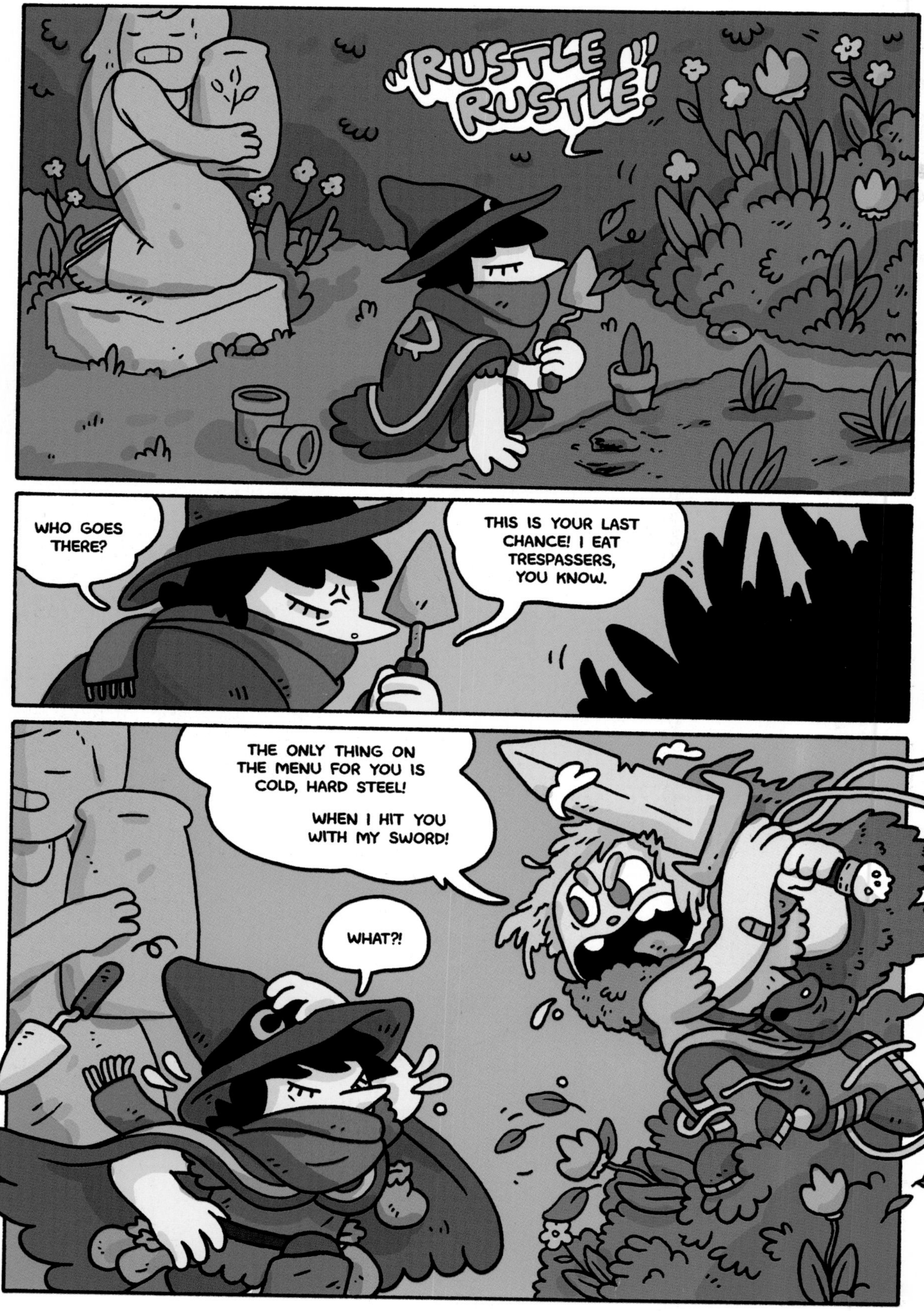
RUSTLE RUSTLE!
WHO GOES THERE?
THIS IS YOUR LAST CHANCE! I EAT TRESPASSERS, YOU KNOW.
THE ONLY THING ON THE MENU FOR YOU IS COLD, HARD STEEL!
WHEN I HIT YOU WITH MY SWORD!
WHAT?!

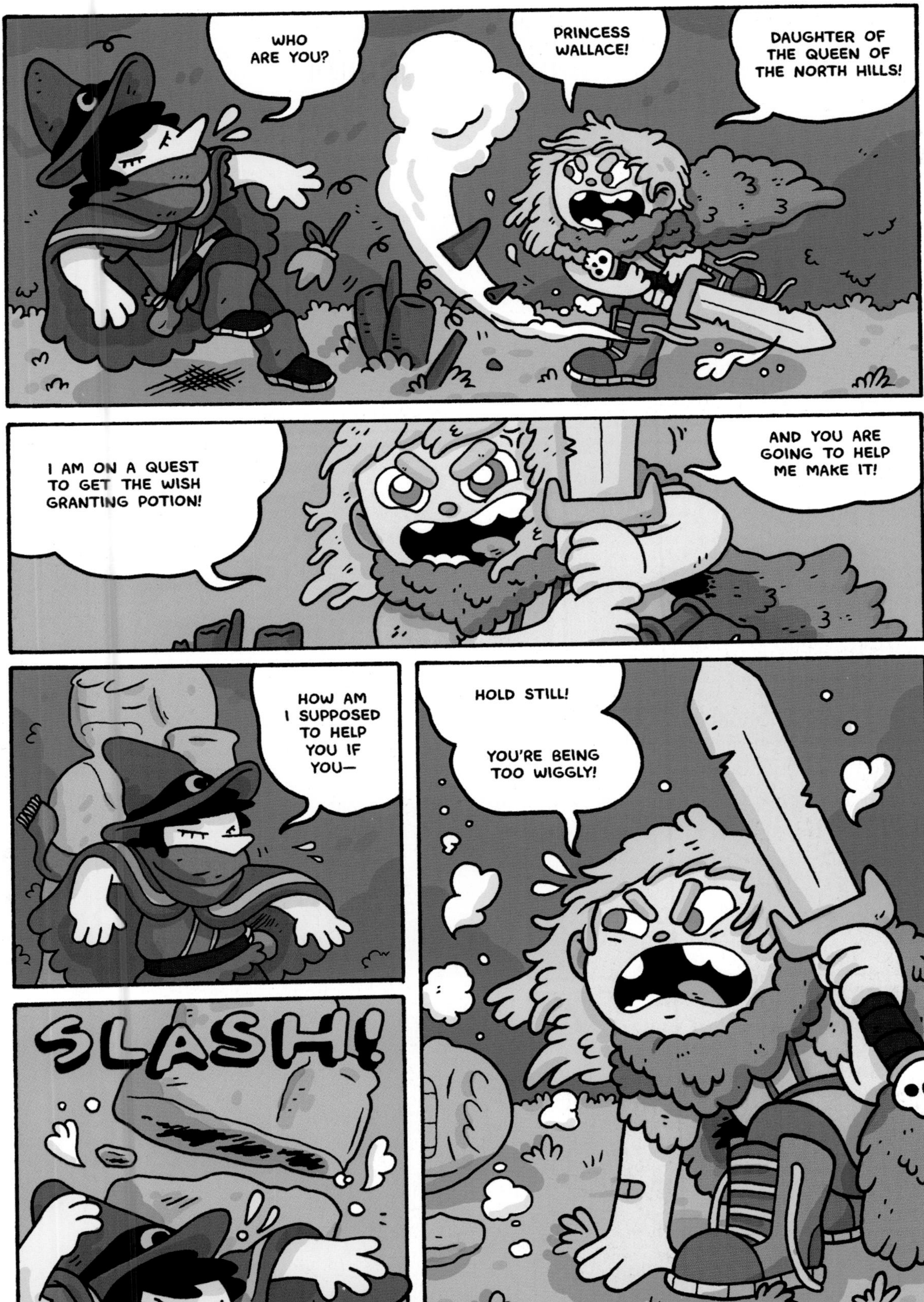
WHO ARE YOU?
PRINCESS WALLACE!
DAUGHTER OF THE QUEEN OF THE NORTH HILLS!
I AM ON A QUEST TO GET THE WISH GRANTING POTION!
AND YOU ARE GOING TO HELP ME MAKE IT!
HOW AM I SUPPOSED TO HELP YOU IF YOU—
SLASH!
HOLD STILL!
YOU'RE BEING TOO WIGGLY!

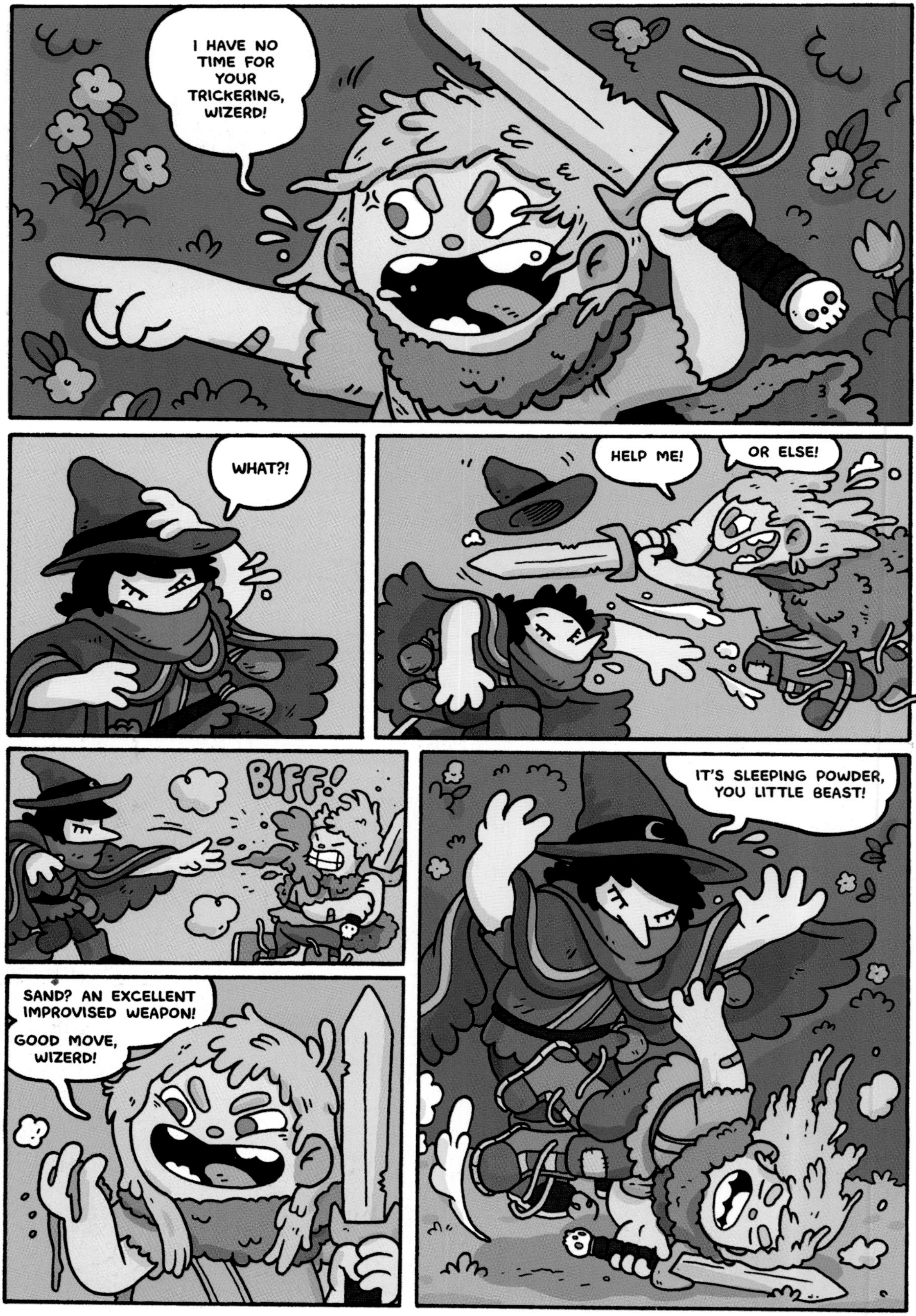
I HAVE NO TIME FOR YOUR TRICKERING, WIZERD!
WHAT?!
HELP ME!
OR ELSE!
BIFF!
IT'S SLEEPING POWDER, YOU LITTLE BEAST!
SAND? AN EXCELLENT IMPROVISED WEAPON!
GOOD MOVE, WIZERD!

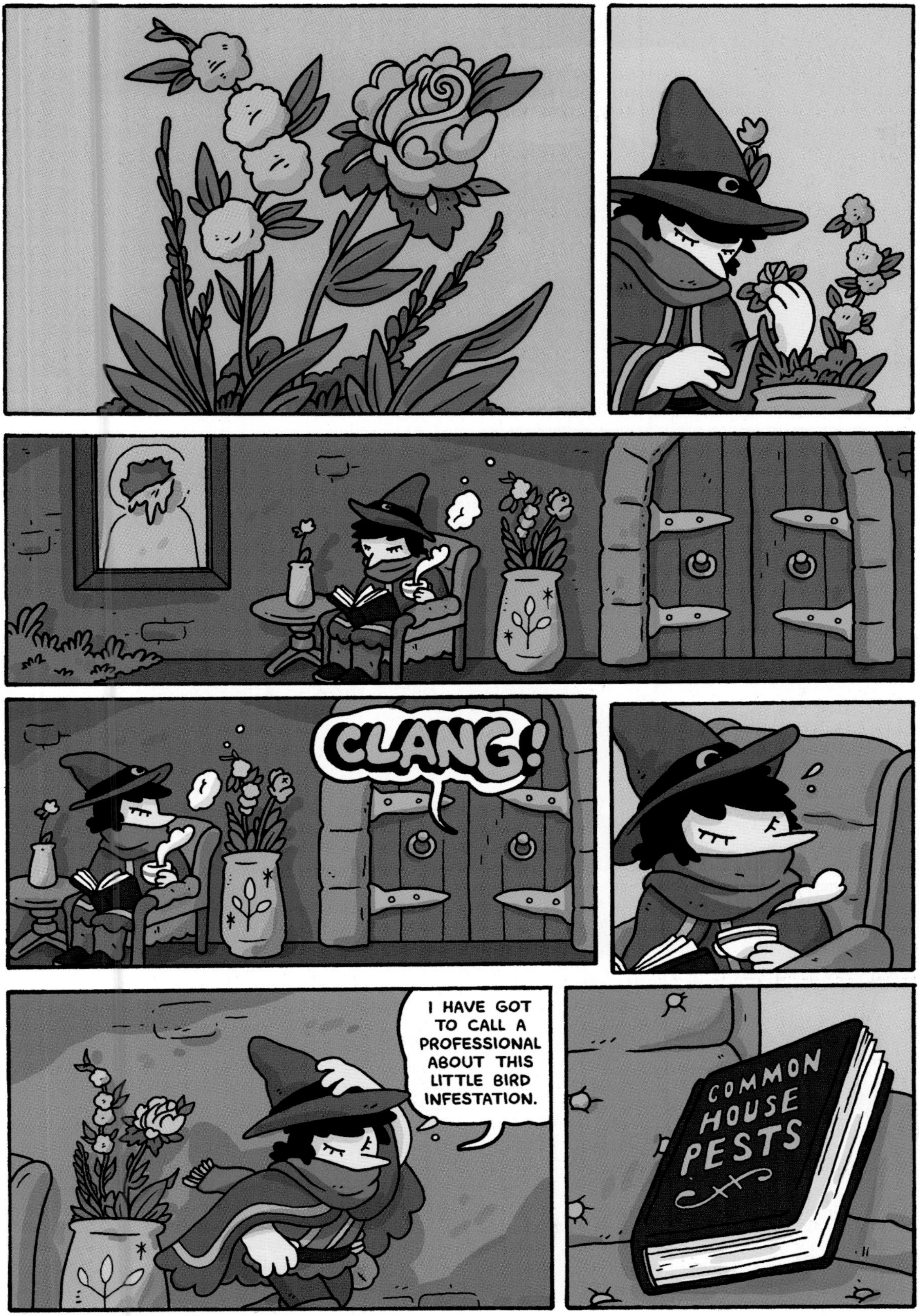
CLANG!
I HAVE GOT TO CALL A PROFESSIONAL ABOUT THIS LITTLE BIRD INFESTATION.
COMMON HOUSE PESTS

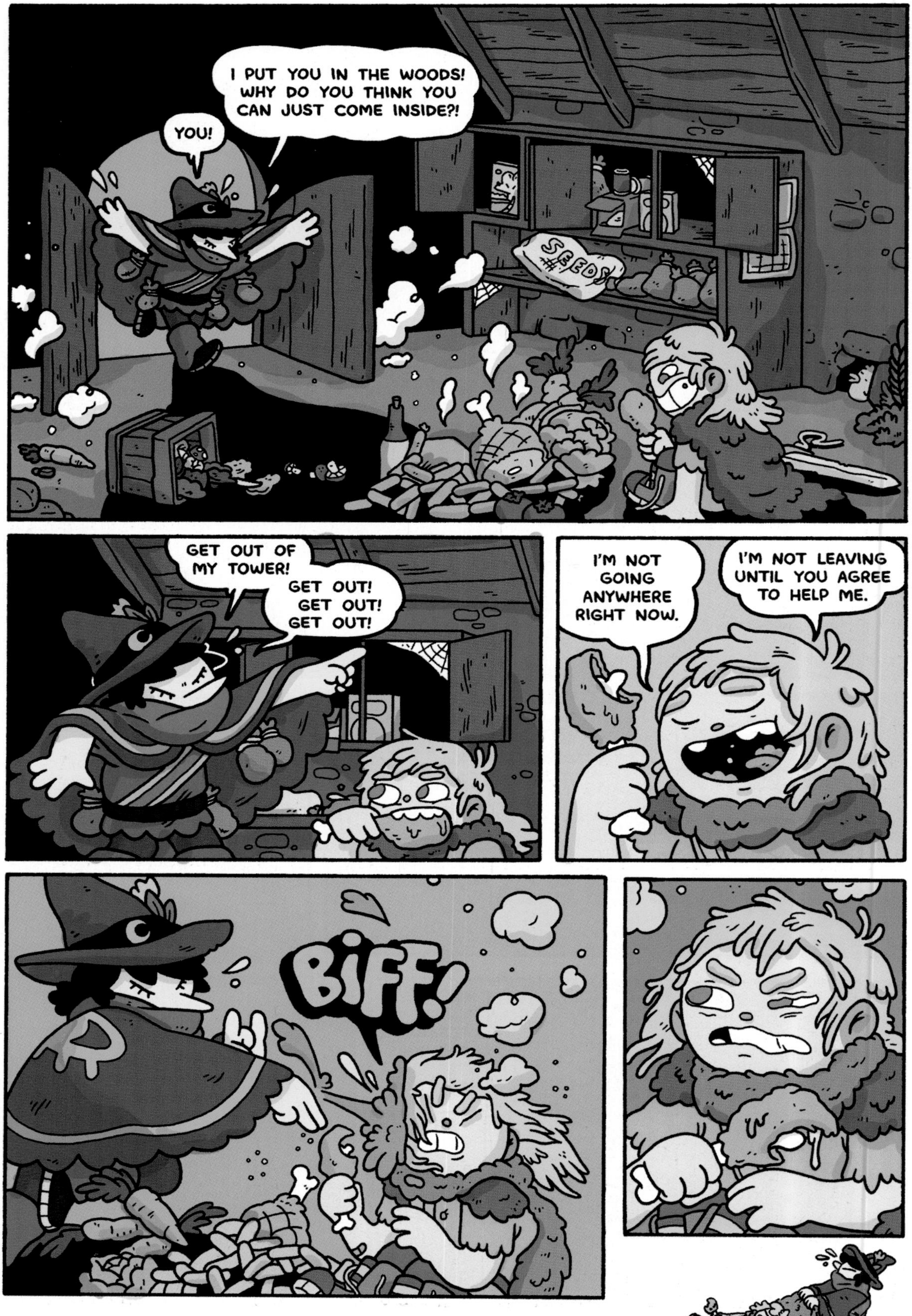
YOU!
I PUT YOU IN THE WOODS! WHY DO YOU THINK YOU CAN JUST COME INSIDE?!
SEEDS
GET OUT OF MY TOWER!
GET OUT! GET OUT! GET OUT!
I'M NOT GOING ANYWHERE RIGHT NOW.
I'M NOT LEAVING UNTIL YOU AGREE TO HELP ME.
BIFF!
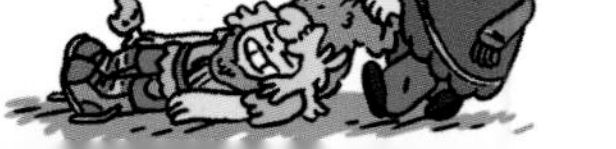

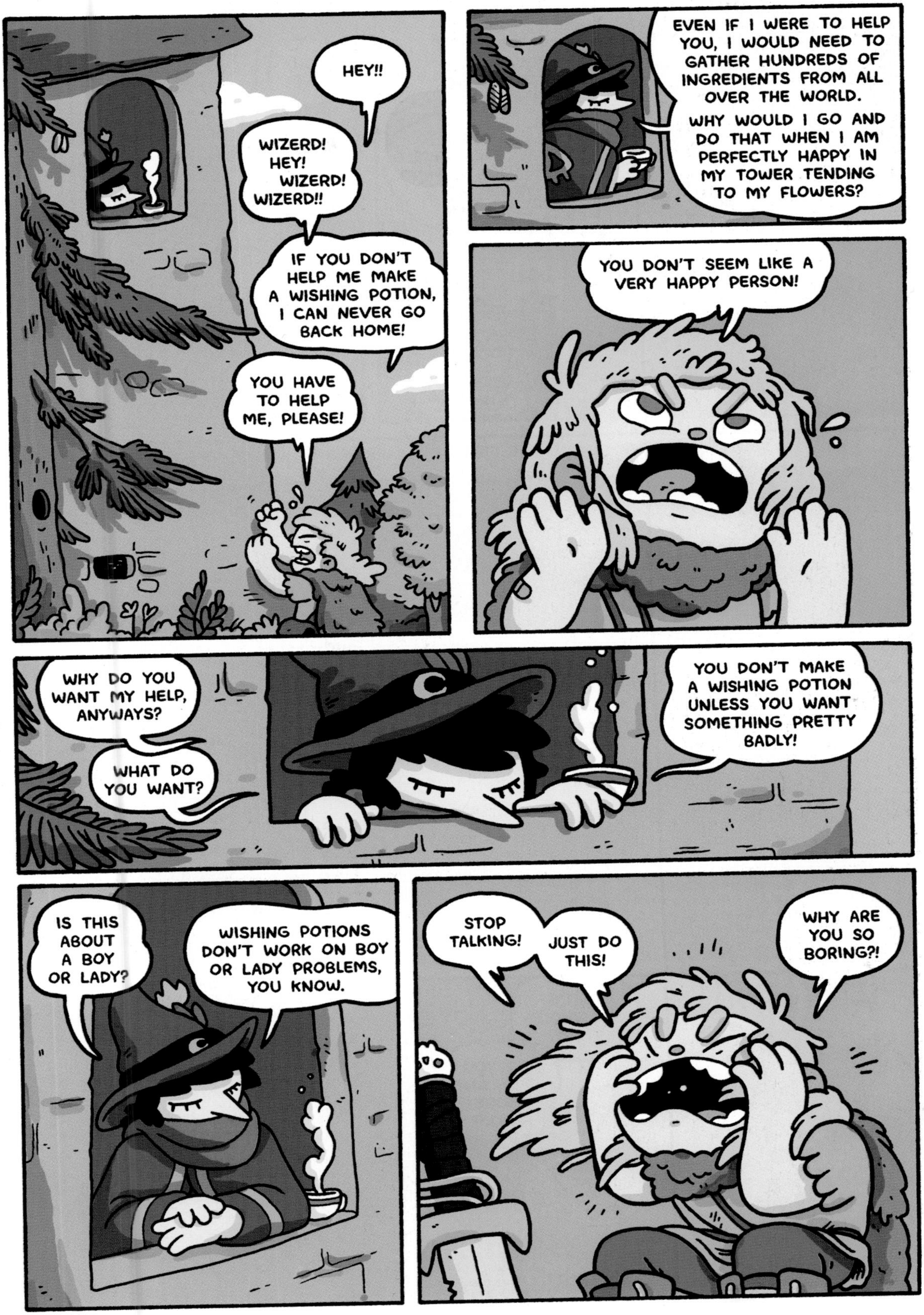
HEY!!
WIZERD! HEY! WIZERD! WIZERD!!
IF YOU DON'T HELP ME MAKE A WISHING POTION, I CAN NEVER GO BACK HOME!
YOU HAVE TO HELP ME, PLEASE!
EVEN IF I WERE TO HELP YOU, I WOULD NEED TO GATHER HUNDREDS OF INGREDIENTS FROM ALL OVER THE WORLD.
WHY WOULD I GO AND DO THAT WHEN I AM PERFECTLY HAPPY IN MY TOWER TENDING TO MY FLOWERS?
YOU DON'T SEEM LIKE A VERY HAPPY PERSON!
WHY DO YOU WANT MY HELP, ANYWAYS?
WHAT DO YOU WANT?
YOU DON'T MAKE A WISHING POTION UNLESS YOU WANT SOMETHING PRETTY BADLY!
IS THIS ABOUT A BOY OR LADY?
WISHING POTIONS DON'T WORK ON BOY OR LADY PROBLEMS, YOU KNOW.
STOP TALKING!
JUST DO THIS!
WHY ARE YOU SO BORING?!

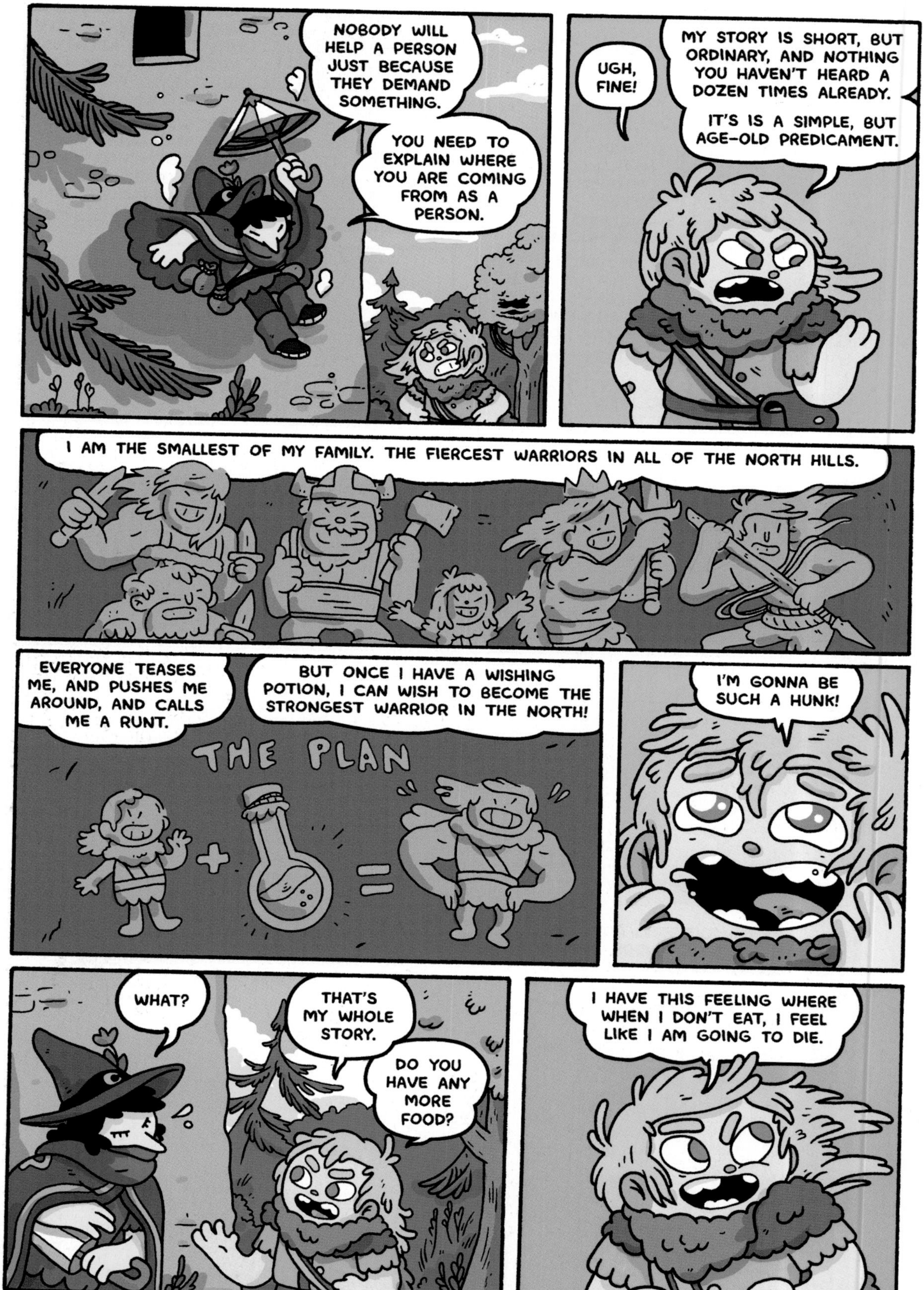
NOBODY WILL HELP A PERSON JUST BECAUSE THEY DEMAND SOMETHING.
YOU NEED TO EXPLAIN WHERE YOU ARE COMING FROM AS A PERSON.
UGH, FINE!
MY STORY IS SHORT, BUT ORDINARY, AND NOTHING YOU HAVEN'T HEARD A DOZEN TIMES ALREADY.
IT'S IS A SIMPLE, BUT AGE-OLD PREDICAMENT.
I AM THE SMALLEST OF MY FAMILY. THE FIERCEST WARRIORS IN ALL OF THE NORTH HILLS.
EVERYONE TEASES ME, AND PUSHES ME AROUND, AND CALLS ME A RUNT.
BUT ONCE I HAVE A WISHING POTION, I CAN WISH TO BECOME THE STRONGEST WARRIOR IN THE NORTH!
THE PLAN
I'M GONNA BE SUCH A HUNK!
WHAT?
THAT'S MY WHOLE STORY.
DO YOU HAVE ANY MORE FOOD?
I HAVE THIS FEELING WHERE WHEN I DON'T EAT, I FEEL LIKE I AM GOING TO DIE.

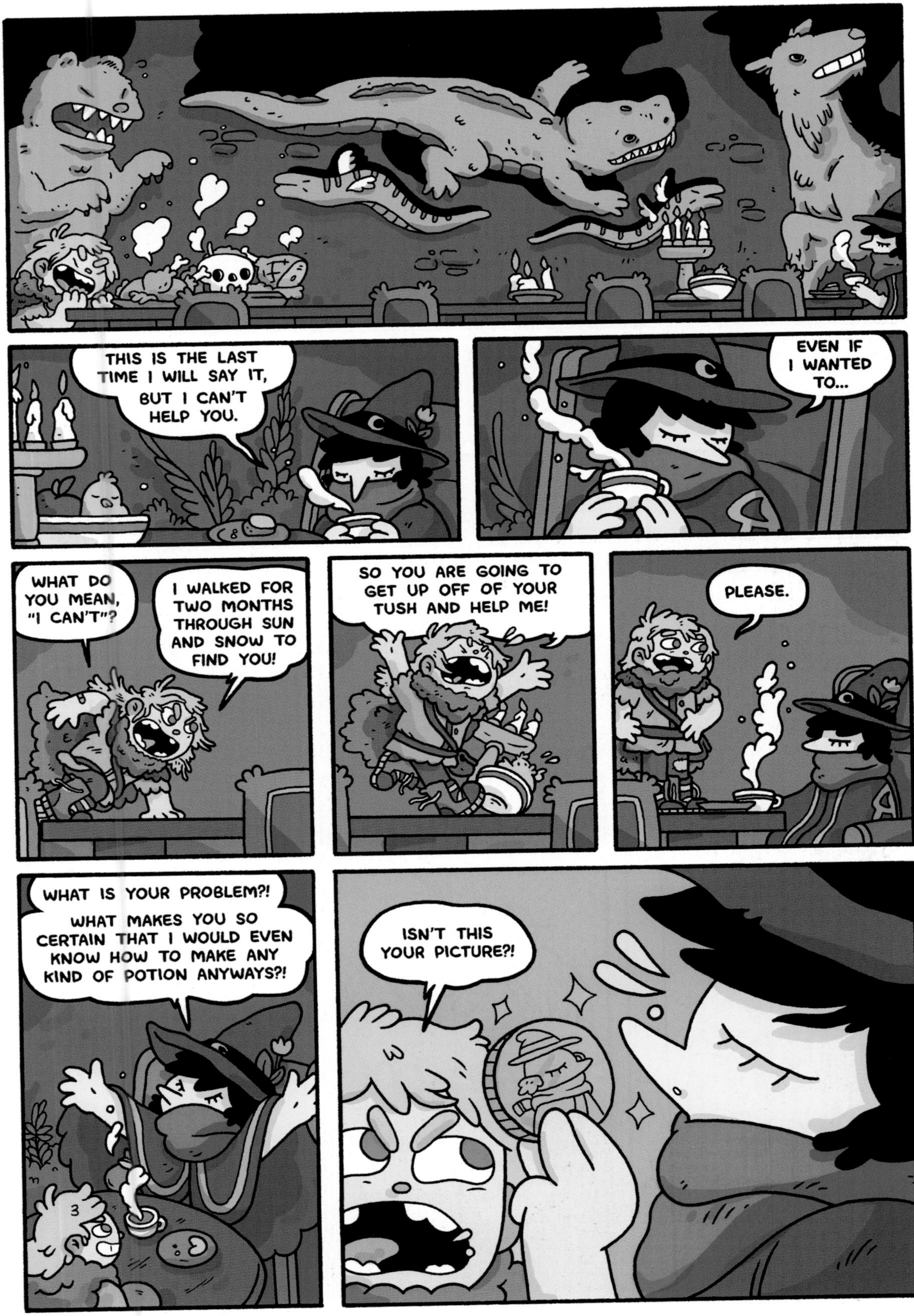

THIS IS THE LAST TIME I WILL SAY IT, BUT I CAN'T HELP YOU.
EVEN IF I WANTED TO...
WHAT DO YOU MEAN, "I CAN'T"?
I WALKED FOR TWO MONTHS THROUGH SUN AND SNOW TO FIND YOU!
SO YOU ARE GOING TO GET UP OFF OF YOUR TUSH AND HELP ME!
PLEASE.
WHAT IS YOUR PROBLEM?!
WHAT MAKES YOU SO CERTAIN THAT I WOULD EVEN KNOW HOW TO MAKE ANY KIND OF POTION ANYWAYS?!
ISN'T THIS YOUR PICTURE?!

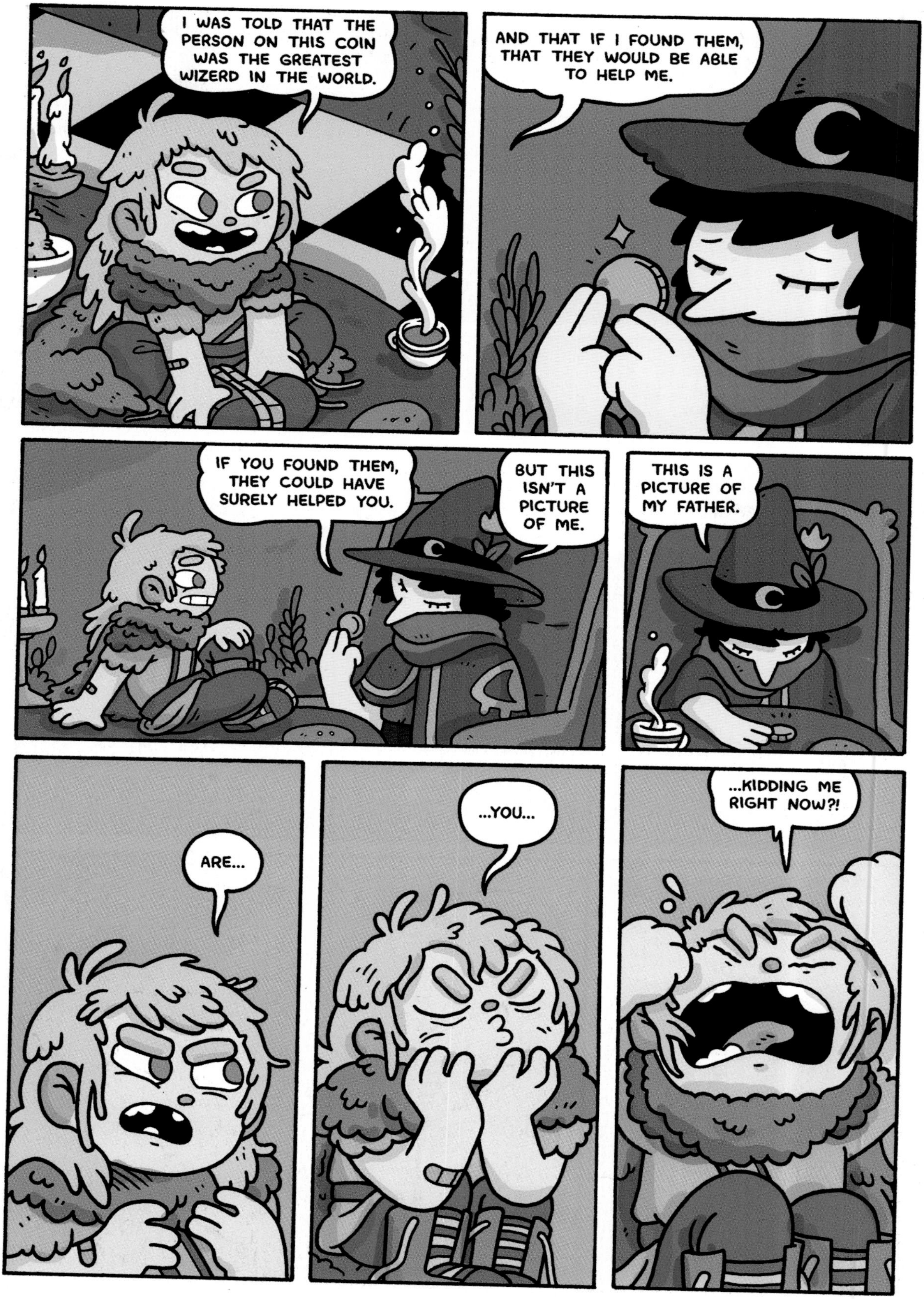
I WAS TOLD THAT THE PERSON ON THIS COIN WAS THE GREATEST WIZERD IN THE WORLD.
AND THAT IF I FOUND THEM, THAT THEY WOULD BE ABLE TO HELP ME.
IF YOU FOUND THEM, THEY COULD HAVE SURELY HELPED YOU.
BUT THIS ISN'T A PICTURE OF ME.
THIS IS A PICTURE OF MY FATHER.
ARE...
...YOU...
...KIDDING ME RIGHT NOW?!

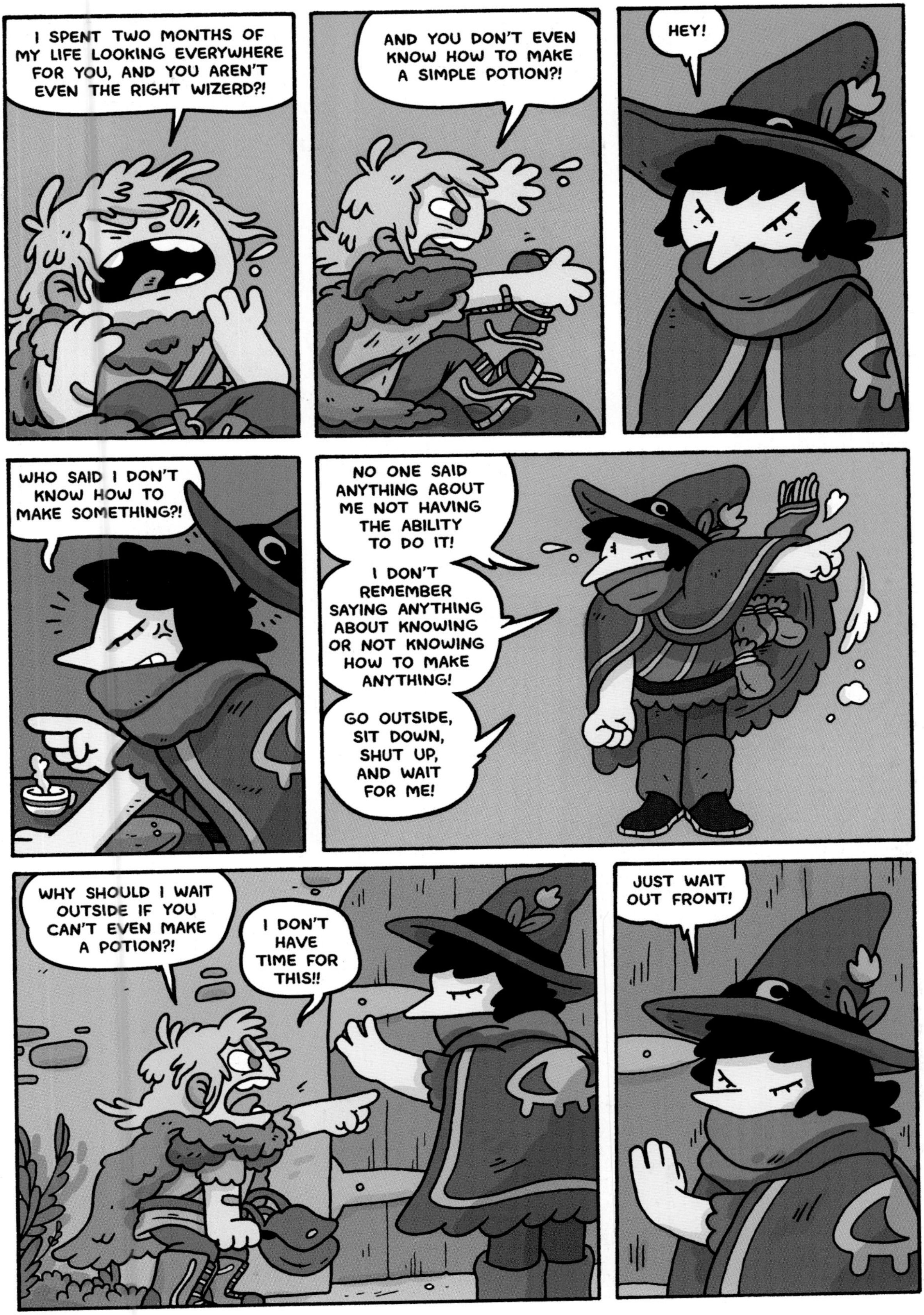
I SPENT TWO MONTHS OF MY LIFE LOOKING EVERYWHERE FOR YOU, AND YOU AREN'T EVEN THE RIGHT WIZERD?!
AND YOU DON'T EVEN KNOW HOW TO MAKE A SIMPLE POTION?!
HEY!
WHO SAID I DON'T KNOW HOW TO MAKE SOMETHING?!
NO ONE SAID ANYTHING ABOUT ME NOT HAVING THE ABILITY TO DO IT!
I DON'T REMEMBER SAYING ANYTHING ABOUT KNOWING OR NOT KNOWING HOW TO MAKE ANYTHING!
GO OUTSIDE, SIT DOWN, SHUT UP, AND WAIT FOR ME!
WHY SHOULD I WAIT OUTSIDE IF YOU CAN'T EVEN MAKE A POTION?!
I DON'T HAVE TIME FOR THIS!!
JUST WAIT OUT FRONT!

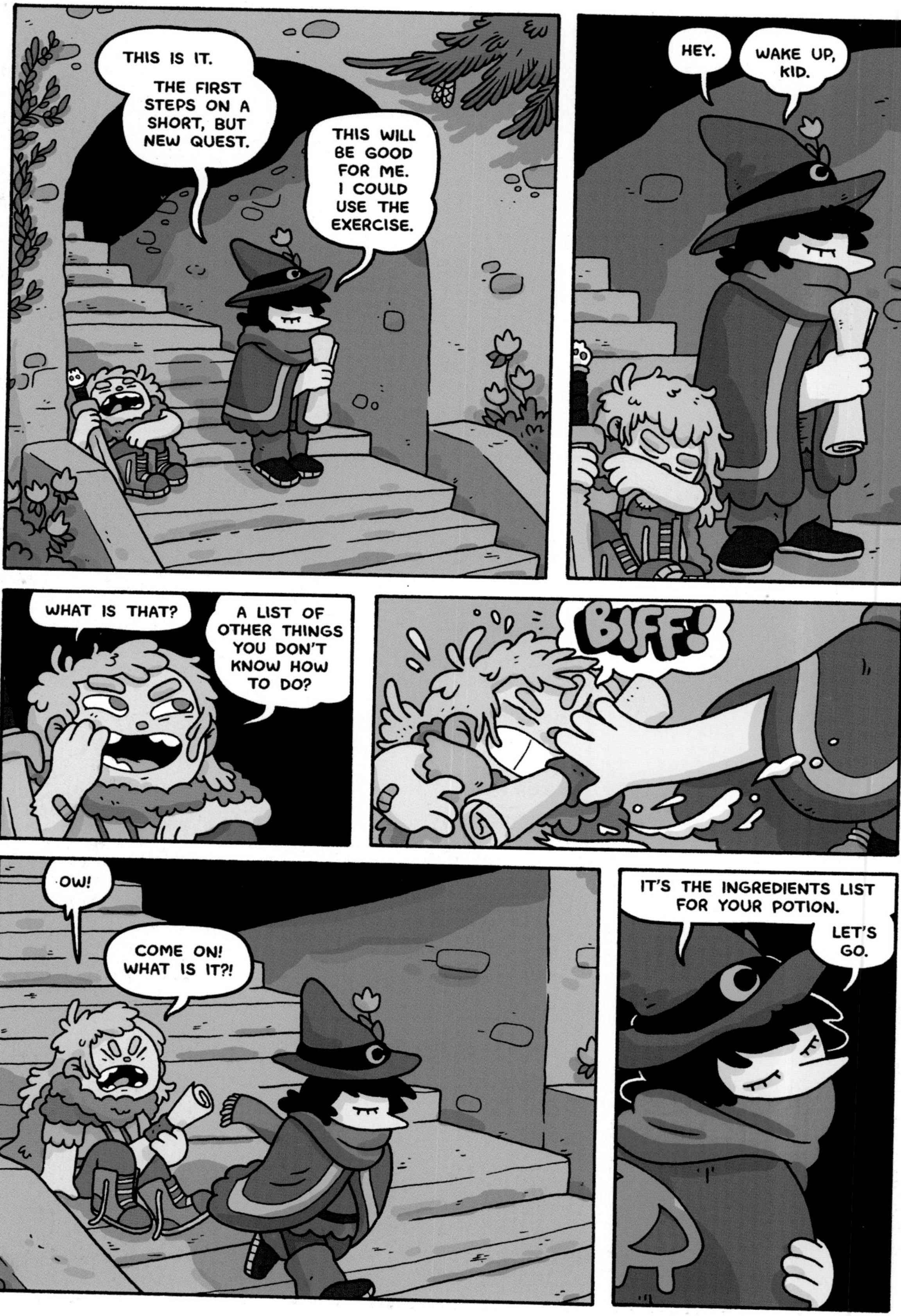
THIS IS IT.
THE FIRST STEPS ON A SHORT, BUT NEW QUEST.
THIS WILL BE GOOD FOR ME. I COULD USE THE EXERCISE.
HEY.
WAKE UP, KID.
WHAT IS THAT?
A LIST OF OTHER THINGS YOU DON'T KNOW HOW TO DO?
BIFF!
OW!
COME ON! WHAT IS IT?!
IT'S THE INGREDIENTS LIST FOR YOUR POTION.
LET'S GO.

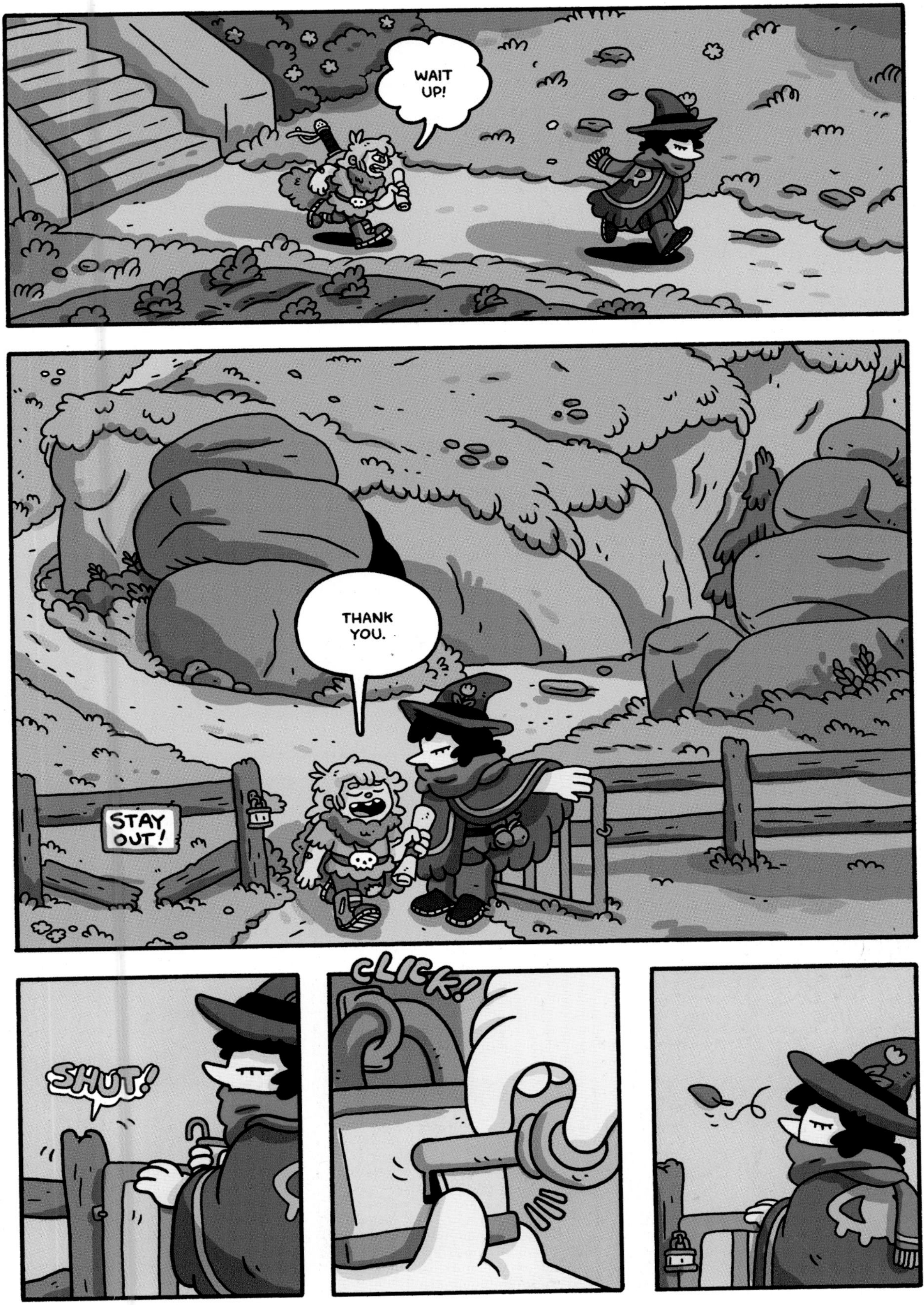
WAIT UP!
THANK YOU.
STAY OUT!
SHUT!
CLICK!

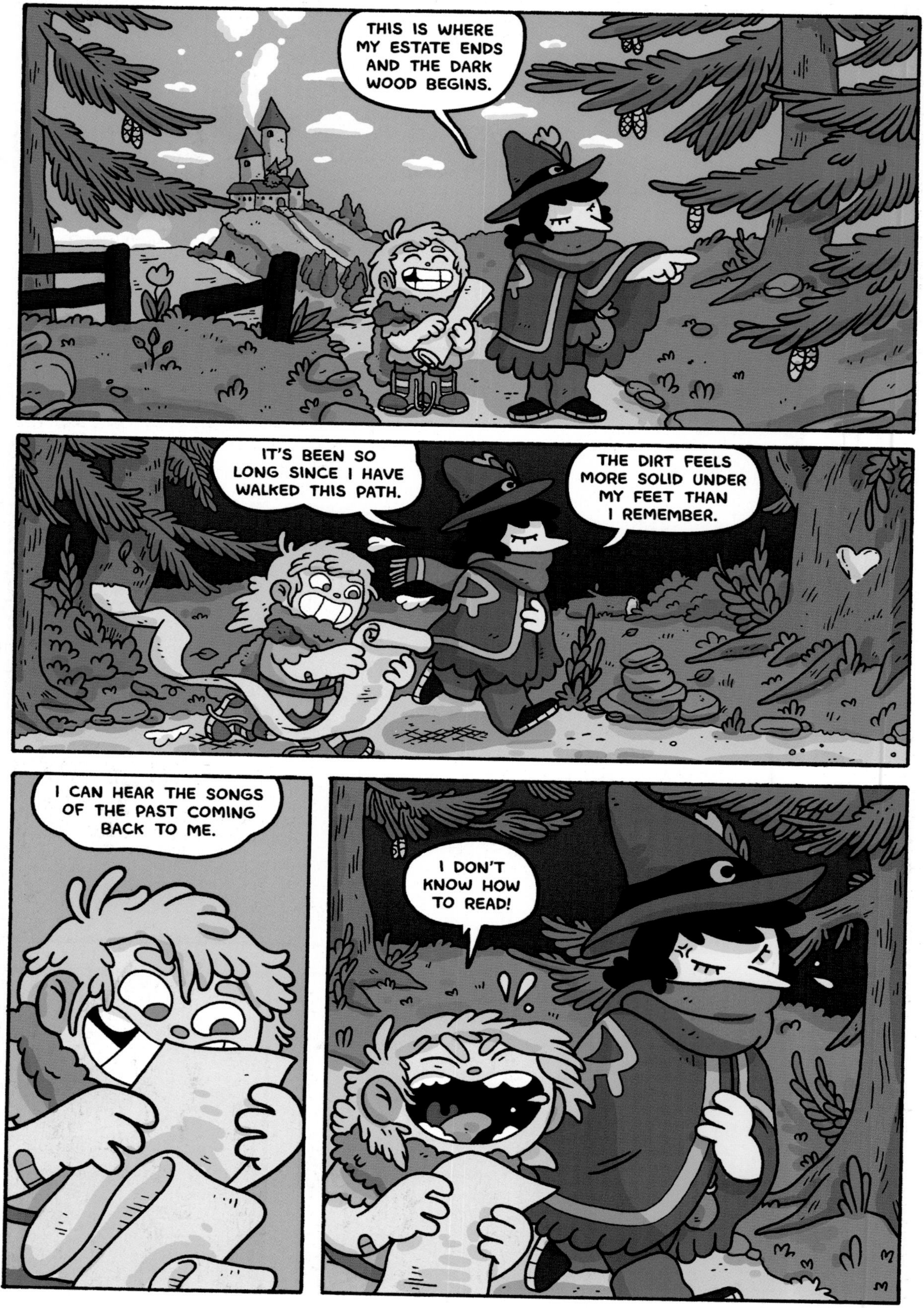
THIS IS WHERE MY ESTATE ENDS AND THE DARK WOOD BEGINS.
IT'S BEEN SO LONG SINCE I HAVE WALKED THIS PATH.
THE DIRT FEELS MORE SOLID UNDER MY FEET THAN I REMEMBER.
I CAN HEAR THE SONGS OF THE PAST COMING BACK TO ME.
I DON'T KNOW HOW TO READ!

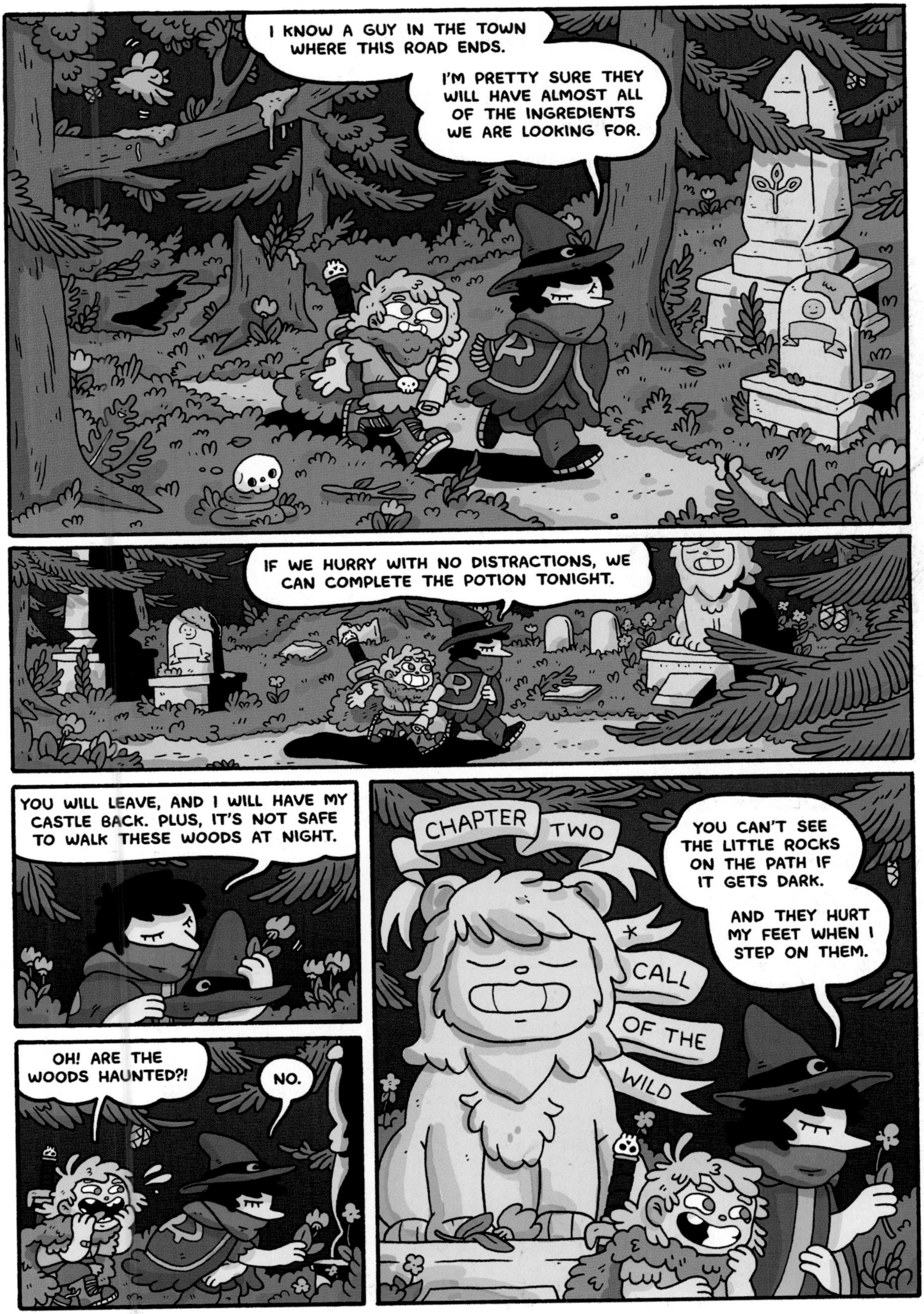
I KNOW A GUY IN THE TOWN WHERE THIS ROAD ENDS.
I'M PRETTY SURE THEY WILL HAVE ALMOST ALL OF THE INGREDIENTS WE ARE LOOKING FOR.
IF WE HURRY WITH NO DISTRACTIONS, WE CAN COMPLETE THE POTION TONIGHT.
YOU WILL LEAVE, AND I WILL HAVE MY CASTLE BACK. PLUS, IT'S NOT SAFE TO WALK THESE WOODS AT NIGHT.
OH! ARE THE WOODS HAUNTED?!
NO.
CHAPTER TWO
CALL OF THE WILD
YOU CAN'T SEE THE LITTLE ROCKS ON THE PATH IF IT GETS DARK.
AND THEY HURT MY FEET WHEN I STEP ON THEM.

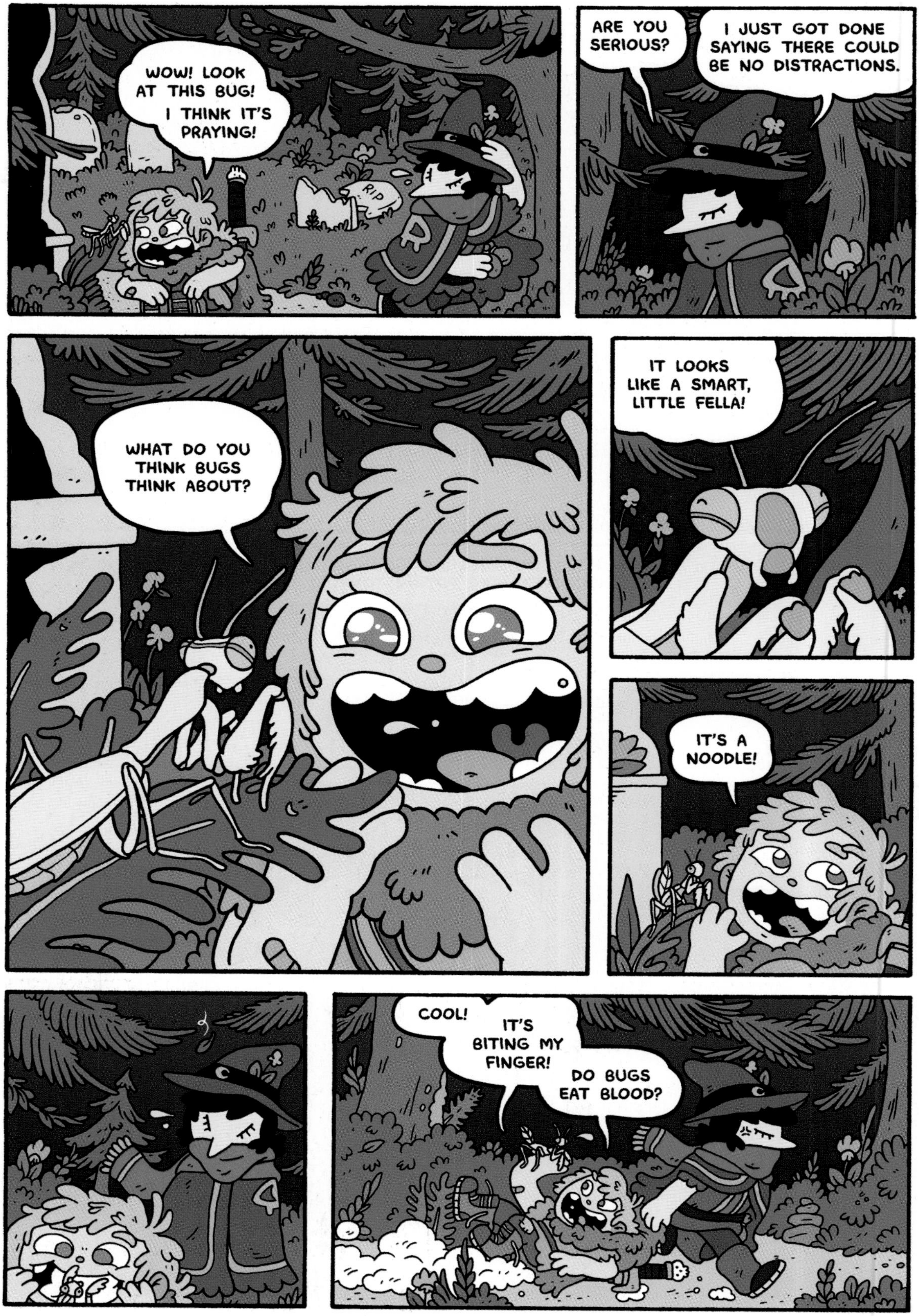
WOW! LOOK AT THIS BUG!
I THINK IT'S PRAYING!
RIP
ARE YOU SERIOUS?
I JUST GOT DONE SAYING THERE COULD BE NO DISTRACTIONS.
WHAT DO YOU THINK BUGS THINK ABOUT?
IT LOOKS LIKE A SMART, LITTLE FELLA!
IT'S A NOODLE!
COOL!
IT'S BITING MY FINGER!
DO BUGS EAT BLOOD?

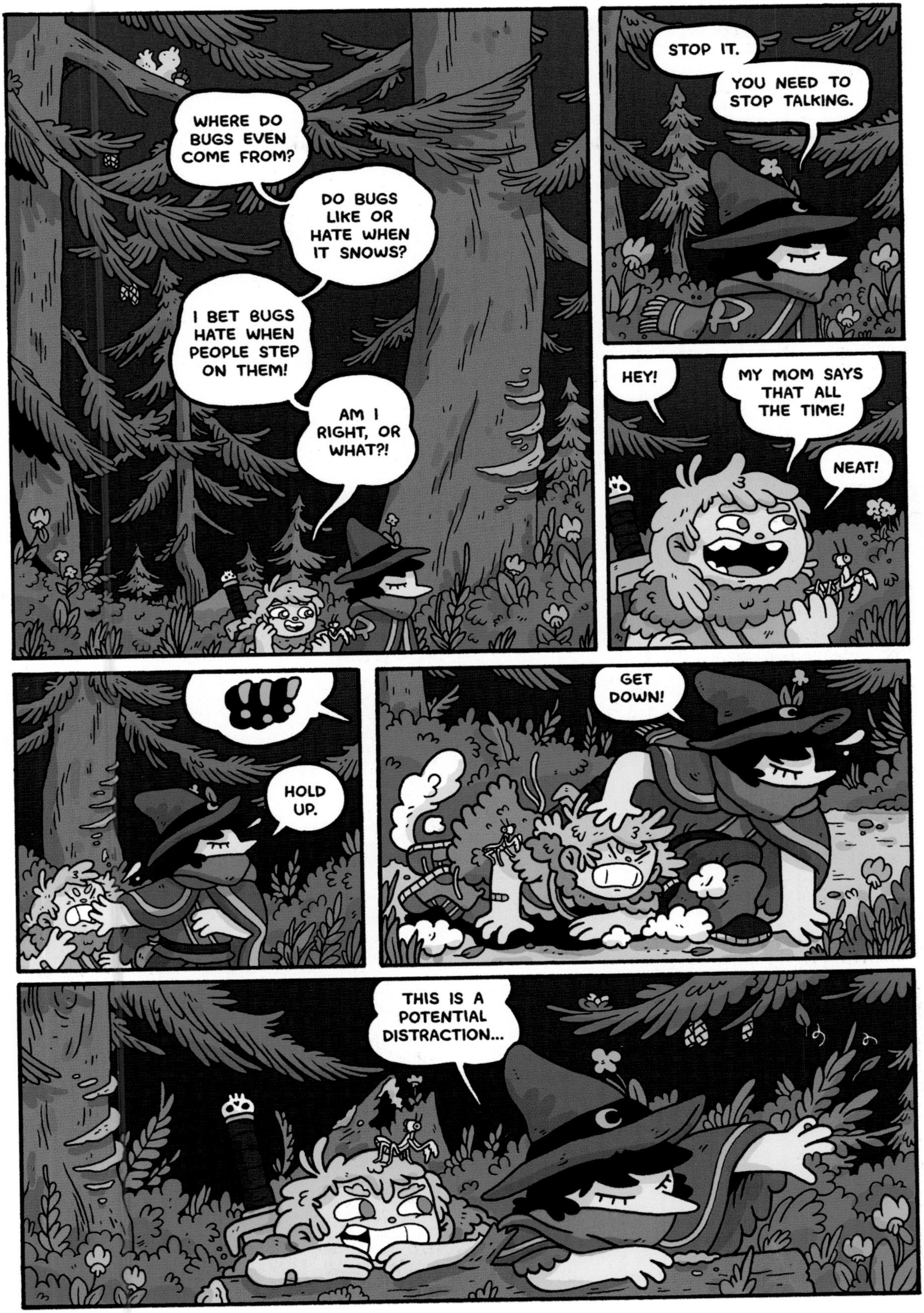
WHERE DO BUGS EVEN COME FROM?
DO BUGS LIKE OR HATE WHEN IT SNOWS?
I BET BUGS HATE WHEN PEOPLE STEP ON THEM!
AM I RIGHT, OR WHAT?!
STOP IT.
YOU NEED TO STOP TALKING.
HEY!
MY MOM SAYS THAT ALL THE TIME!
NEAT!
!!
HOLD UP.
GET DOWN!
THIS IS A POTENTIAL DISTRACTION...

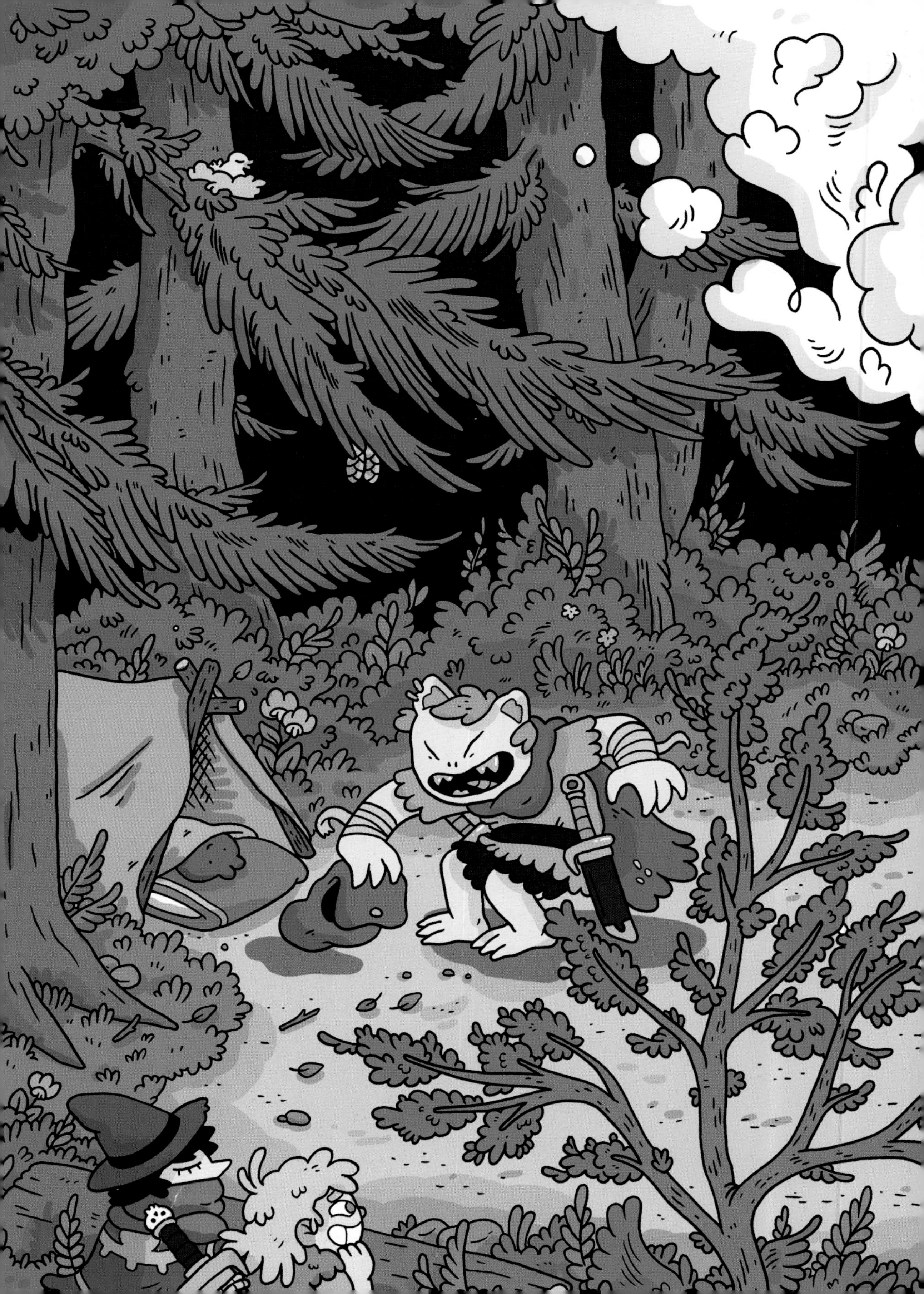

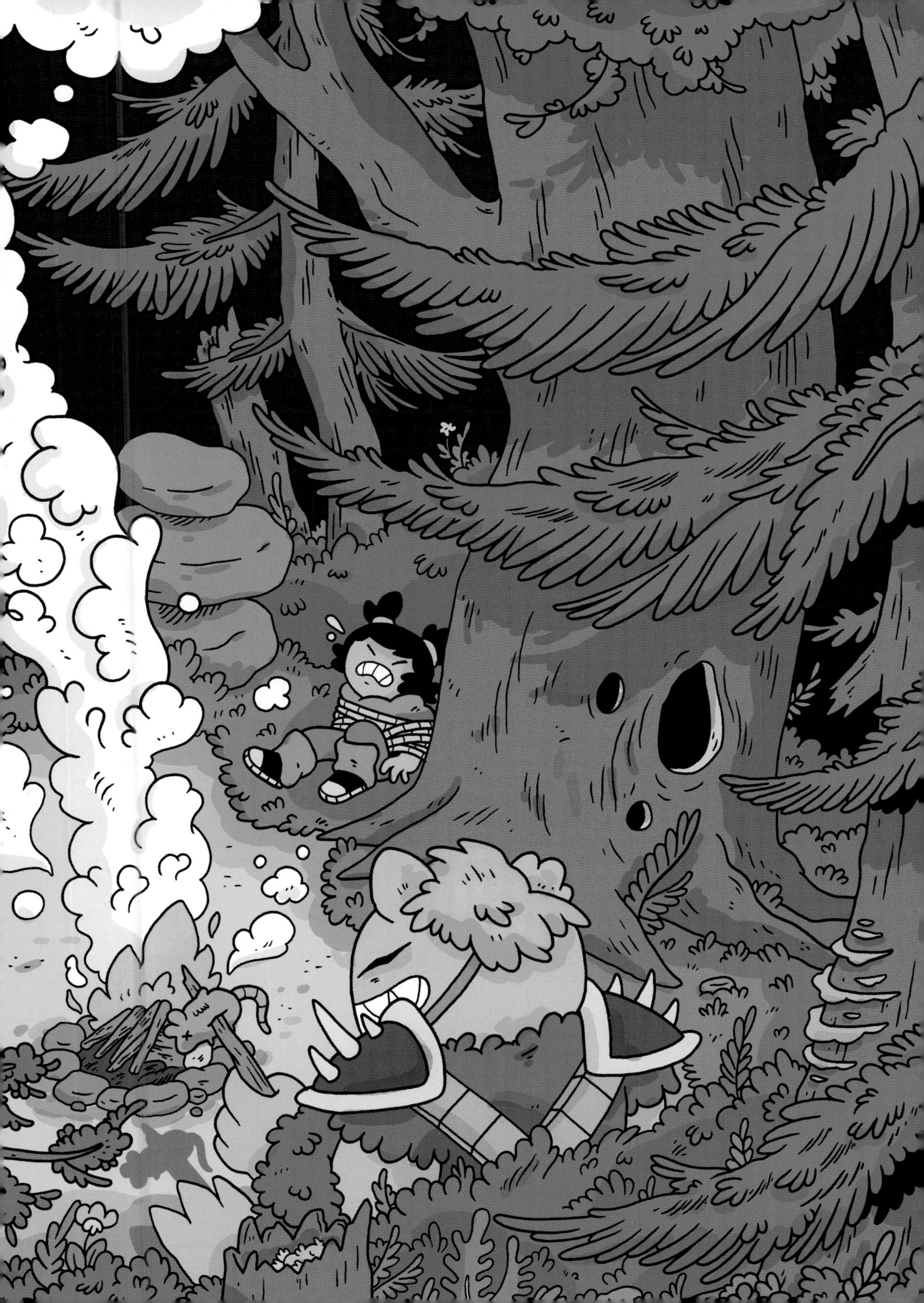

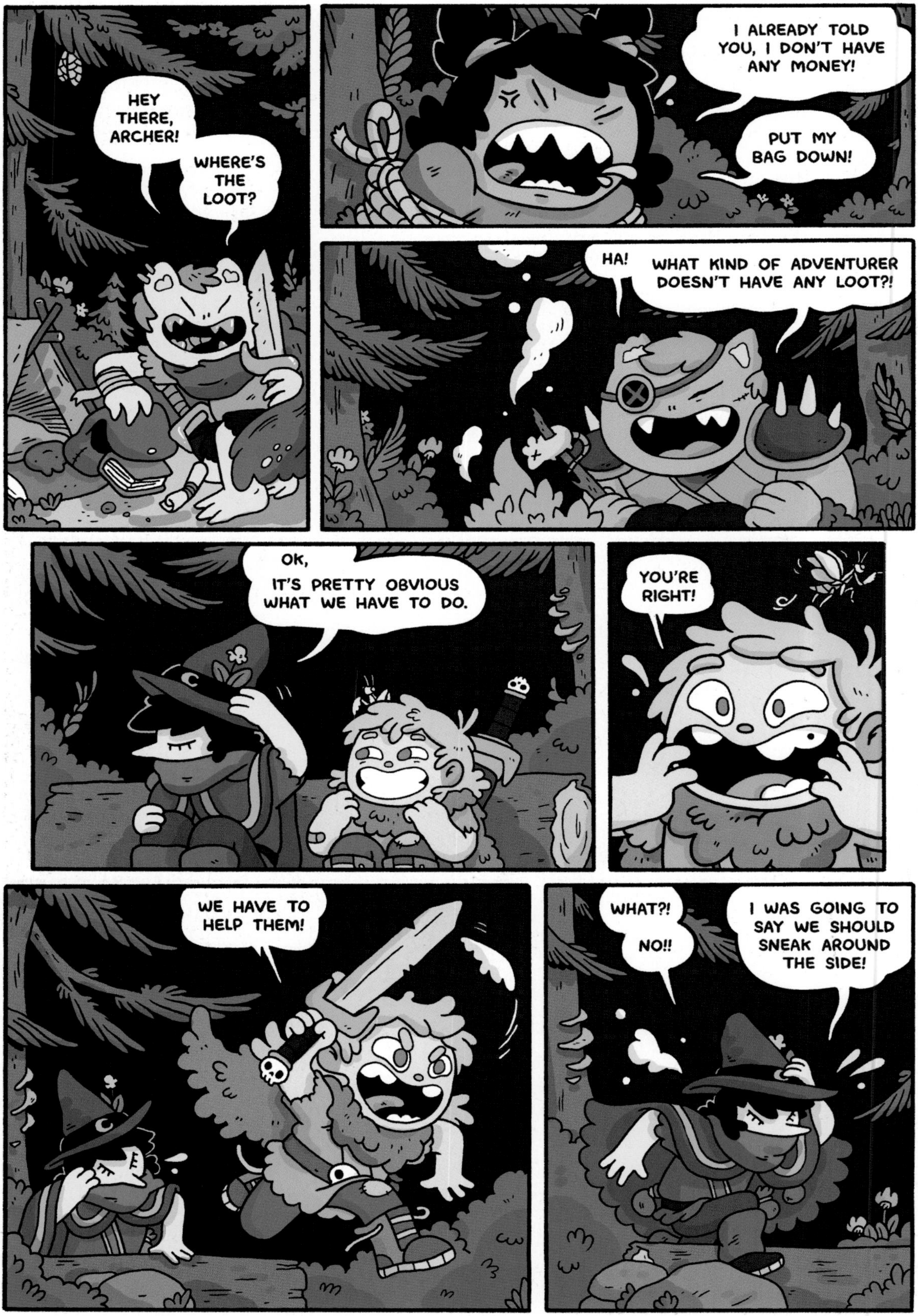
HEY THERE, ARCHER!
WHERE'S THE LOOT?
I ALREADY TOLD YOU, I DON'T HAVE ANY MONEY!
PUT MY BAG DOWN!
HA!
WHAT KIND OF ADVENTURER DOESN'T HAVE ANY LOOT?!
OK,
IT'S PRETTY OBVIOUS WHAT WE HAVE TO DO.
YOU'RE RIGHT!
WE HAVE TO HELP THEM!
WHAT?!
NO!!
I WAS GOING TO SAY WE SHOULD SNEAK AROUND THE SIDE!

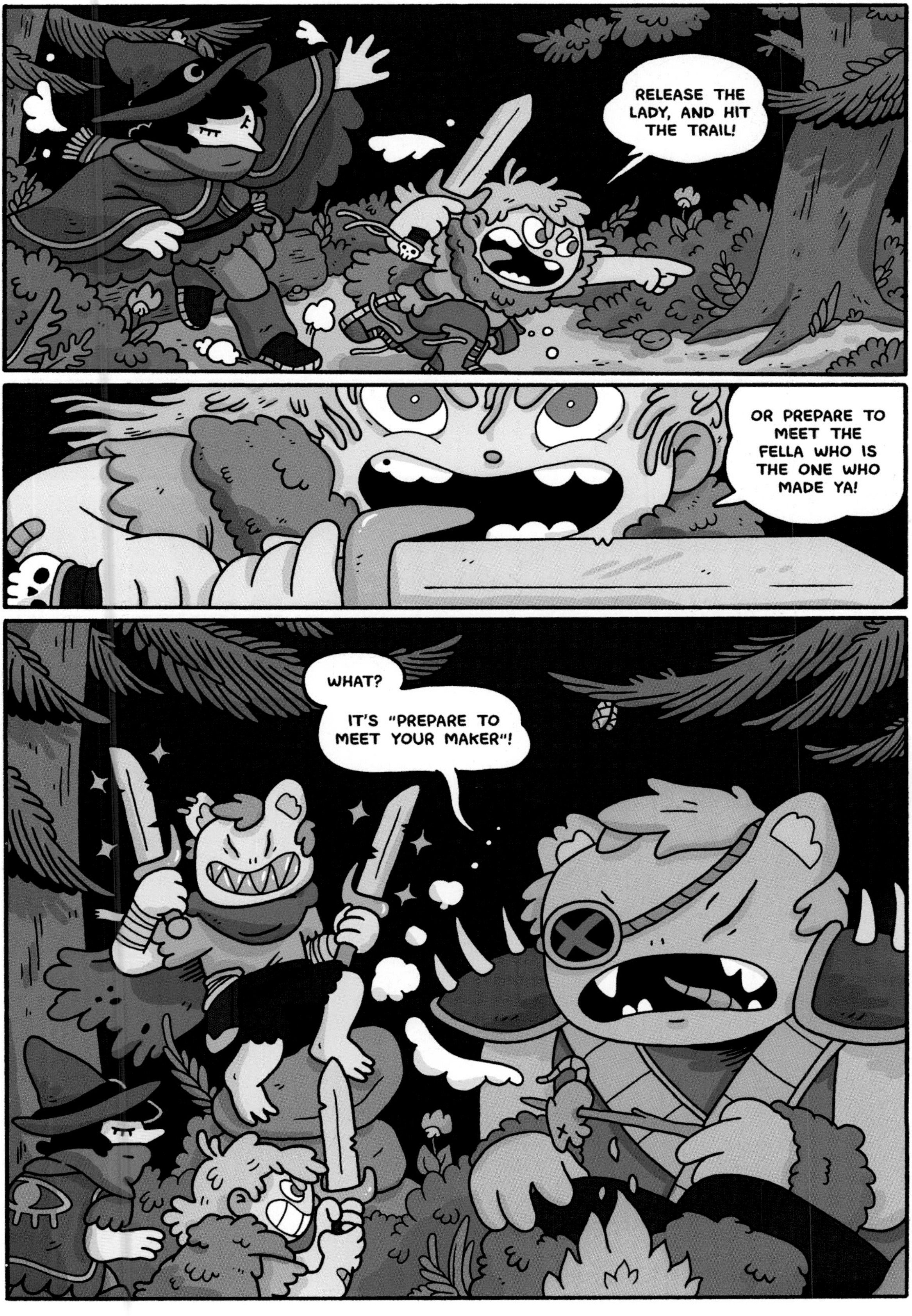
RELEASE THE LADY, AND HIT THE TRAIL!
OR PREPARE TO MEET THE FELLA WHO IS THE ONE WHO MADE YA!
WHAT?
IT'S "PREPARE TO MEET YOUR MAKER"!

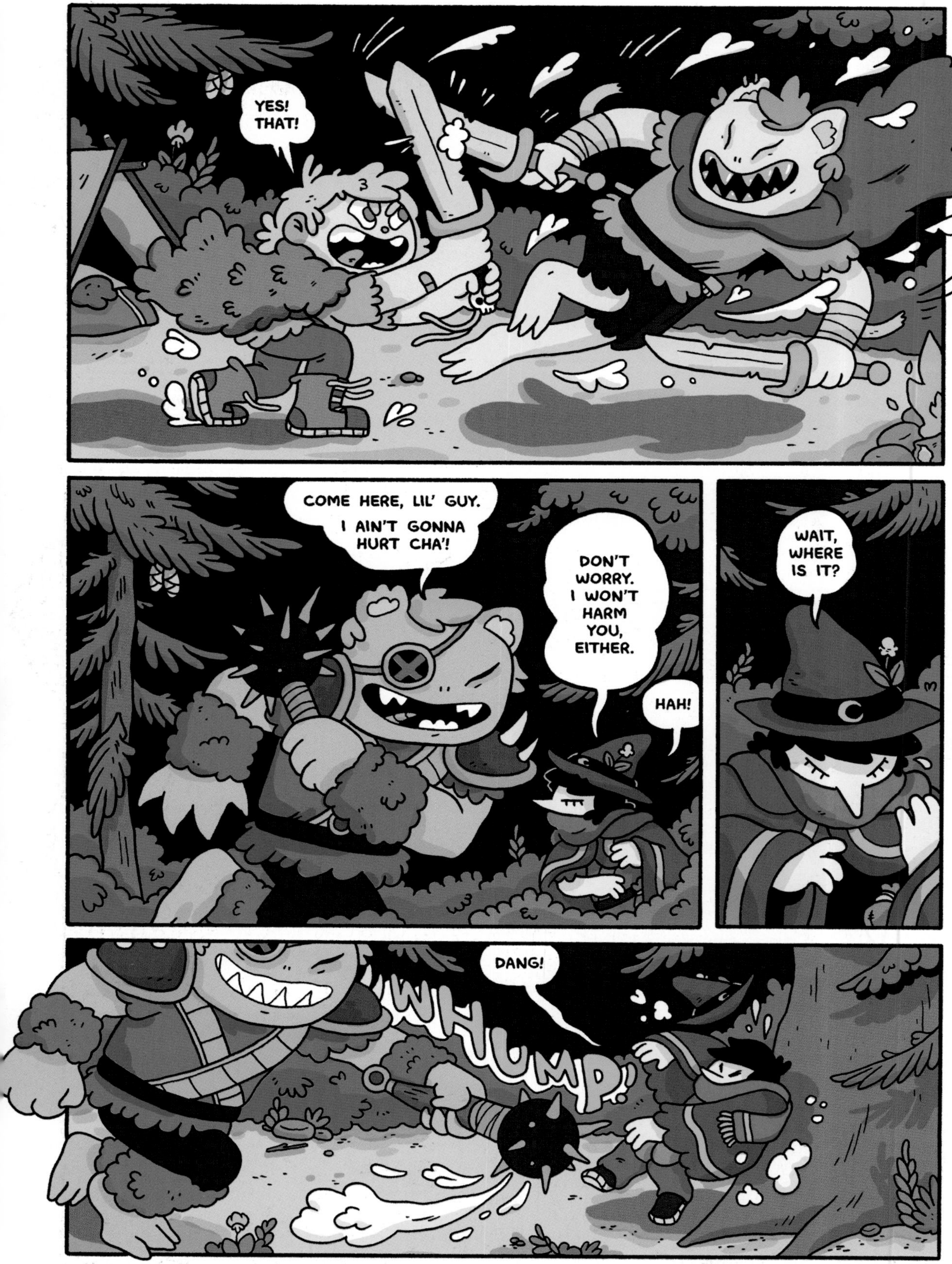
YES! THAT!
COME HERE, LIL' GUY. I AIN'T GONNA HURT CHA'!
DON'T WORRY. I WON'T HARM YOU, EITHER.
HAH!
WAIT, WHERE IS IT?
DANG!
WHUMP

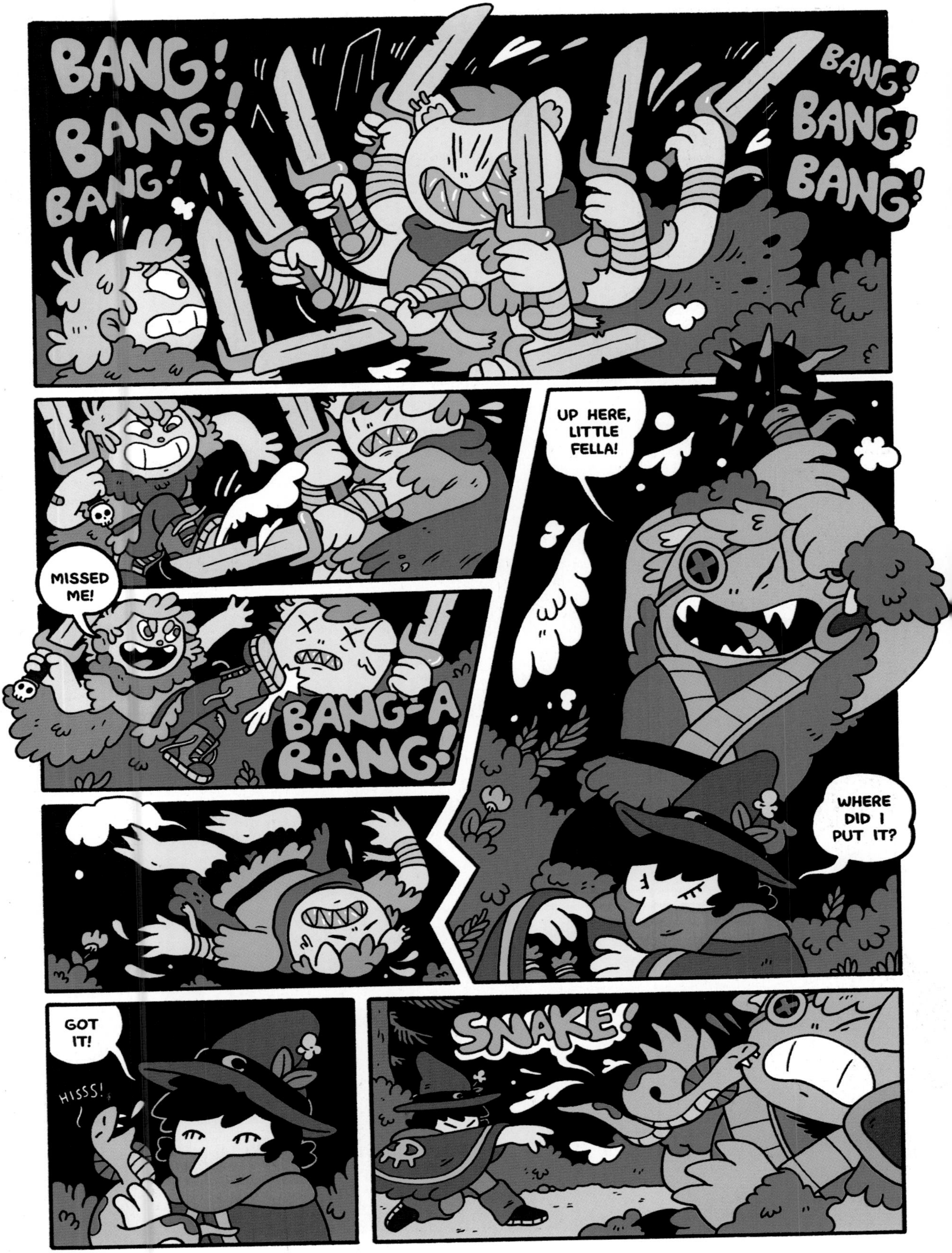
BANG! BANG! BANG!
BANG! BANG! BANG!
MISSED ME!
BANG-A RANG!
UP HERE, LITTLE FELLA!
WHERE DID I PUT IT?
GOT IT!
HISSS!
SNAKE!

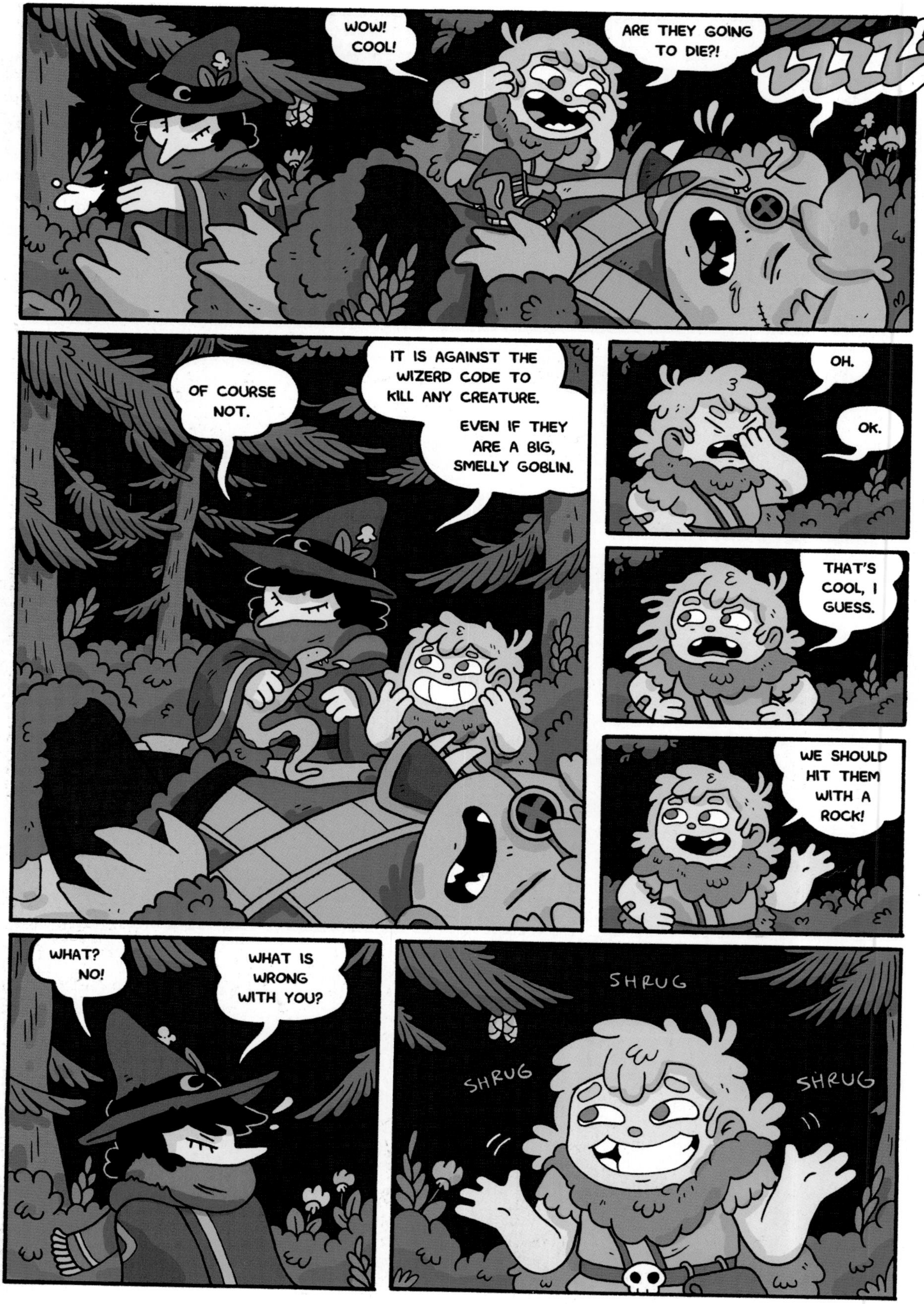

WOW! COOL!
ARE THEY GOING TO DIE?!
ZZZZZ!
OF COURSE NOT.
IT IS AGAINST THE WIZERD CODE TO KILL ANY CREATURE.
EVEN IF THEY ARE A BIG, SMELLY GOBLIN.
OH.
OK.
THAT'S COOL, I GUESS.
WE SHOULD HIT THEM WITH A ROCK!
WHAT? NO!
WHAT IS WRONG WITH YOU?
SHRUG
SHRUG
SHRUG

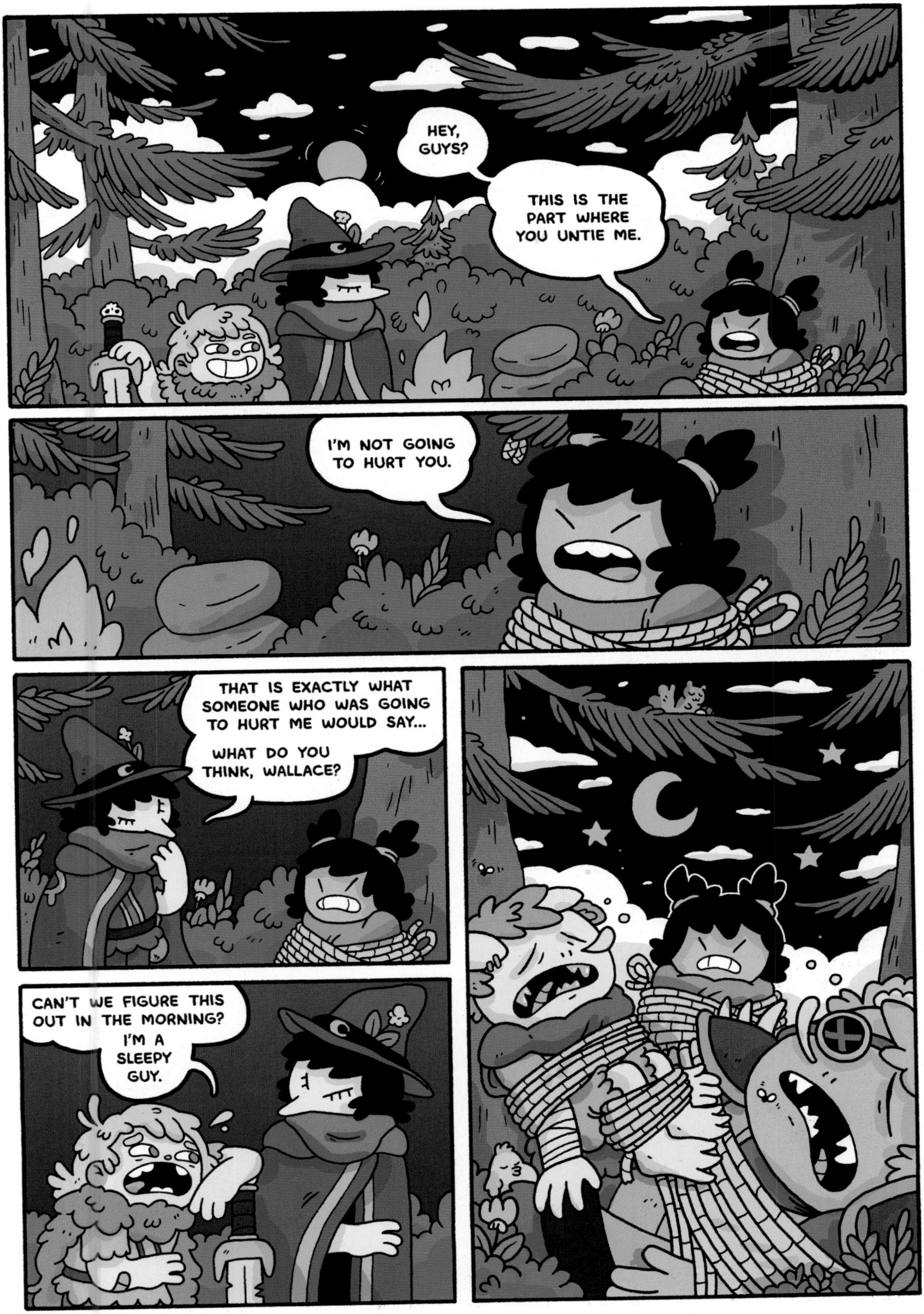
HEY, GUYS?
THIS IS THE PART WHERE YOU UNTIE ME.
I'M NOT GOING TO HURT YOU.
THAT IS EXACTLY WHAT SOMEONE WHO WAS GOING TO HURT ME WOULD SAY...
WHAT DO YOU THINK, WALLACE?
CAN'T WE FIGURE THIS OUT IN THE MORNING?
I'M A SLEEPY GUY.

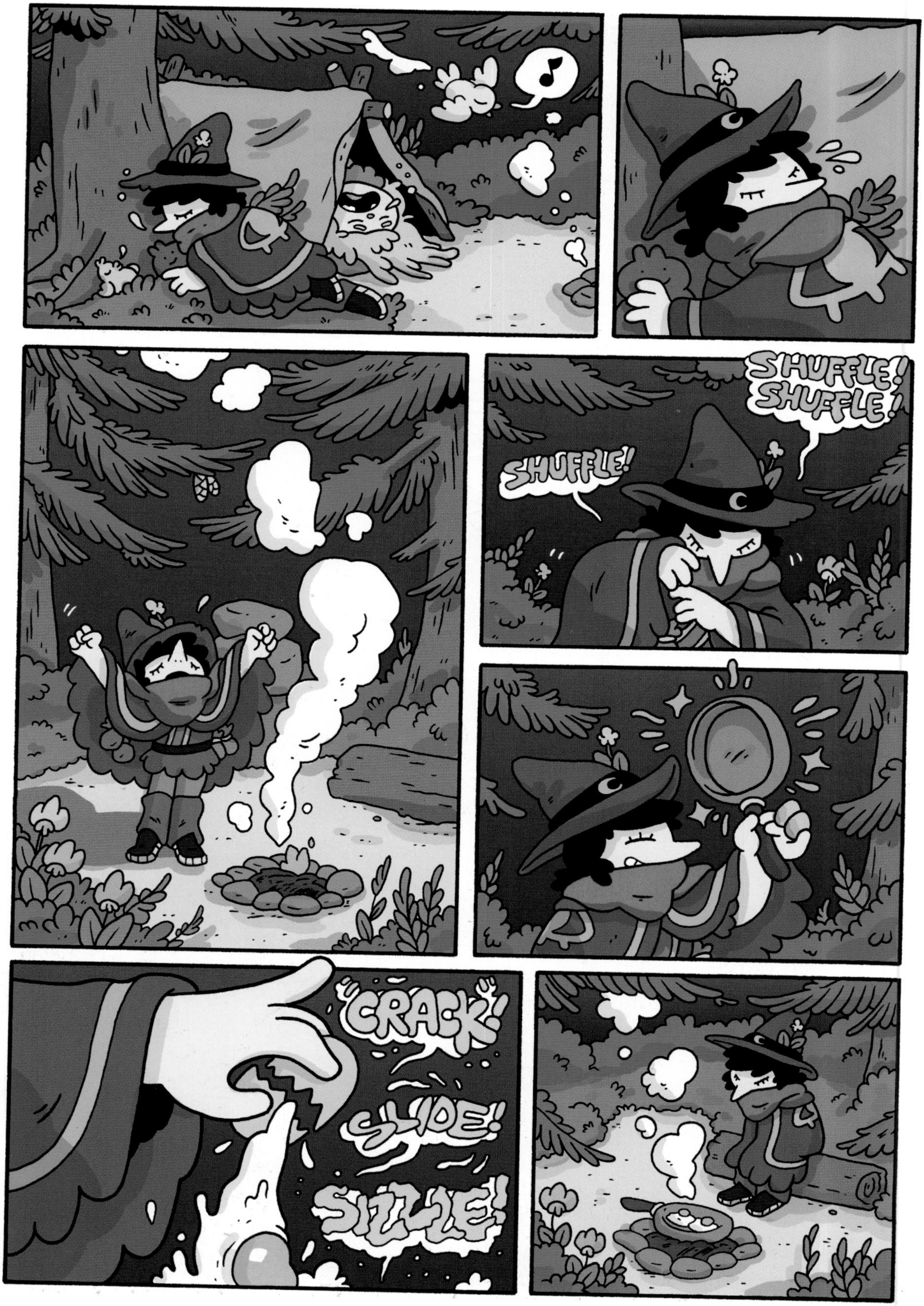

SHUFFLE! SHUFFLE!
SHUFFLE!
CRACK!
SLIDE!
SIZZLE!

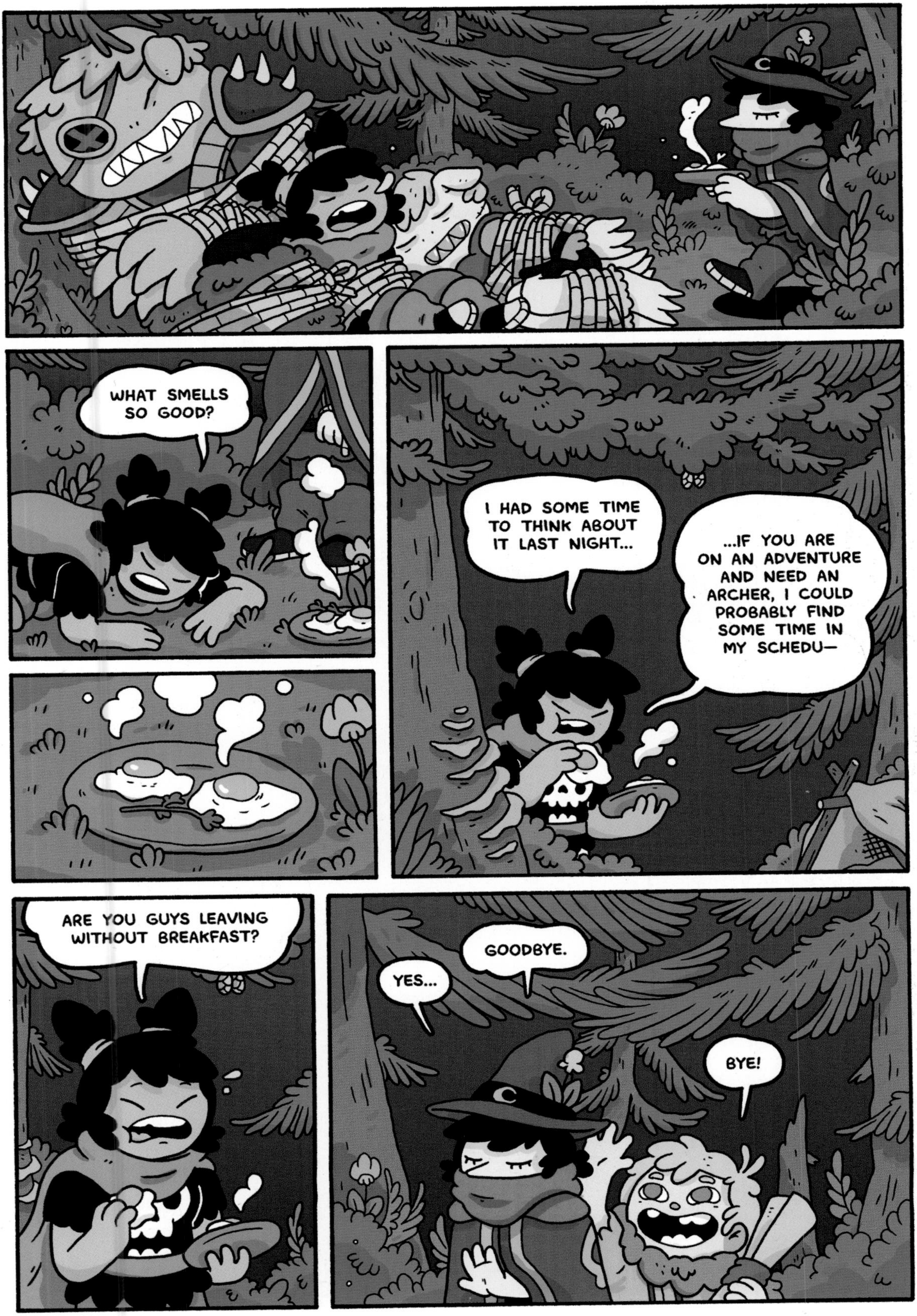
WHAT SMELLS SO GOOD?
I HAD SOME TIME TO THINK ABOUT IT LAST NIGHT...
...IF YOU ARE ON AN ADVENTURE AND NEED AN ARCHER, I COULD PROBABLY FIND SOME TIME IN MY SCHEDU—
ARE YOU GUYS LEAVING WITHOUT BREAKFAST?
YES...
GOODBYE.
BYE!

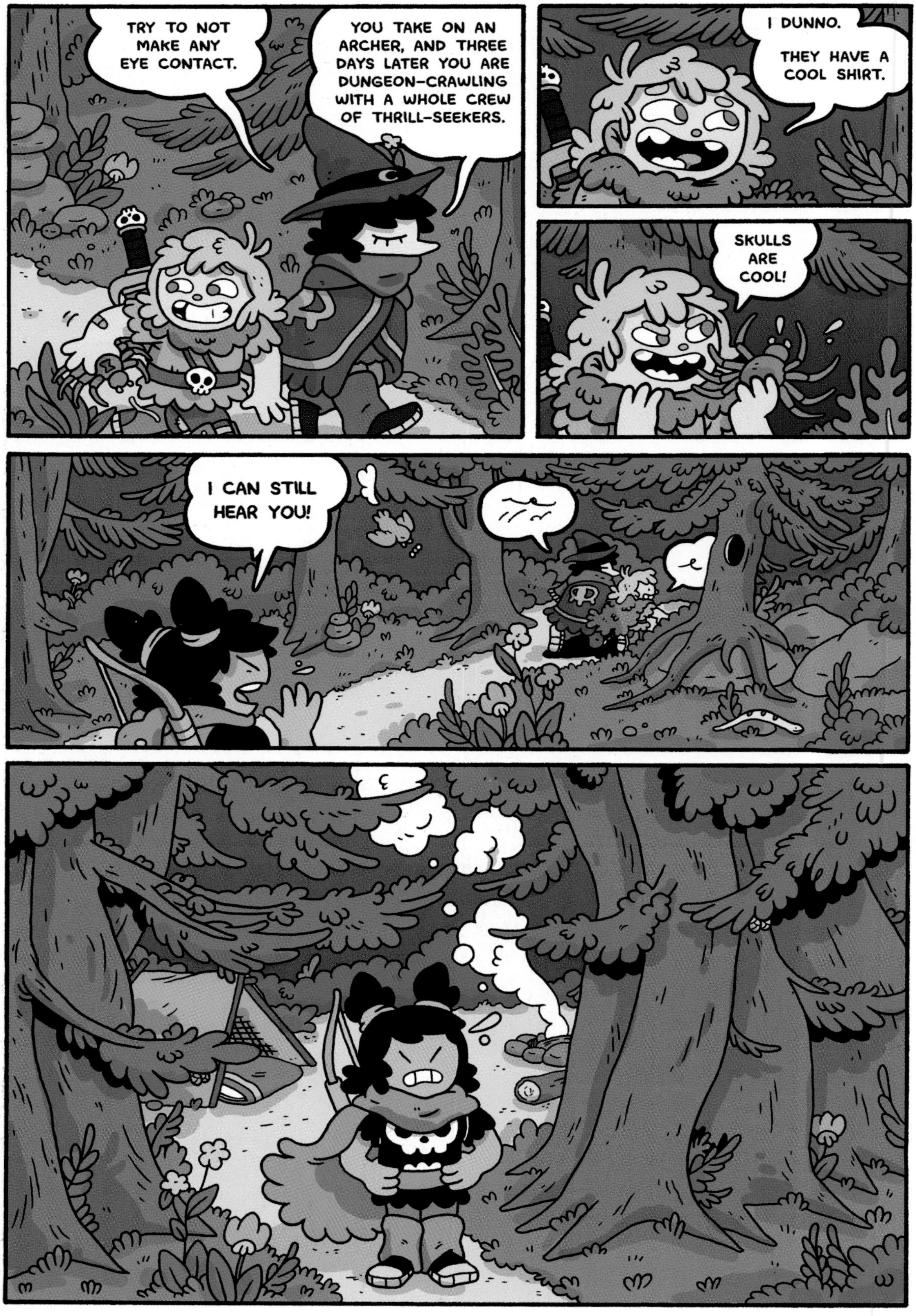
TRY TO NOT MAKE ANY EYE CONTACT.
YOU TAKE ON AN ARCHER, AND THREE DAYS LATER YOU ARE DUNGEON-CRAWLING WITH A WHOLE CREW OF THRILL-SEEKERS.
I DUNNO.
THEY HAVE A COOL SHIRT.
SKULLS ARE COOL!
I CAN STILL HEAR YOU!

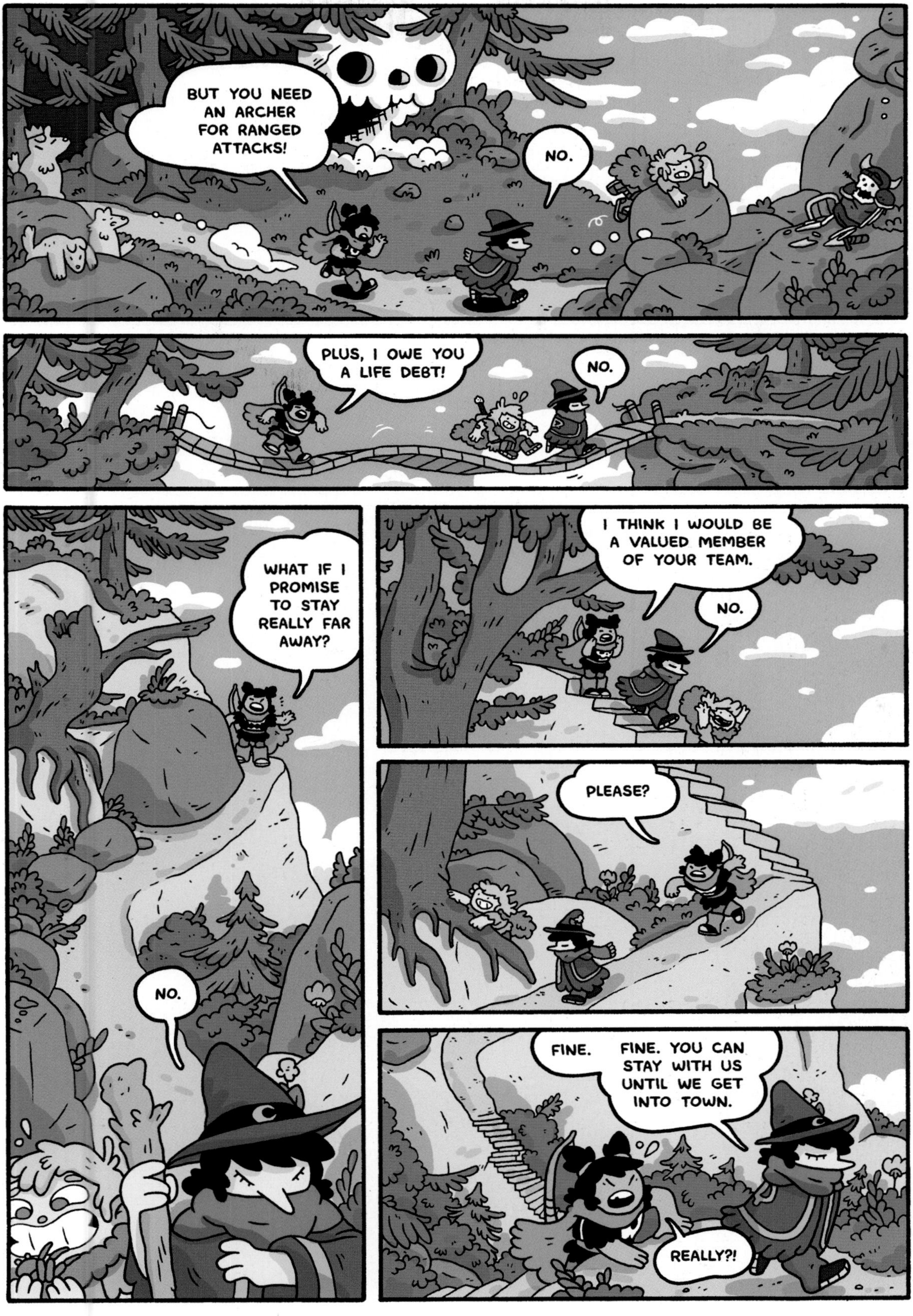
BUT YOU NEED AN ARCHER FOR RANGED ATTACKS!
NO.
PLUS, I OWE YOU A LIFE DEBT!
NO.
WHAT IF I PROMISE TO STAY REALLY FAR AWAY?
NO.
I THINK I WOULD BE A VALUED MEMBER OF YOUR TEAM.
NO.
PLEASE?
FINE.
FINE. YOU CAN STAY WITH US UNTIL WE GET INTO TOWN.
REALLY?!

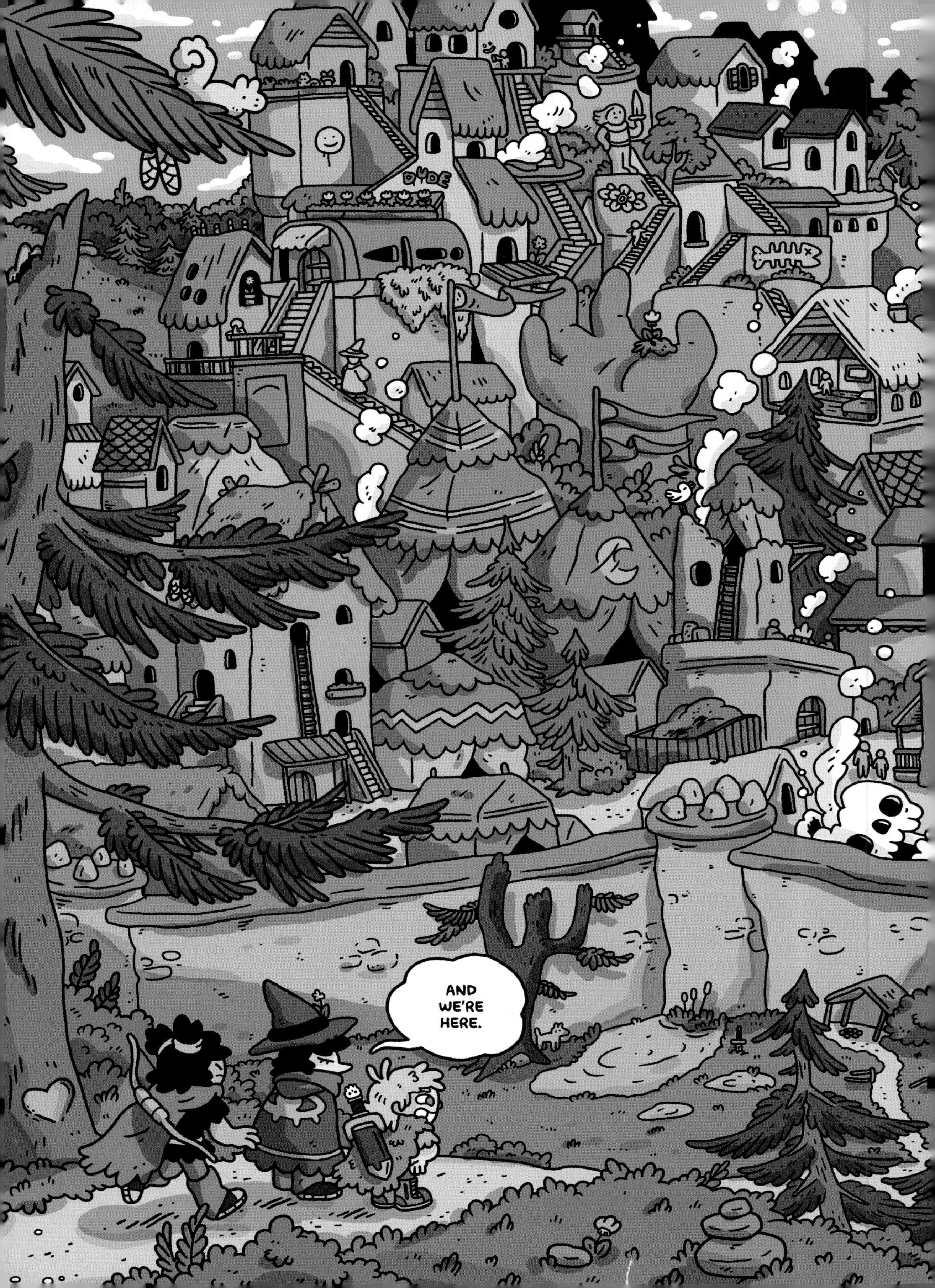
DUDE
AND WE'RE HERE.

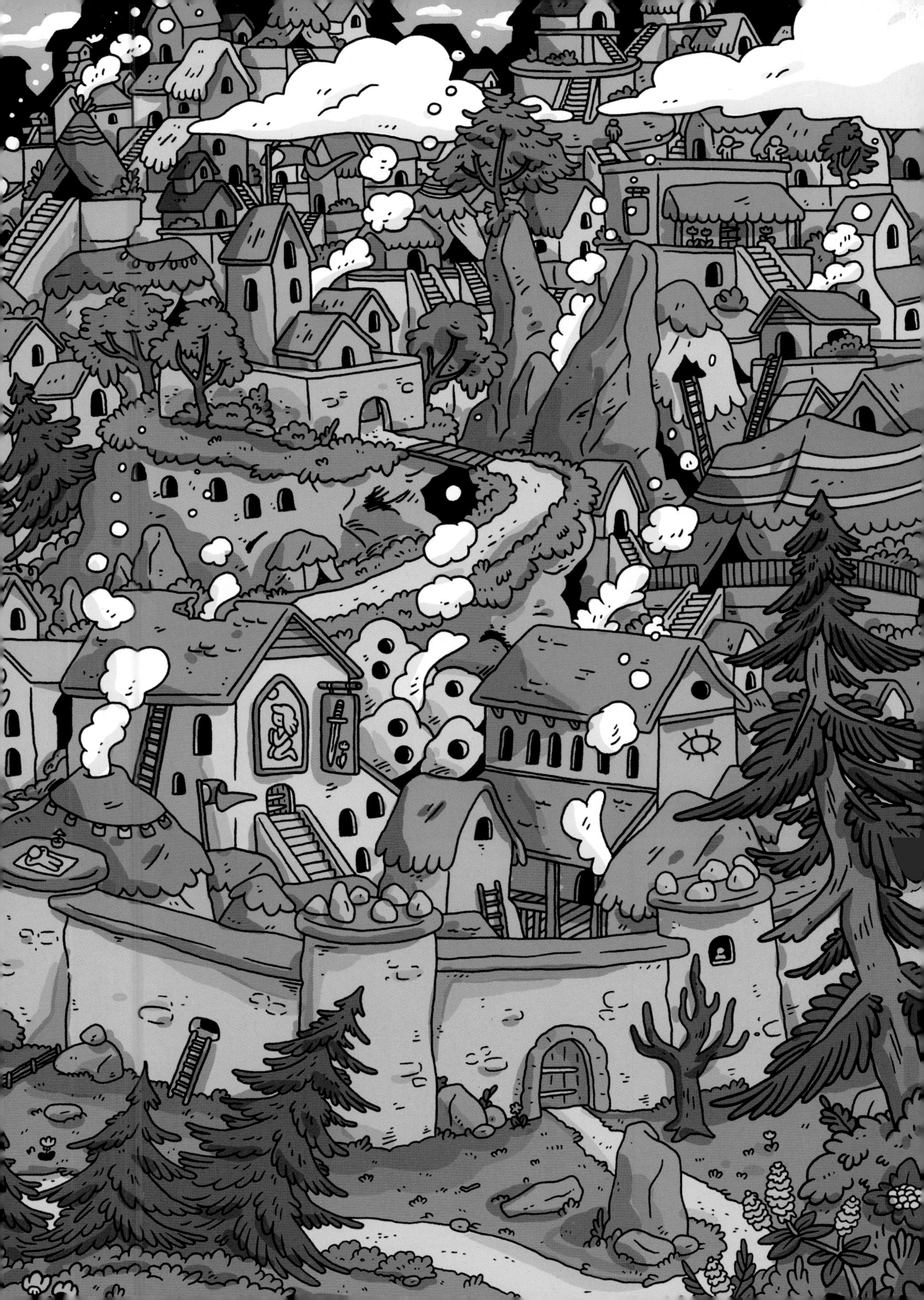

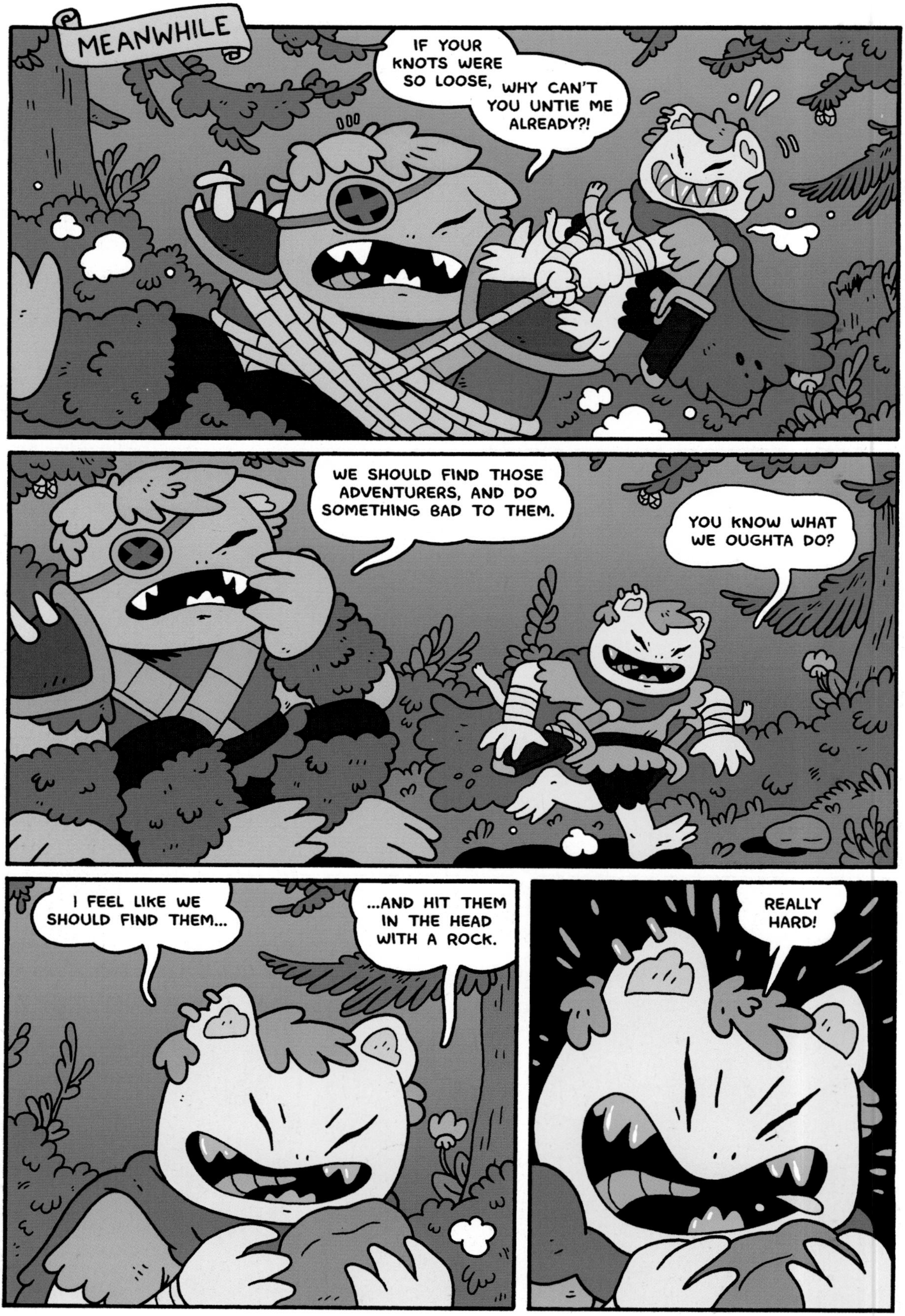
MEANWHILE
IF YOUR KNOTS WERE SO LOOSE,
WHY CAN'T YOU UNTIE ME ALREADY?!
WE SHOULD FIND THOSE ADVENTURERS, AND DO SOMETHING BAD TO THEM.
YOU KNOW WHAT WE OUGHTA DO?
I FEEL LIKE WE SHOULD FIND THEM...
...AND HIT THEM IN THE HEAD WITH A ROCK.
REALLY HARD!

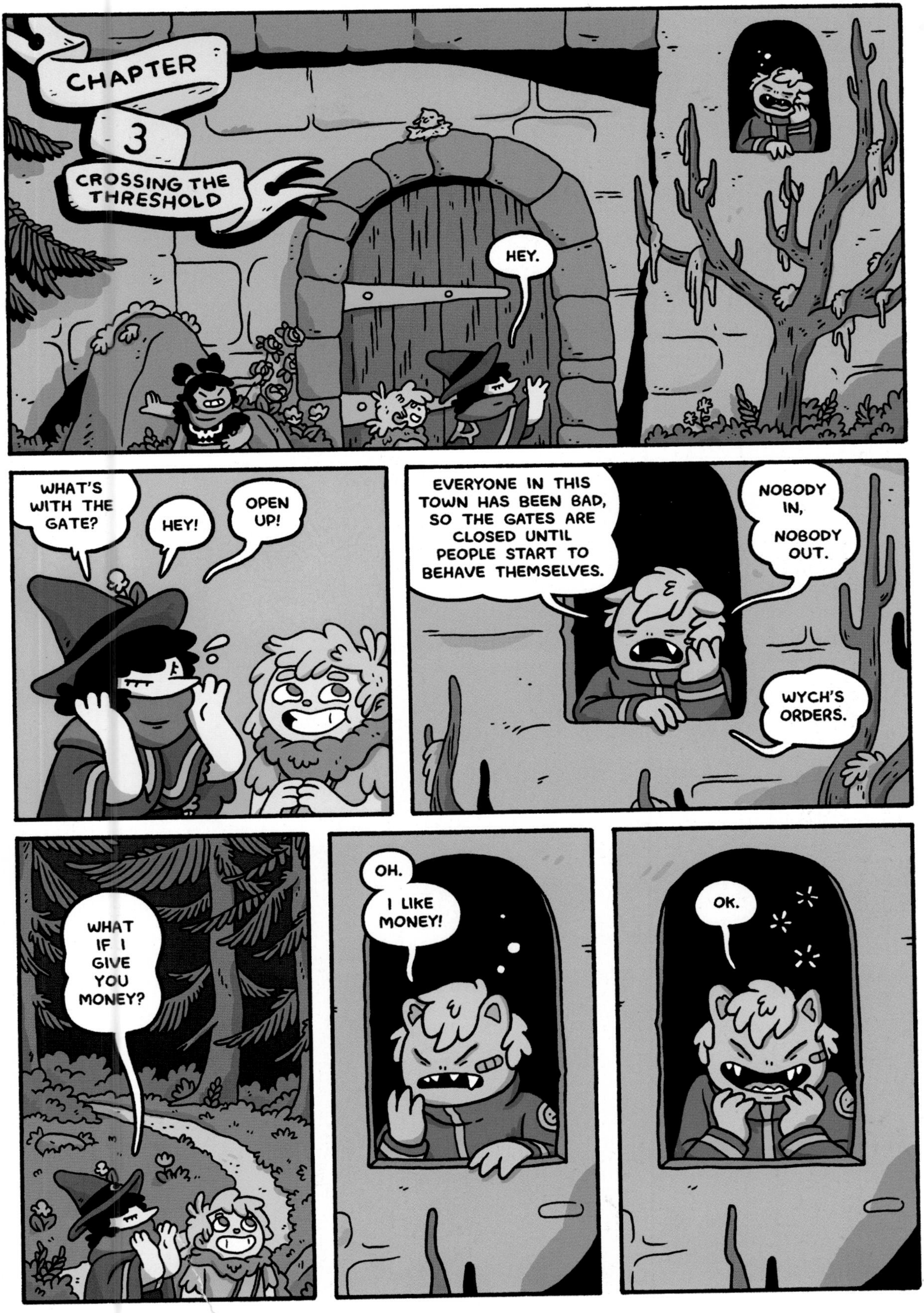

CHAPTER 3
CROSSING THE THRESHOLD
HEY.
WHAT'S WITH THE GATE?
HEY!
OPEN UP!
EVERYONE IN THIS TOWN HAS BEEN BAD, SO THE GATES ARE CLOSED UNTIL PEOPLE START TO BEHAVE THEMSELVES.
NOBODY IN,
NOBODY OUT.
WYCH'S ORDERS.
WHAT IF I GIVE YOU MONEY?
OH.
I LIKE MONEY!
OK.

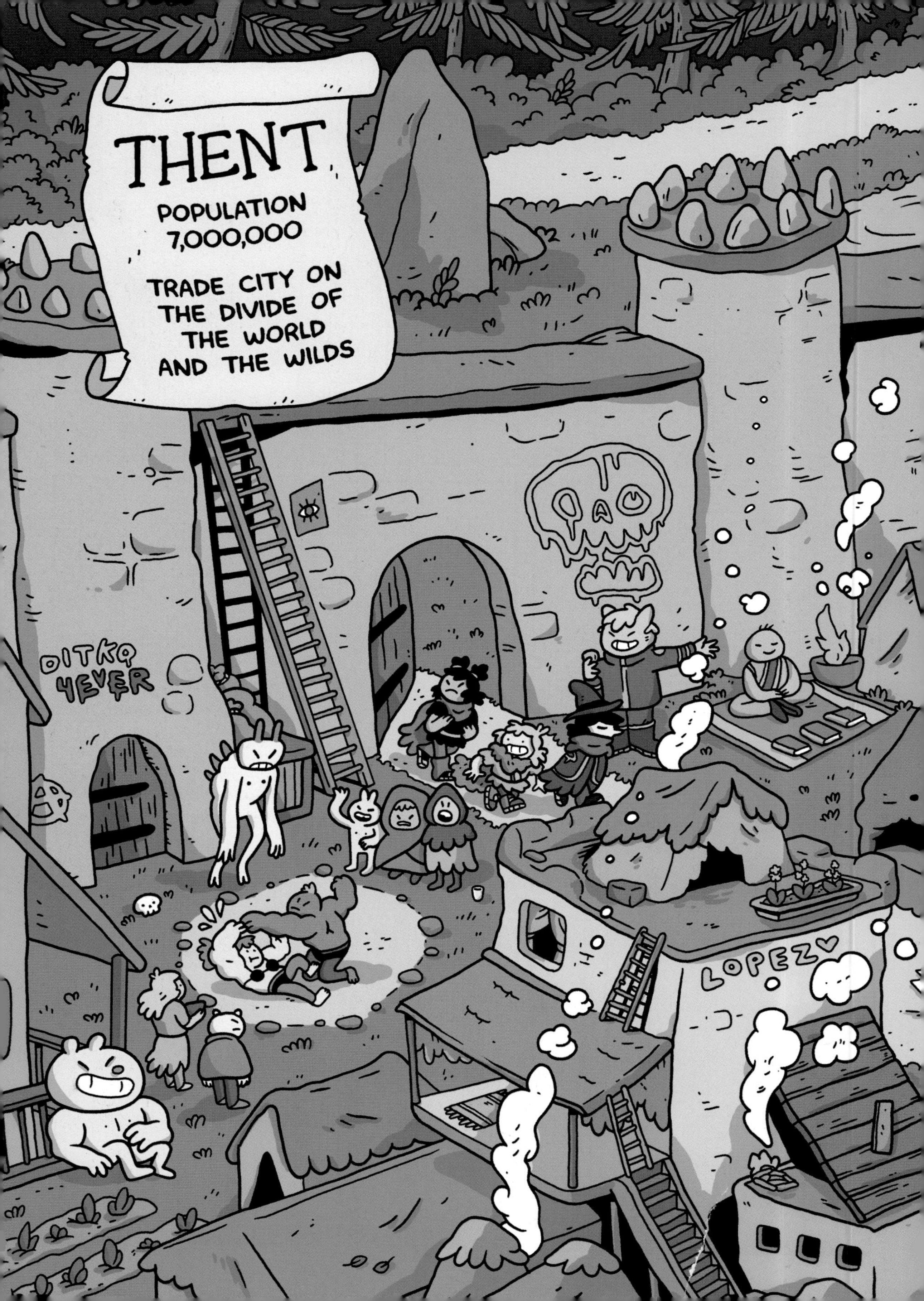
THENT
POPULATION
7,000,000
TRADE CITY ON
THE DIVIDE OF
THE WORLD
AND THE WILDS
DITKO
4EVER
LOPEZ

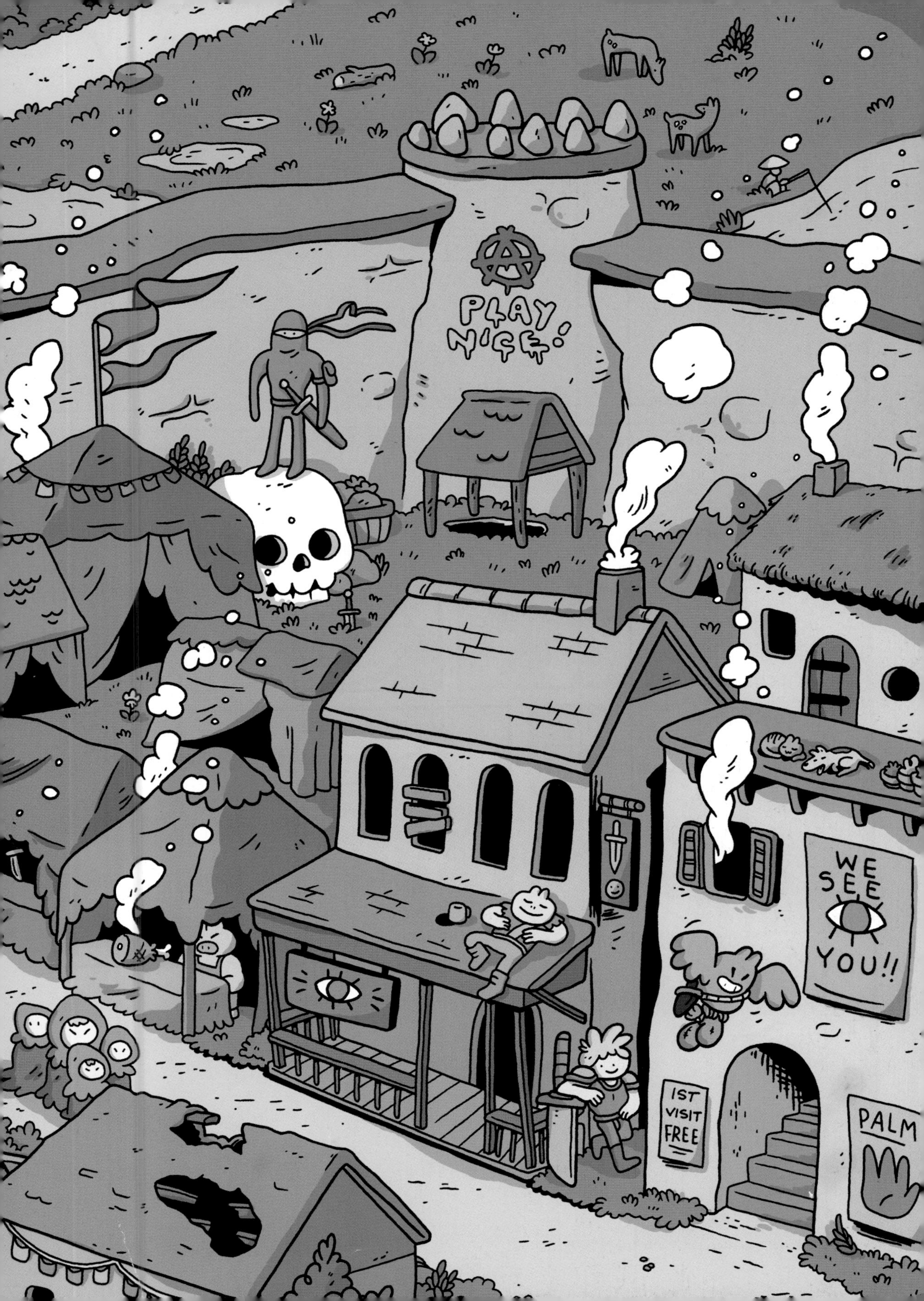
PLAY NICE!
WE SEE YOU!!
1ST VISIT FREE
PALM

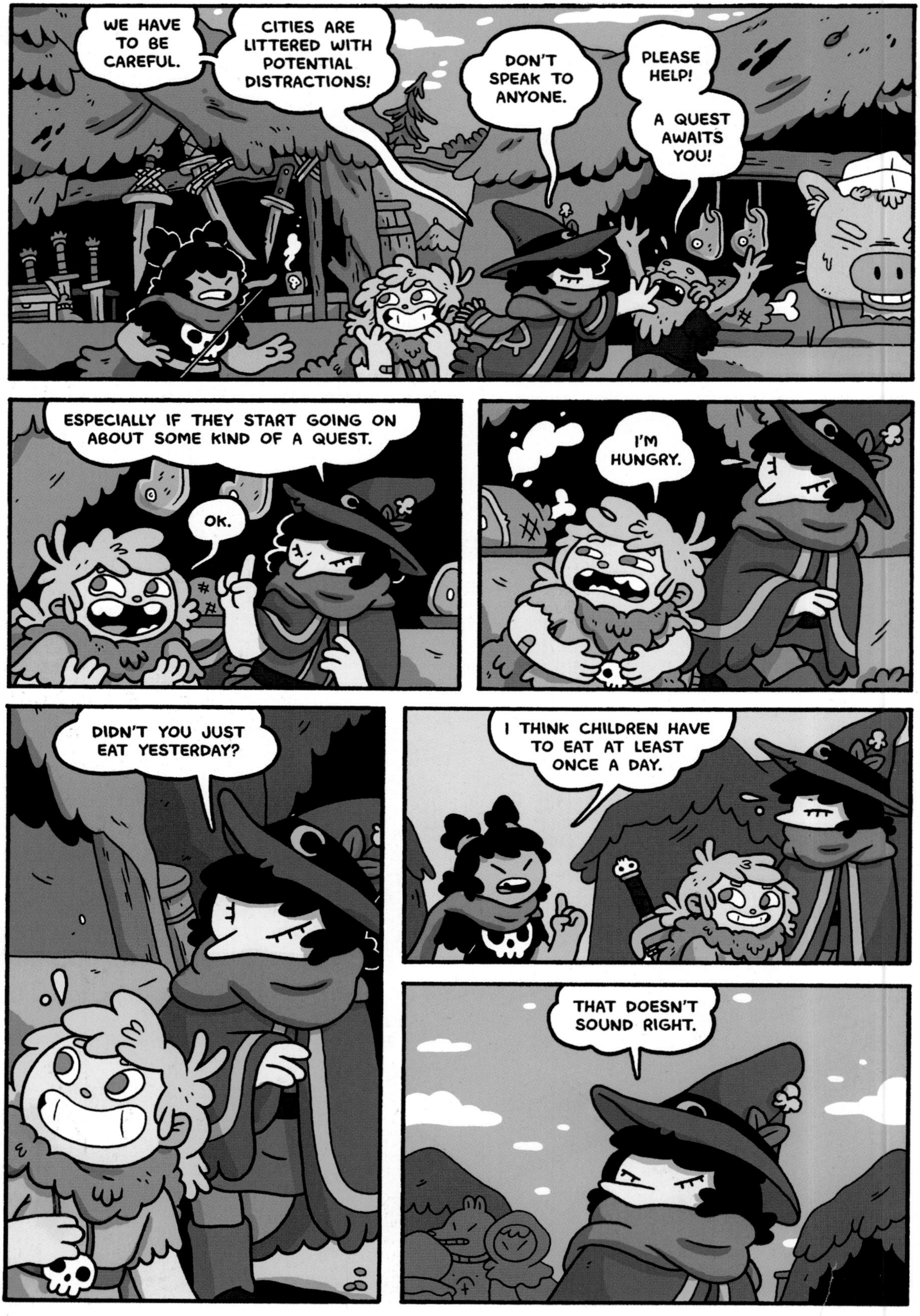
WE HAVE TO BE CAREFUL.
CITIES ARE LITTERED WITH POTENTIAL DISTRACTIONS!
DON'T SPEAK TO ANYONE.
PLEASE HELP!
A QUEST AWAITS YOU!
ESPECIALLY IF THEY START GOING ON ABOUT SOME KIND OF A QUEST.
OK.
I'M HUNGRY.
DIDN'T YOU JUST EAT YESTERDAY?
I THINK CHILDREN HAVE TO EAT AT LEAST ONCE A DAY.
THAT DOESN'T SOUND RIGHT.

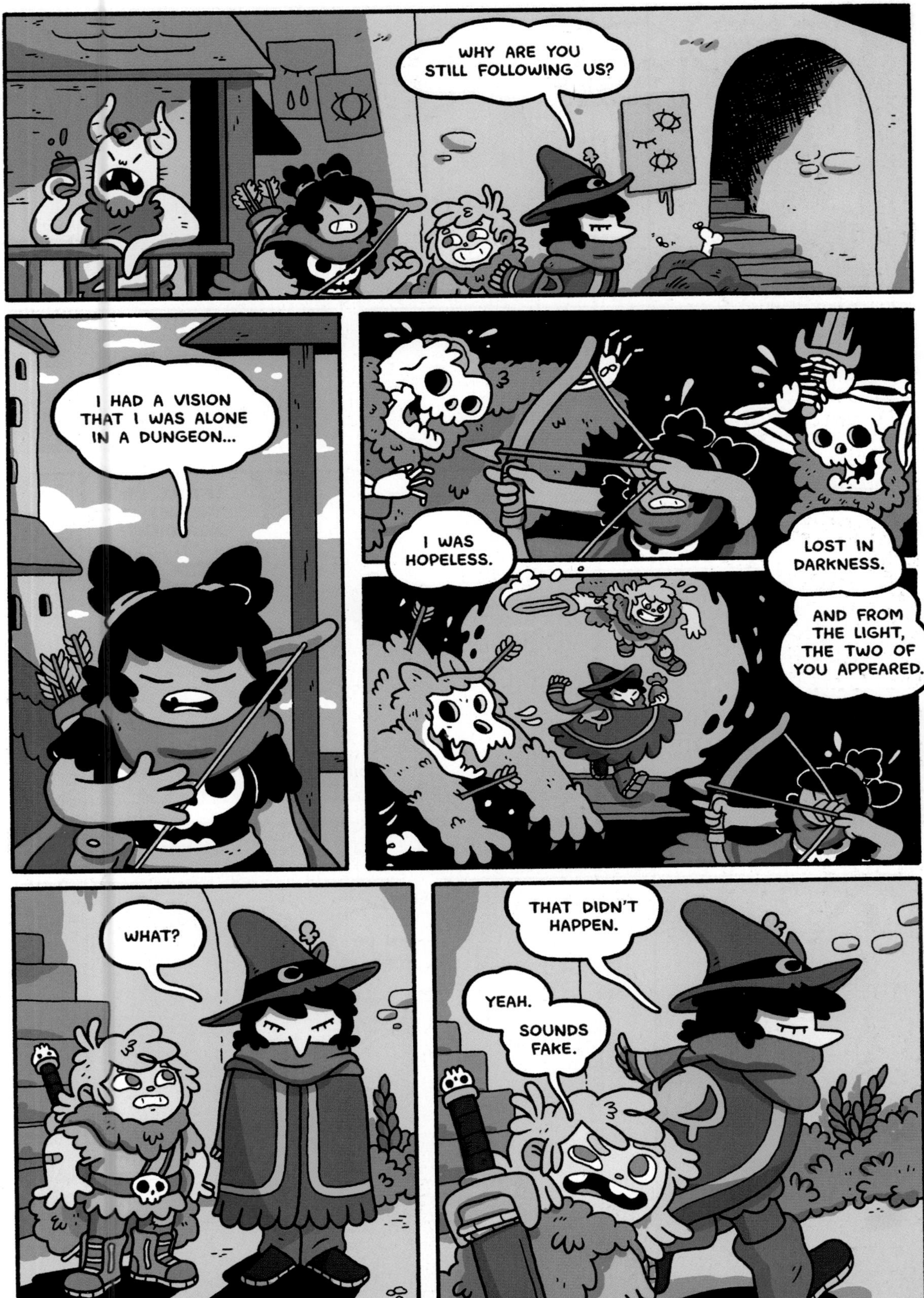
WHY ARE YOU STILL FOLLOWING US?
I HAD A VISION THAT I WAS ALONE IN A DUNGEON...
I WAS HOPELESS.
LOST IN DARKNESS.
AND FROM THE LIGHT, THE TWO OF YOU APPEARED.
WHAT?
THAT DIDN'T HAPPEN.
YEAH.
SOUNDS FAKE.

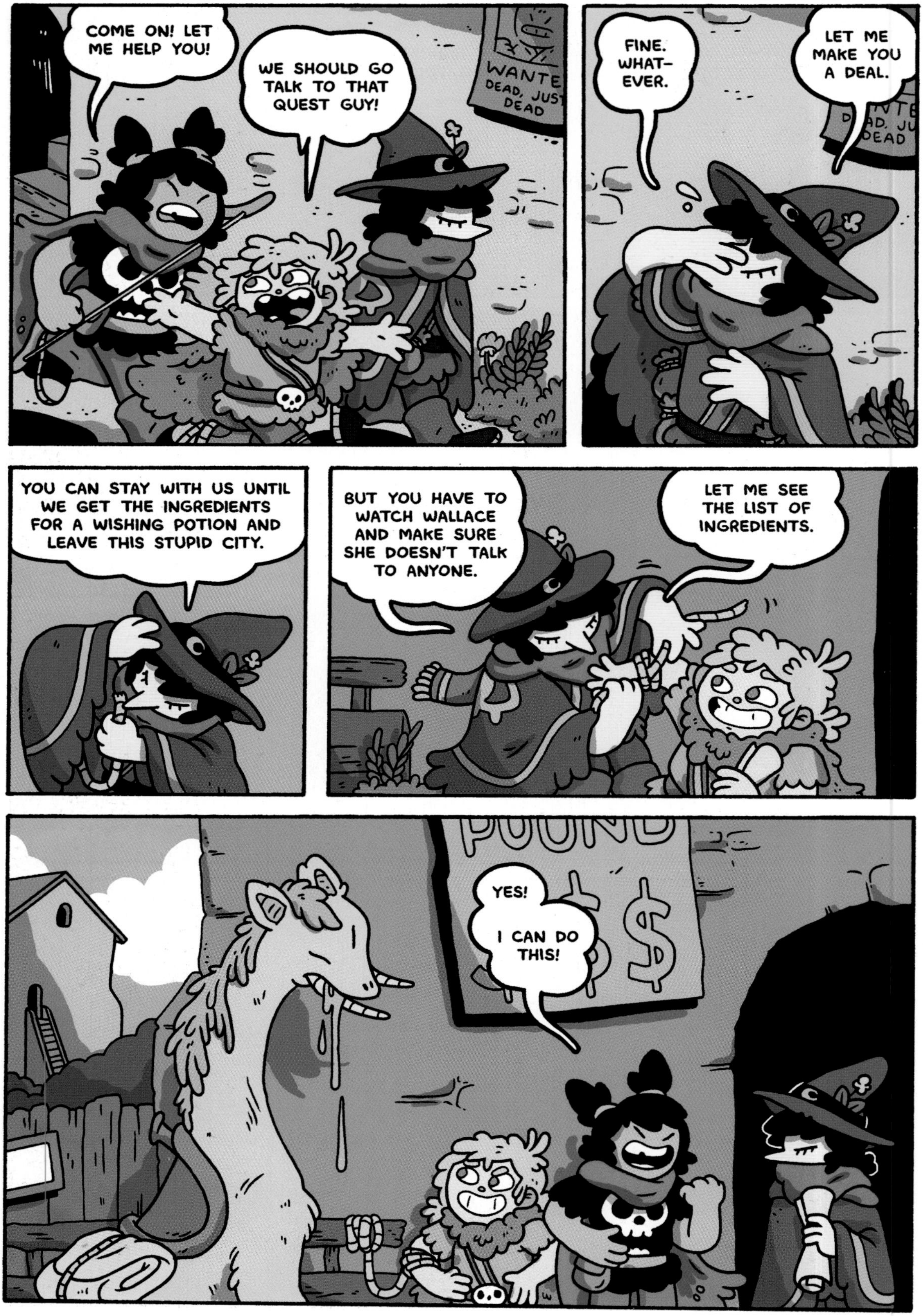
WANTED DEAD, JUST DEAD
COME ON! LET ME HELP YOU!
WE SHOULD GO TALK TO THAT QUEST GUY!
FINE. WHAT-EVER.
LET ME MAKE YOU A DEAL.
YOU CAN STAY WITH US UNTIL WE GET THE INGREDIENTS FOR A WISHING POTION AND LEAVE THIS STUPID CITY.
BUT YOU HAVE TO WATCH WALLACE AND MAKE SURE SHE DOESN'T TALK TO ANYONE.
LET ME SEE THE LIST OF INGREDIENTS.
POUND
$ $
YES!
I CAN DO THIS!

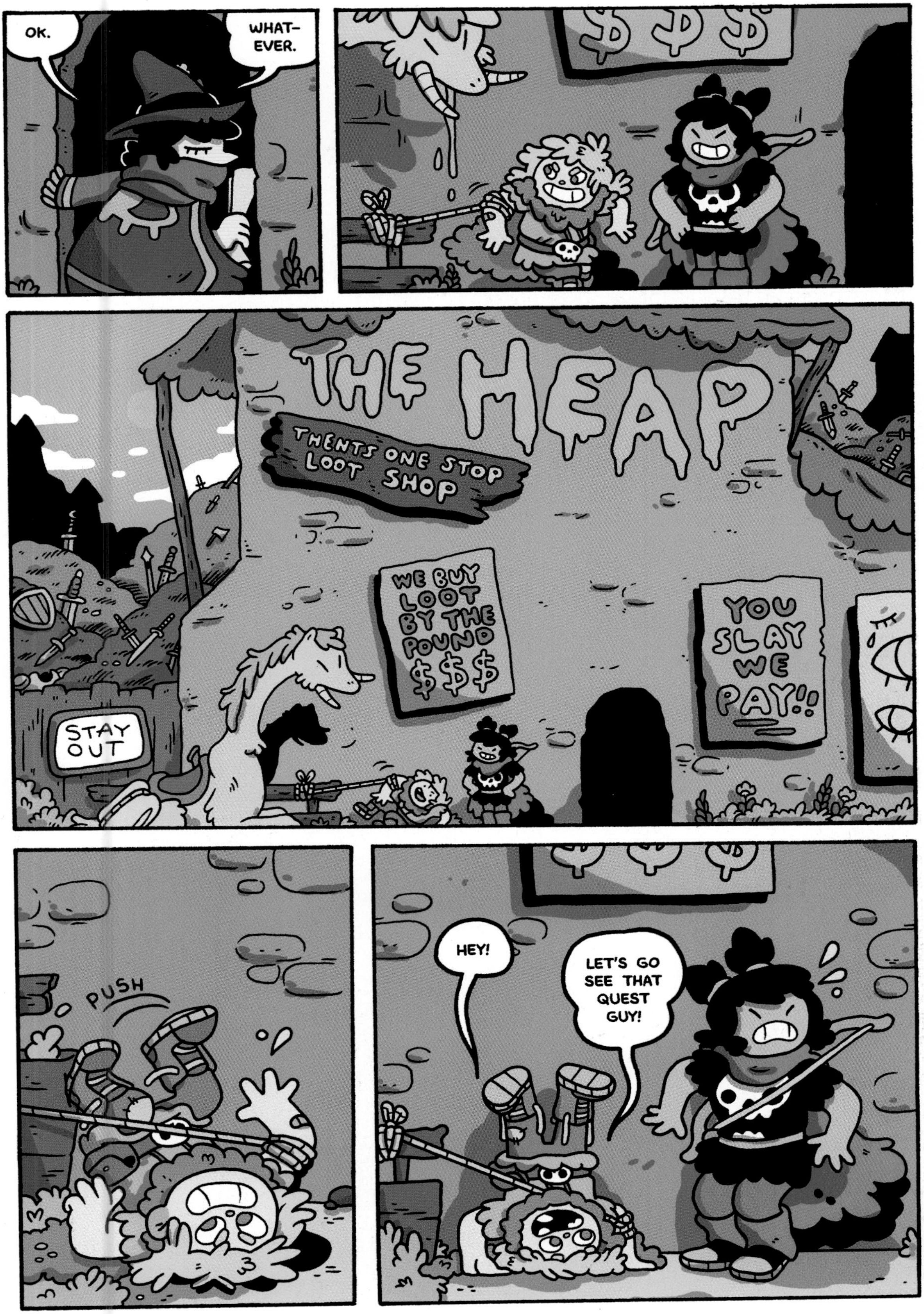
OK.
WHAT-EVER.
$ $ $
THE HEAP
THENTS ONE STOP LOOT SHOP
WE BUY LOOT BY THE POUND $$$
YOU SLAY WE PAY!!
STAY OUT
PUSH
HEY!
LET'S GO SEE THAT QUEST GUY!

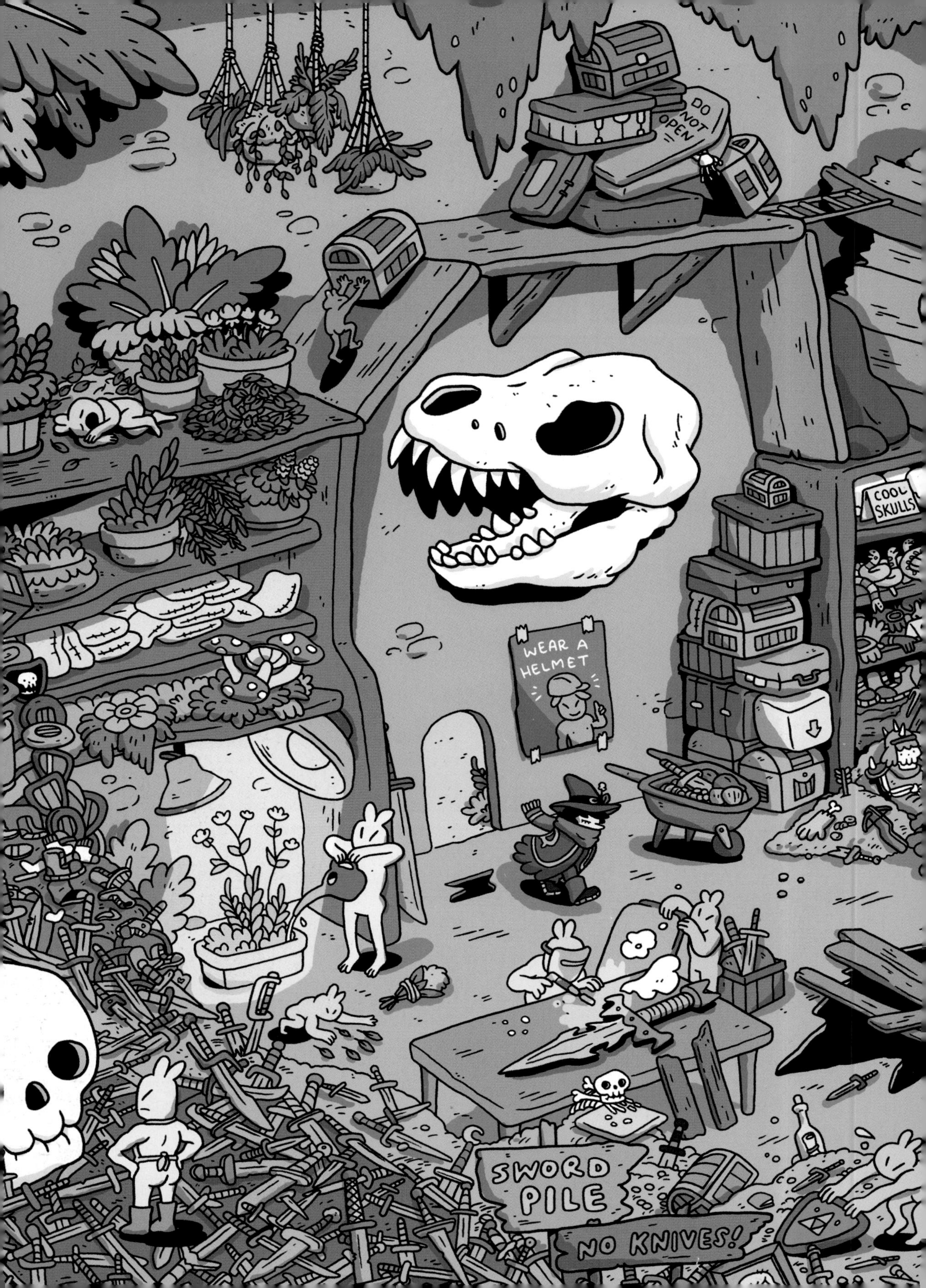
DO NOT OPEN
COOL SKULLS
WEAR A HELMET
SWORD PILE
NO KNIVES!

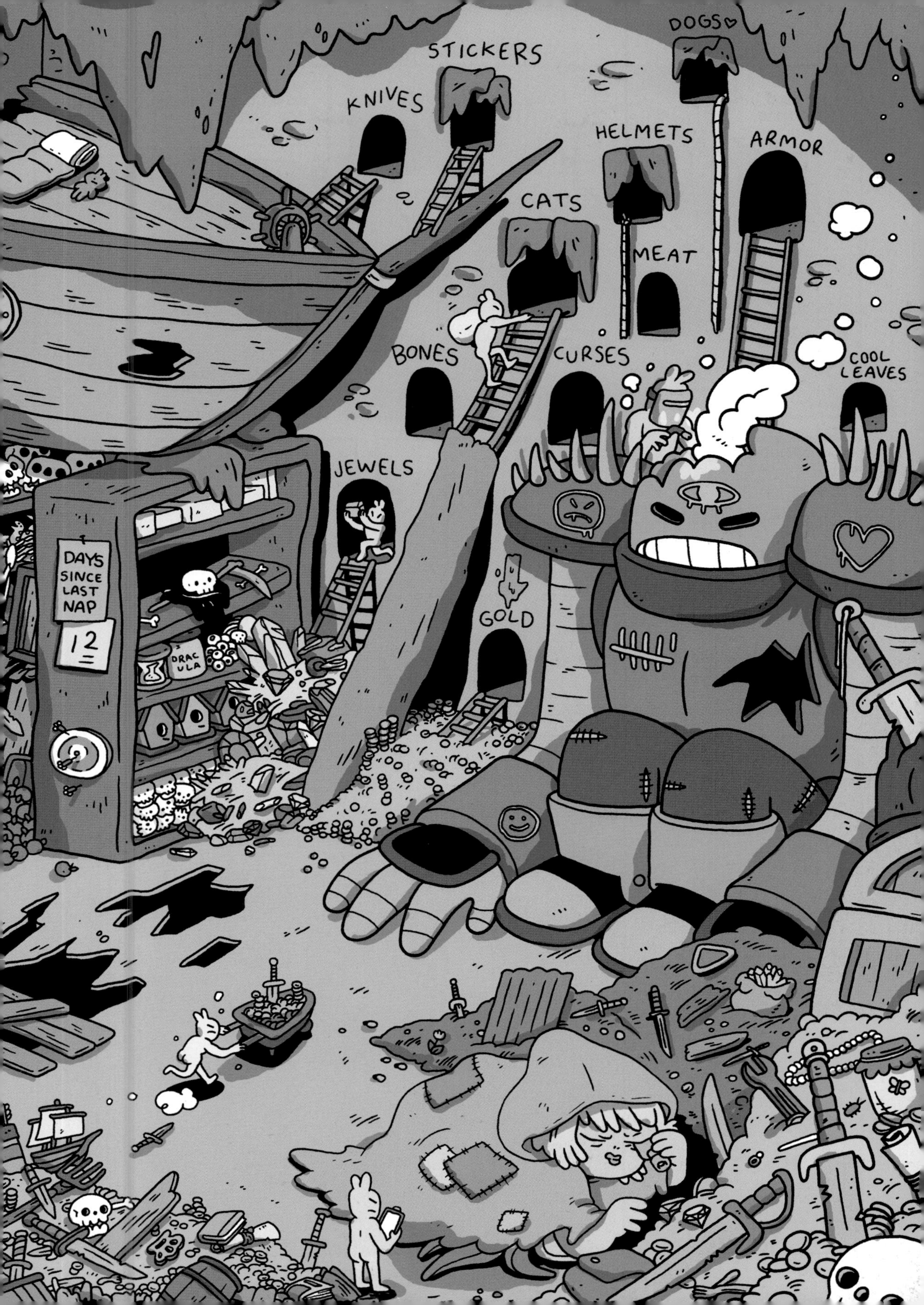

DOGS
STICKERS
KNIVES
HELMETS
ARMOR
CATS
MEAT
BONES
CURSES
COOL LEAVES
JEWELS
GOLD
DAYS SINCE LAST NAP
12
DRAC ULA

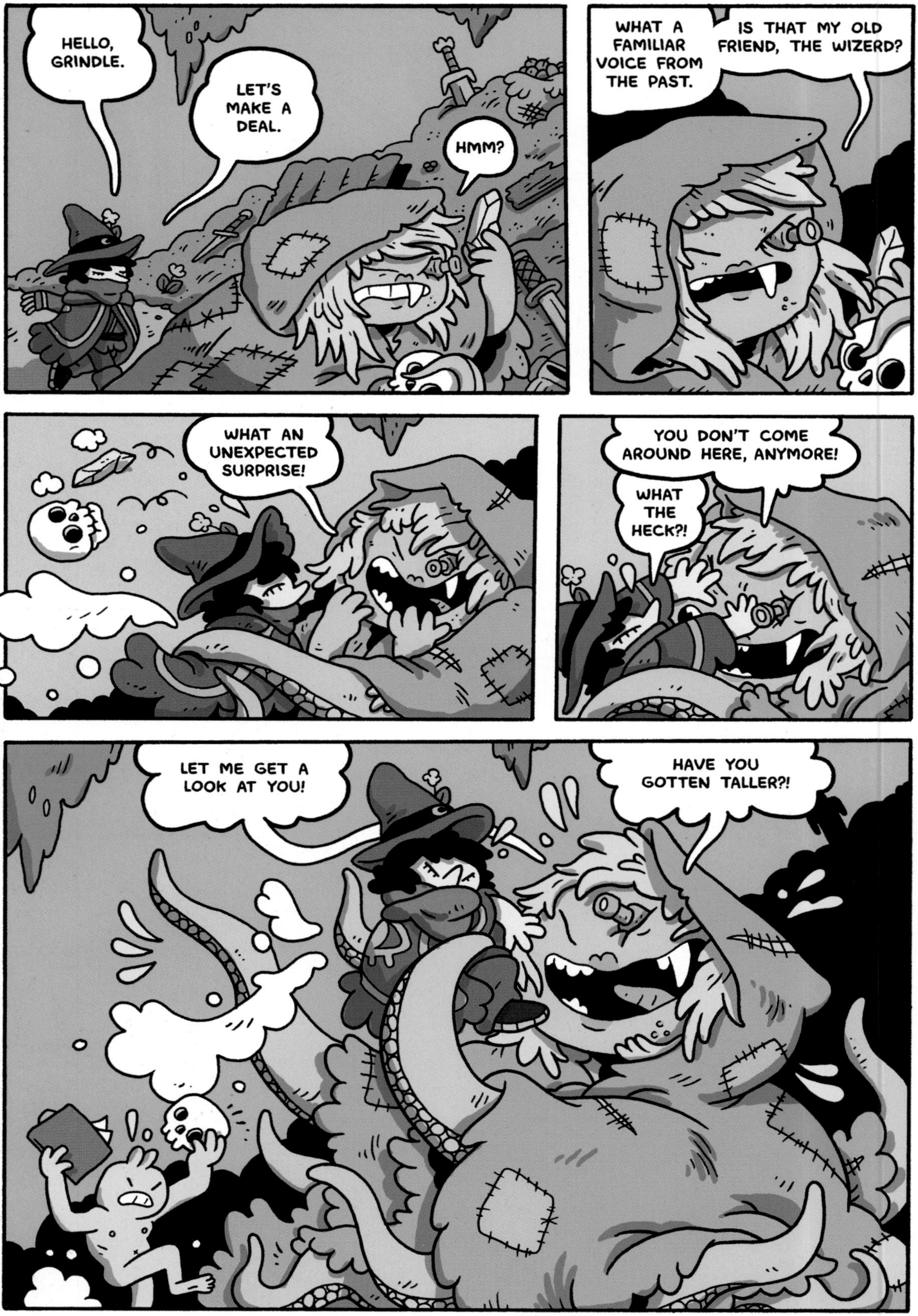

HELLO, GRINDLE.
LET'S MAKE A DEAL.
HMM?
WHAT A FAMILIAR VOICE FROM THE PAST.
IS THAT MY OLD FRIEND, THE WIZERD?
WHAT AN UNEXPECTED SURPRISE!
YOU DON'T COME AROUND HERE, ANYMORE!
WHAT THE HECK?!
LET ME GET A LOOK AT YOU!
HAVE YOU GOTTEN TALLER?!

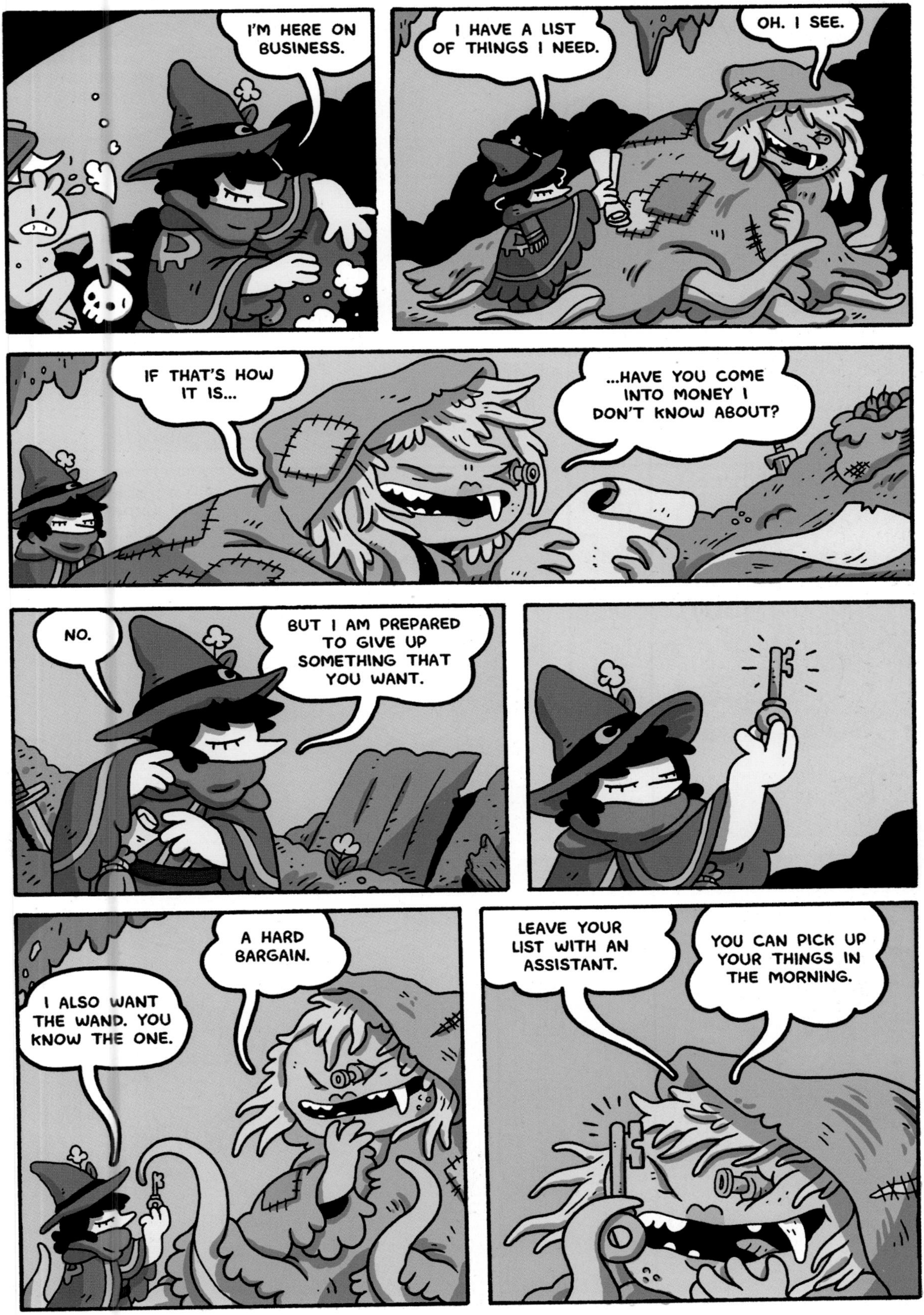

I'M HERE ON BUSINESS.
I HAVE A LIST OF THINGS I NEED.
OH. I SEE.
IF THAT'S HOW IT IS...
...HAVE YOU COME INTO MONEY I DON'T KNOW ABOUT?
NO.
BUT I AM PREPARED TO GIVE UP SOMETHING THAT YOU WANT.
I ALSO WANT THE WAND. YOU KNOW THE ONE.
A HARD BARGAIN.
LEAVE YOUR LIST WITH AN ASSISTANT.
YOU CAN PICK UP YOUR THINGS IN THE MORNING.

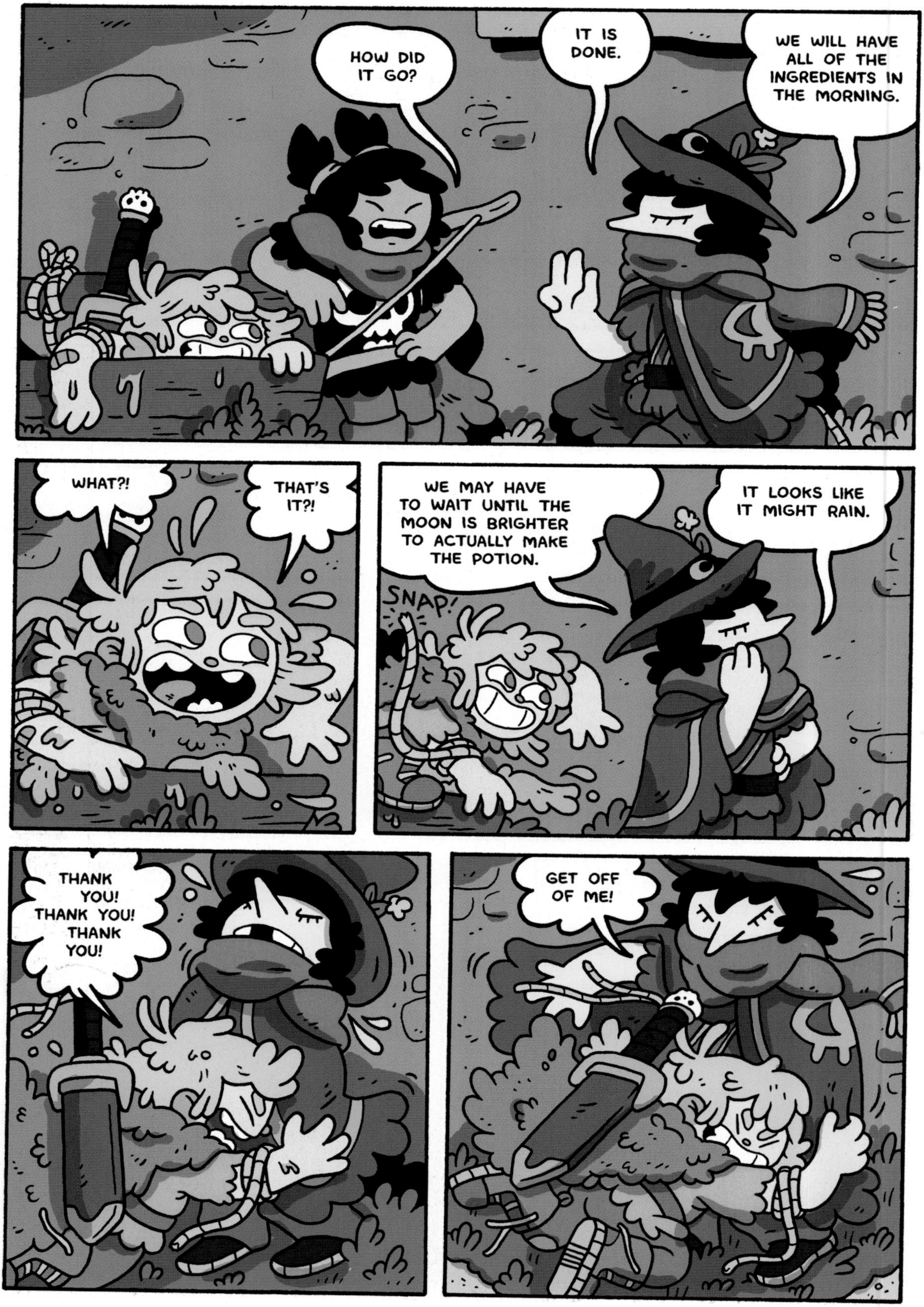
HOW DID IT GO?
IT IS DONE.
WE WILL HAVE ALL OF THE INGREDIENTS IN THE MORNING.
WHAT?!
THAT'S IT?!
WE MAY HAVE TO WAIT UNTIL THE MOON IS BRIGHTER TO ACTUALLY MAKE THE POTION.
SNAP!
IT LOOKS LIKE IT MIGHT RAIN.
THANK YOU! THANK YOU! THANK YOU!
GET OFF OF ME!

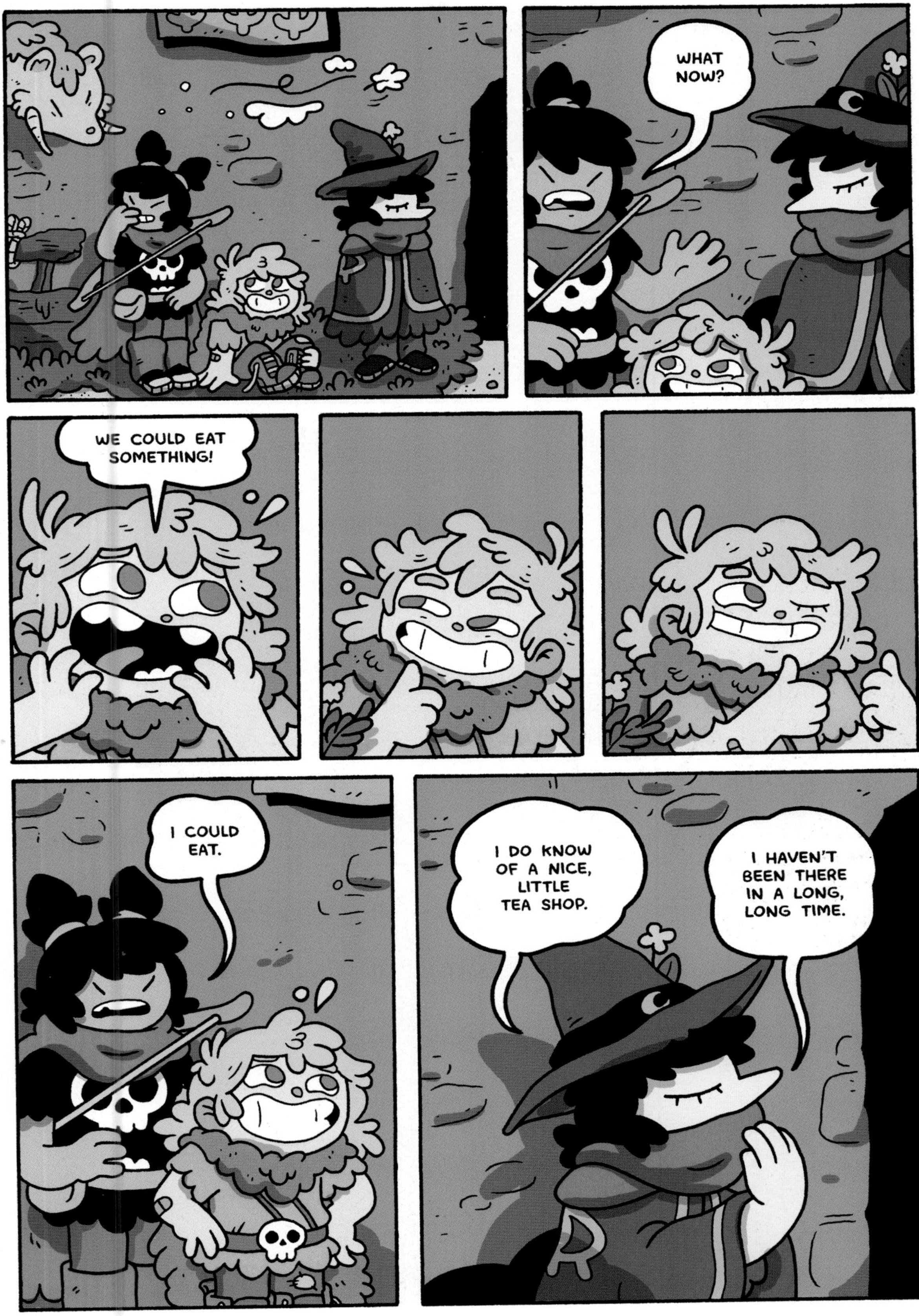
WHAT NOW?
WE COULD EAT SOMETHING!
I COULD EAT.
I DO KNOW OF A NICE, LITTLE TEA SHOP.
I HAVEN'T BEEN THERE IN A LONG, LONG TIME.

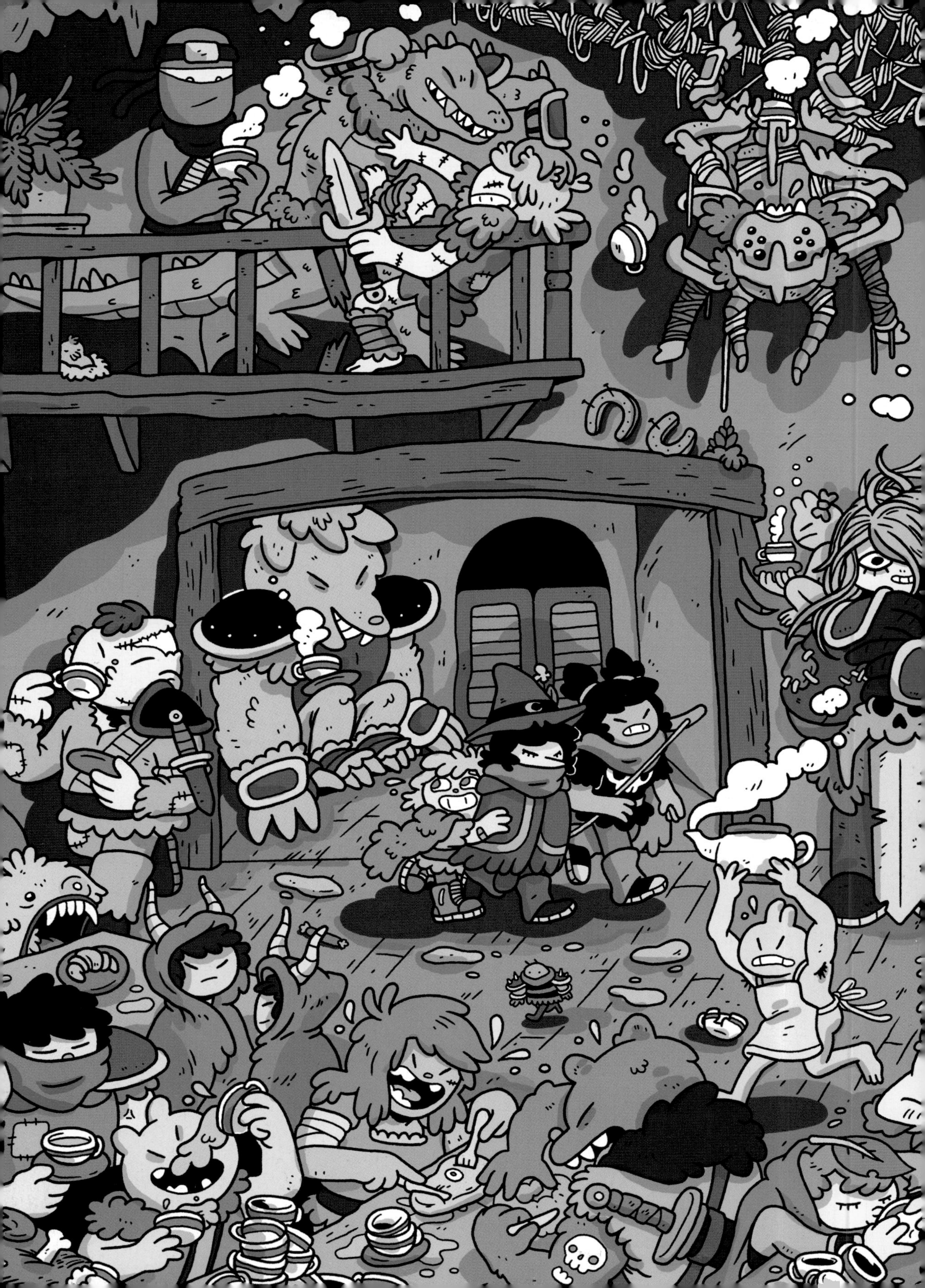

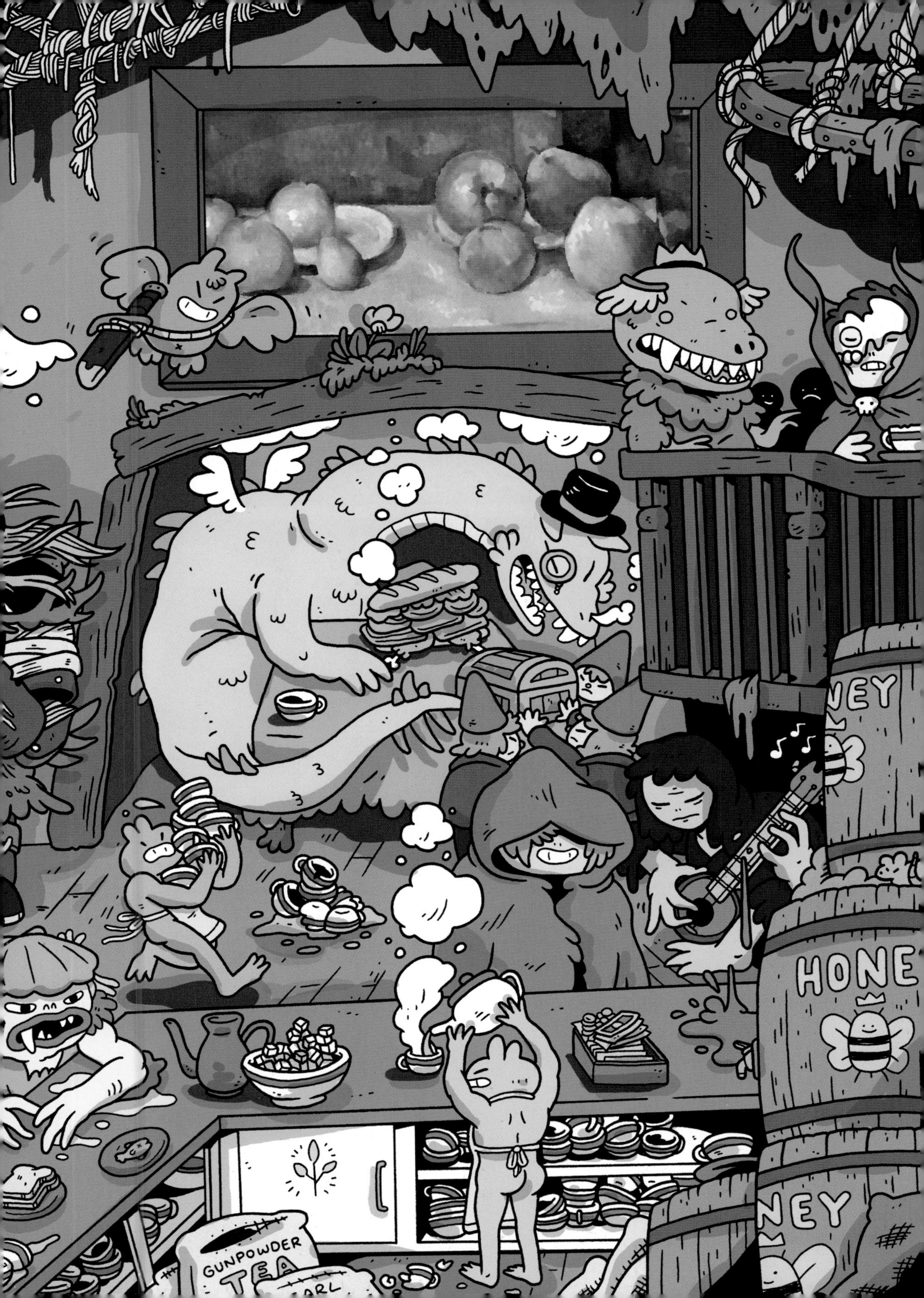
NEY
HONE
NEY
GUNPOWDER TEA
ARL

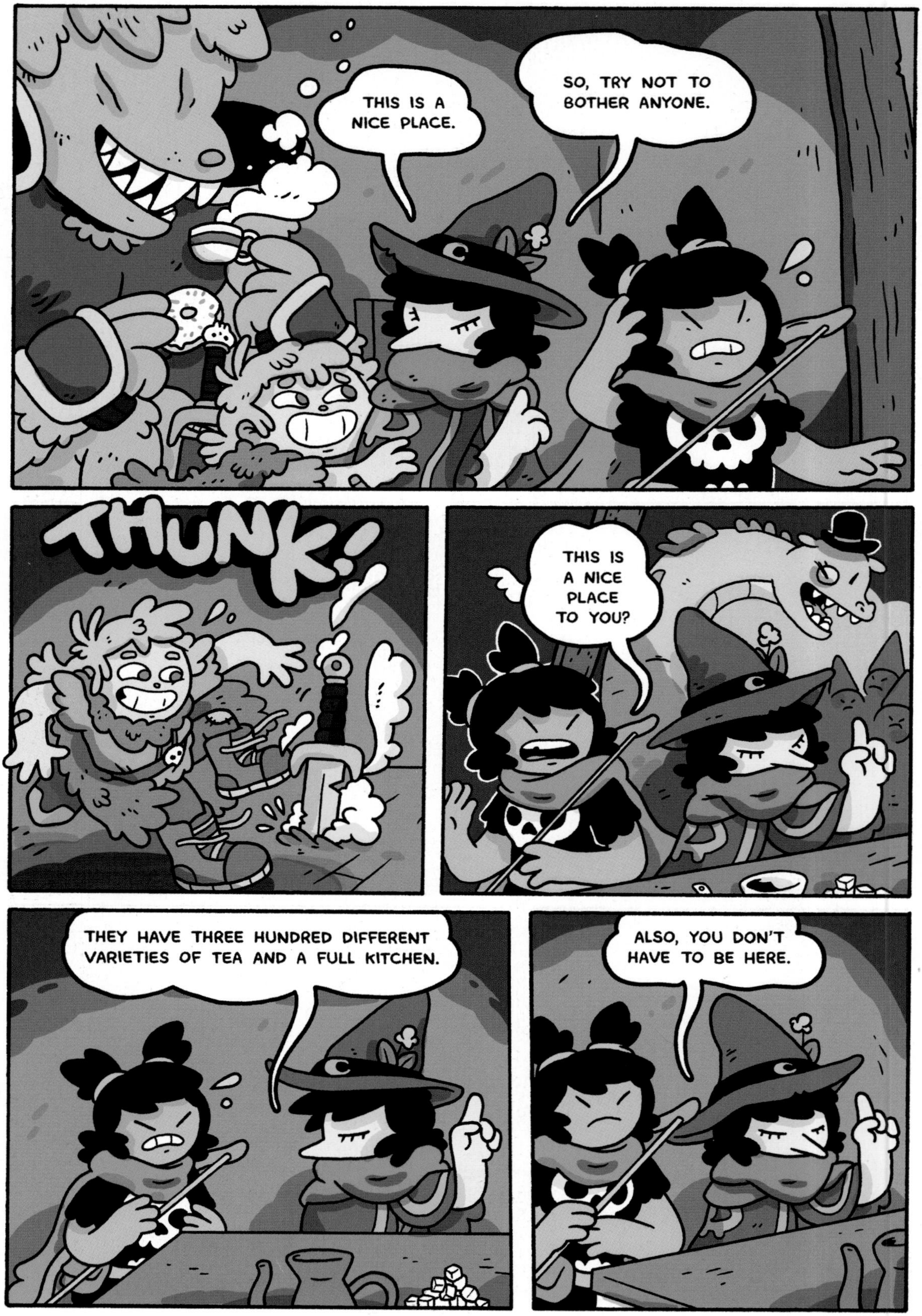
THIS IS A NICE PLACE.
SO, TRY NOT TO BOTHER ANYONE.
THUNK!
THIS IS A NICE PLACE TO YOU?
THEY HAVE THREE HUNDRED DIFFERENT VARIETIES OF TEA AND A FULL KITCHEN.
ALSO, YOU DON'T HAVE TO BE HERE.

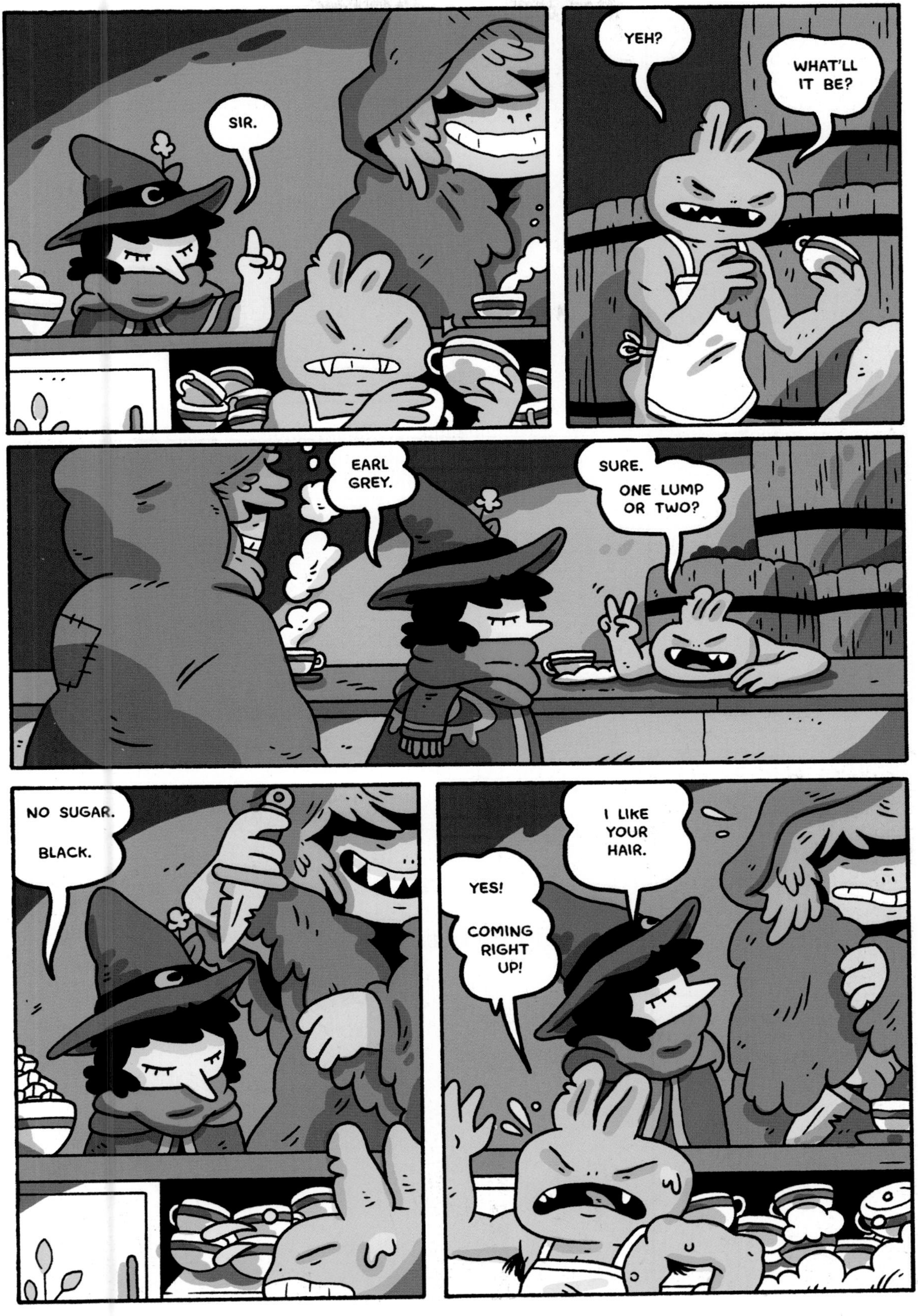
SIR.
YEH?
WHAT'LL IT BE?
EARL GREY.
SURE.
ONE LUMP OR TWO?
NO SUGAR.
BLACK.
I LIKE YOUR HAIR.
YES!
COMING RIGHT UP!

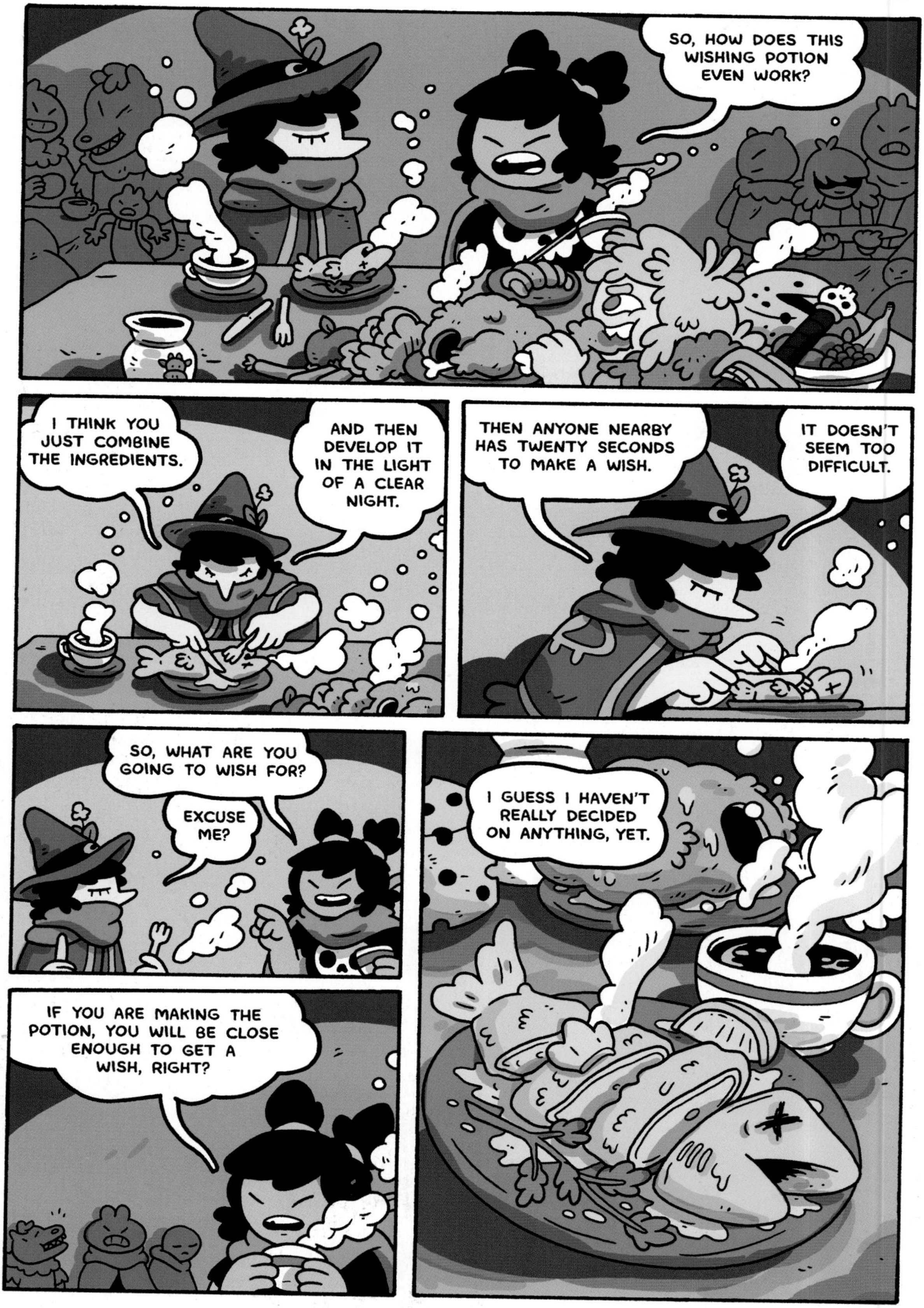
SO, HOW DOES THIS WISHING POTION EVEN WORK?
I THINK YOU JUST COMBINE THE INGREDIENTS.
AND THEN DEVELOP IT IN THE LIGHT OF A CLEAR NIGHT.
THEN ANYONE NEARBY HAS TWENTY SECONDS TO MAKE A WISH.
IT DOESN'T SEEM TOO DIFFICULT.
SO, WHAT ARE YOU GOING TO WISH FOR?
EXCUSE ME?
IF YOU ARE MAKING THE POTION, YOU WILL BE CLOSE ENOUGH TO GET A WISH, RIGHT?
I GUESS I HAVEN'T REALLY DECIDED ON ANYTHING, YET.

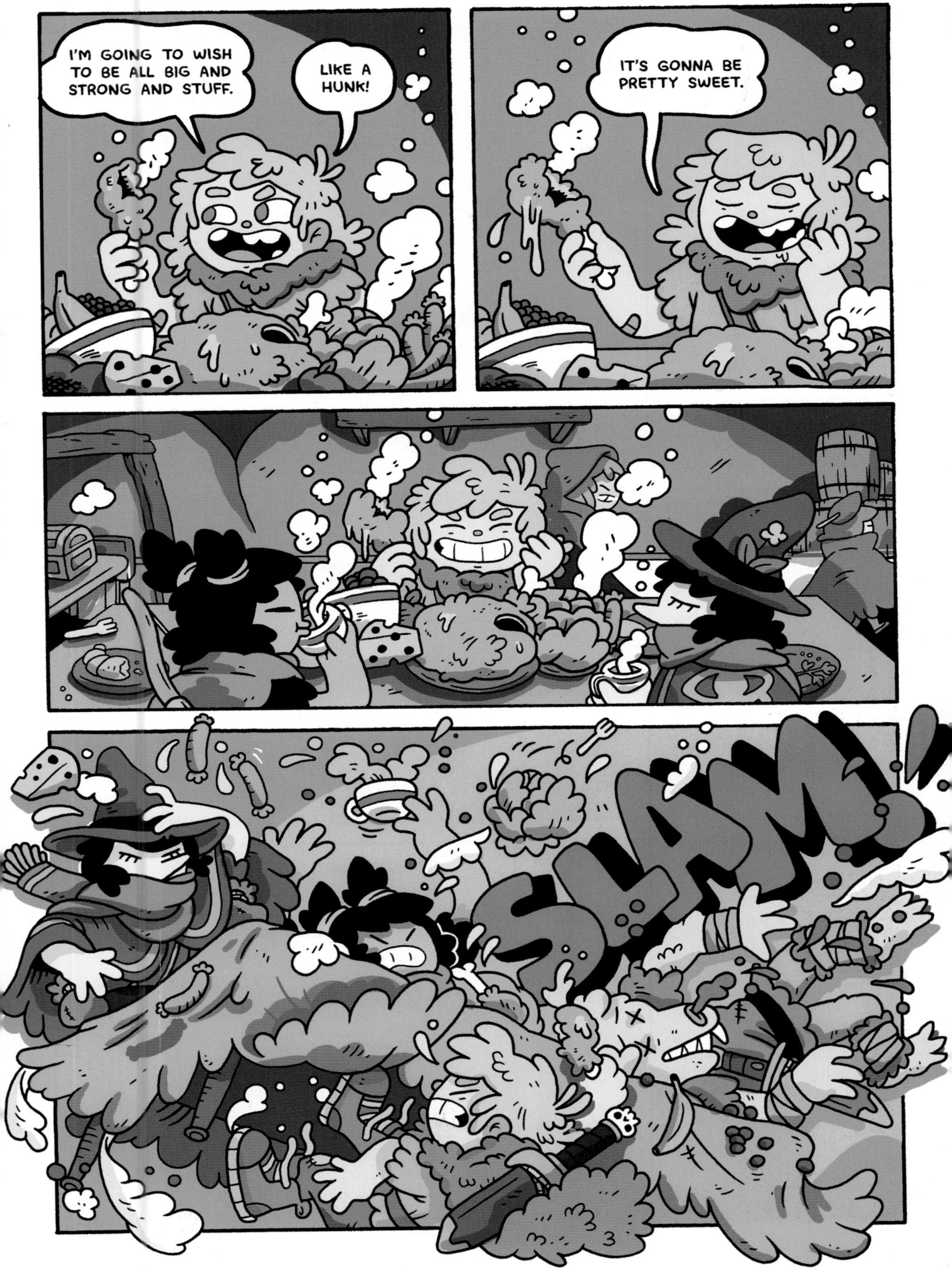

I'M GOING TO WISH TO BE ALL BIG AND STRONG AND STUFF.
LIKE A HUNK!
IT'S GONNA BE PRETTY SWEET.
SLAM!!

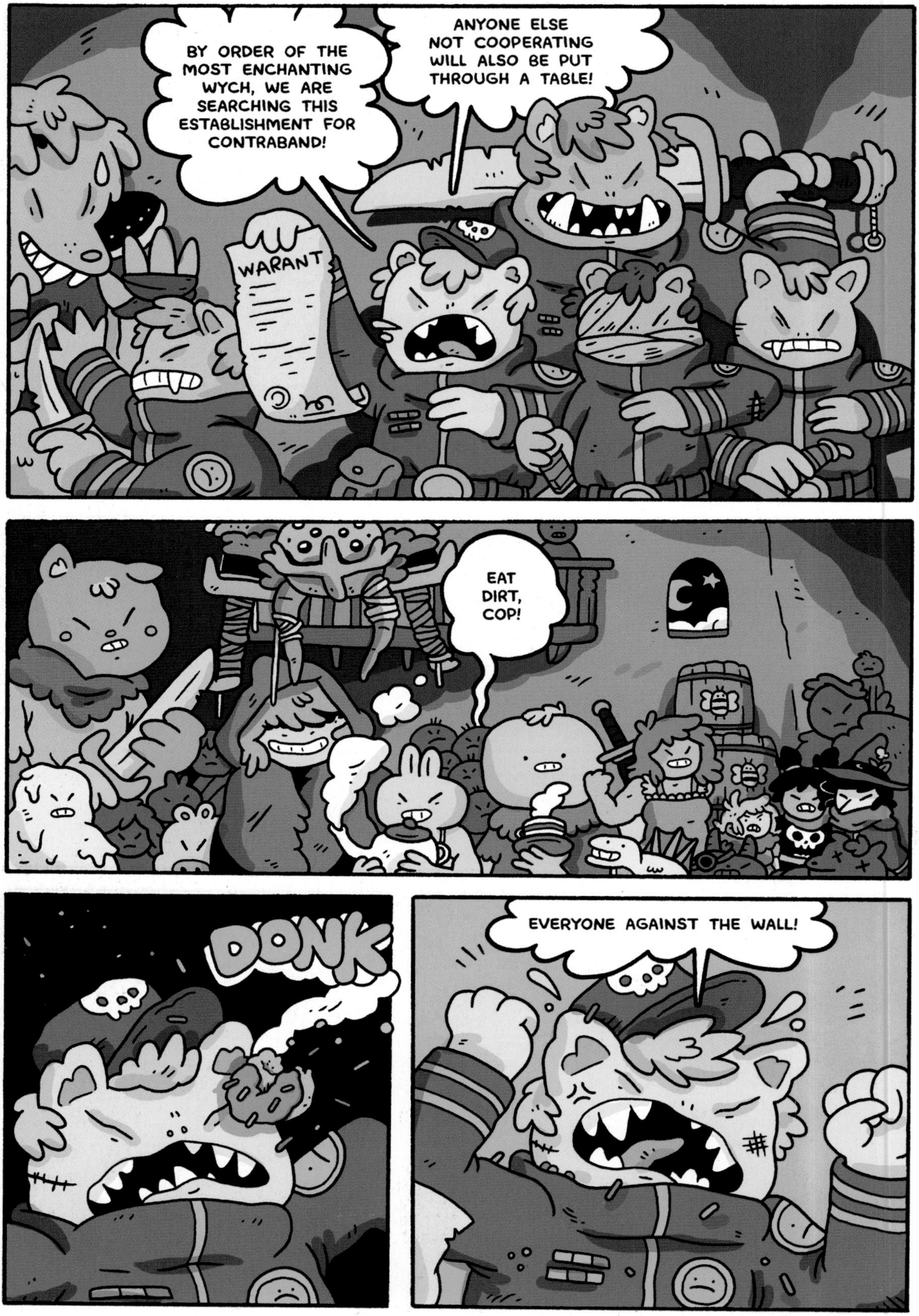
BY ORDER OF THE MOST ENCHANTING WYCH, WE ARE SEARCHING THIS ESTABLISHMENT FOR CONTRABAND!
ANYONE ELSE NOT COOPERATING WILL ALSO BE PUT THROUGH A TABLE!
WARANT
EAT DIRT, COP!
DONK
EVERYONE AGAINST THE WALL!

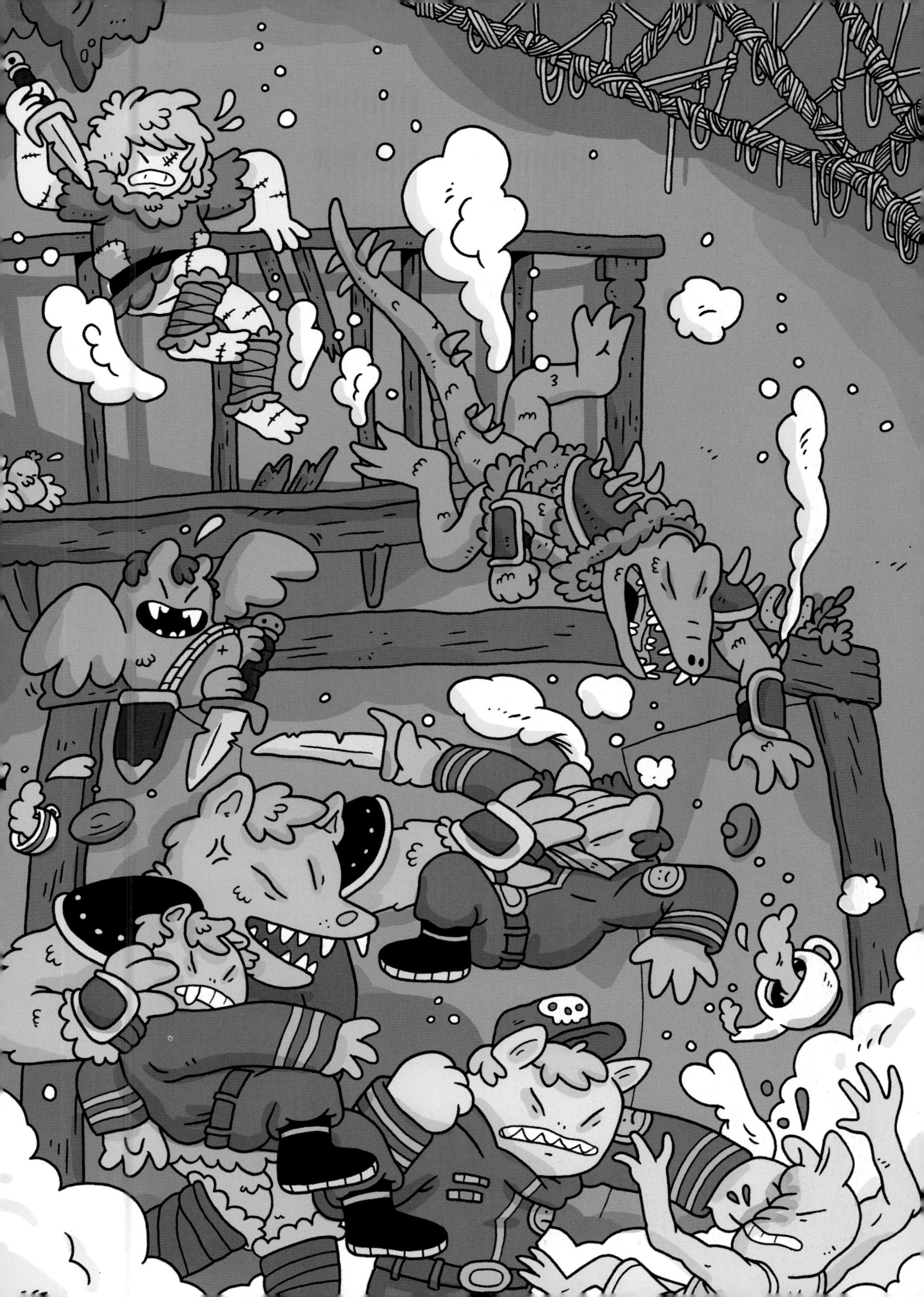

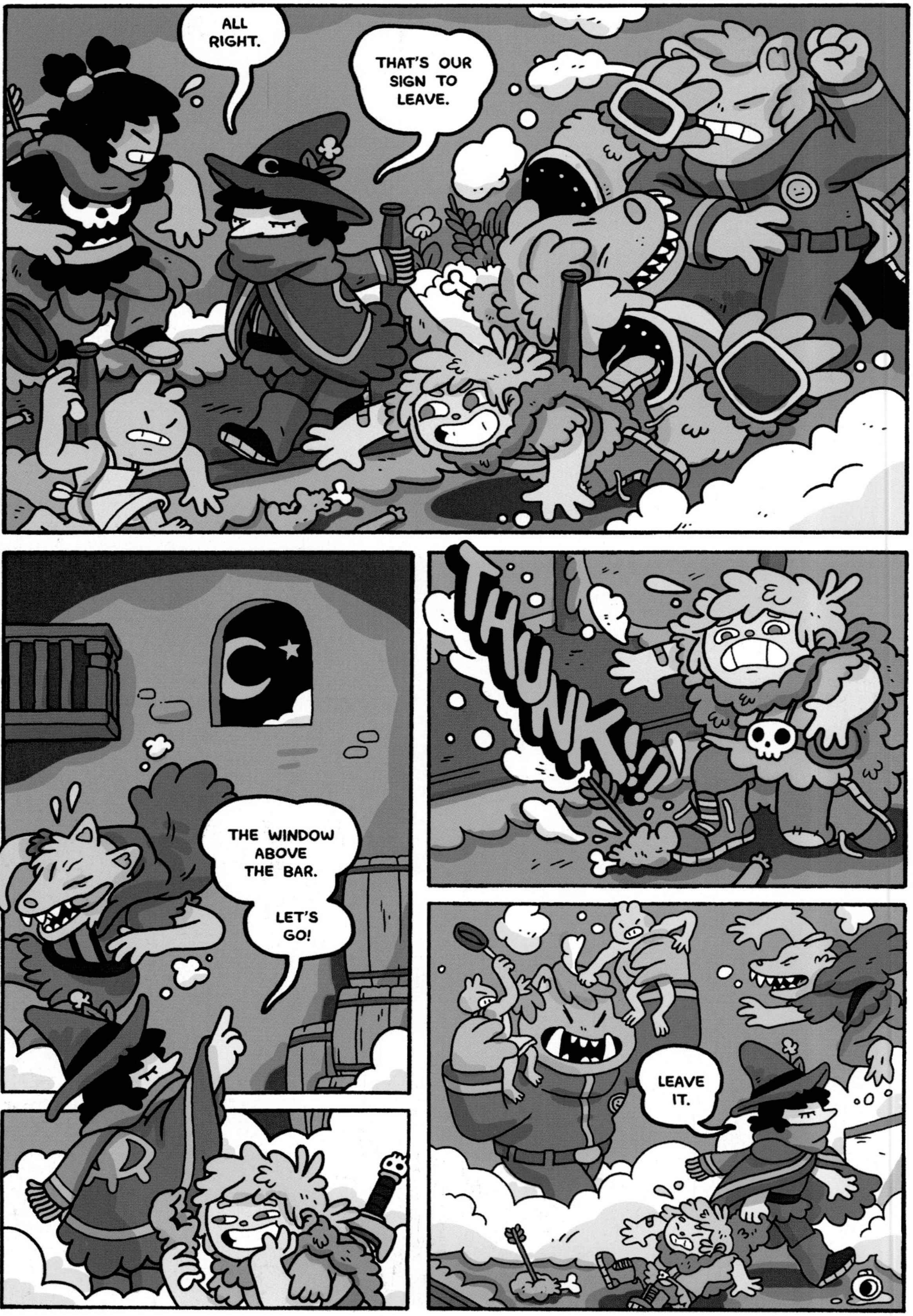
ALL RIGHT.
THAT'S OUR SIGN TO LEAVE.
THUNK!!
THE WINDOW ABOVE THE BAR.
LET'S GO!
LEAVE IT.

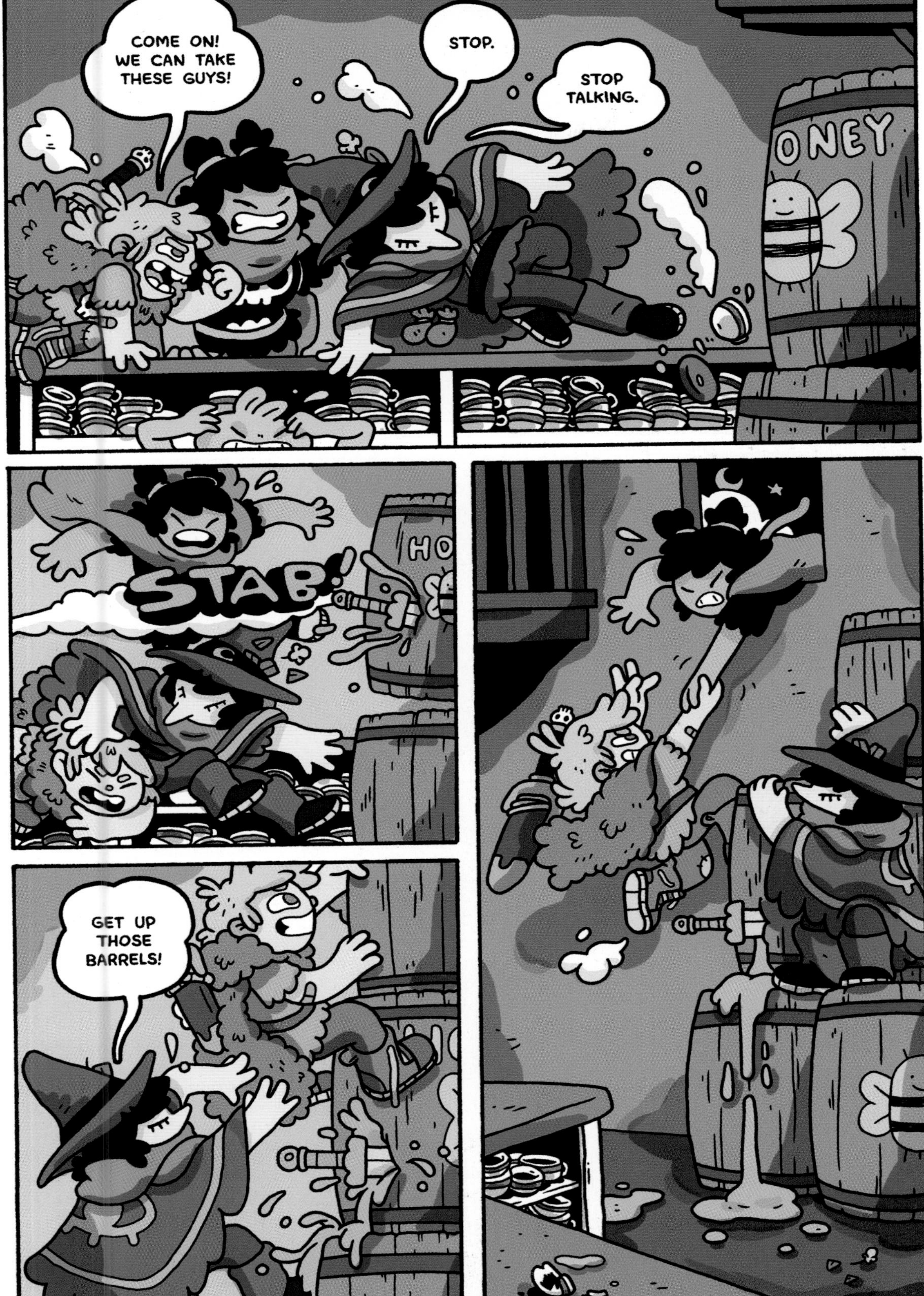
COME ON! WE CAN TAKE THESE GUYS!
STOP.
STOP TALKING.
ONEY
HO
STAB!
GET UP THOSE BARRELS!

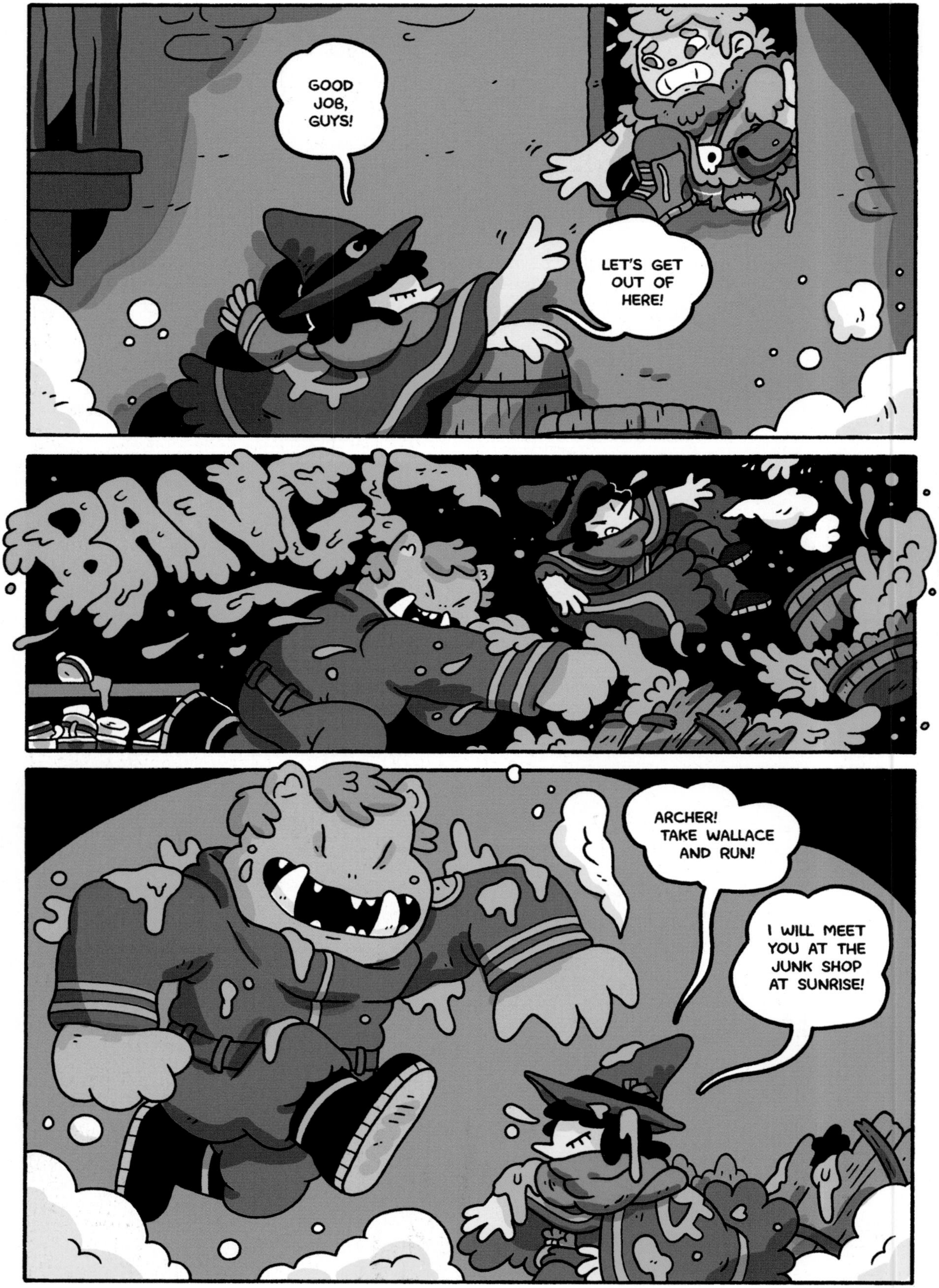
GOOD JOB, GUYS!
LET'S GET OUT OF HERE!
BANG!
ARCHER! TAKE WALLACE AND RUN!
I WILL MEET YOU AT THE JUNK SHOP AT SUNRISE!

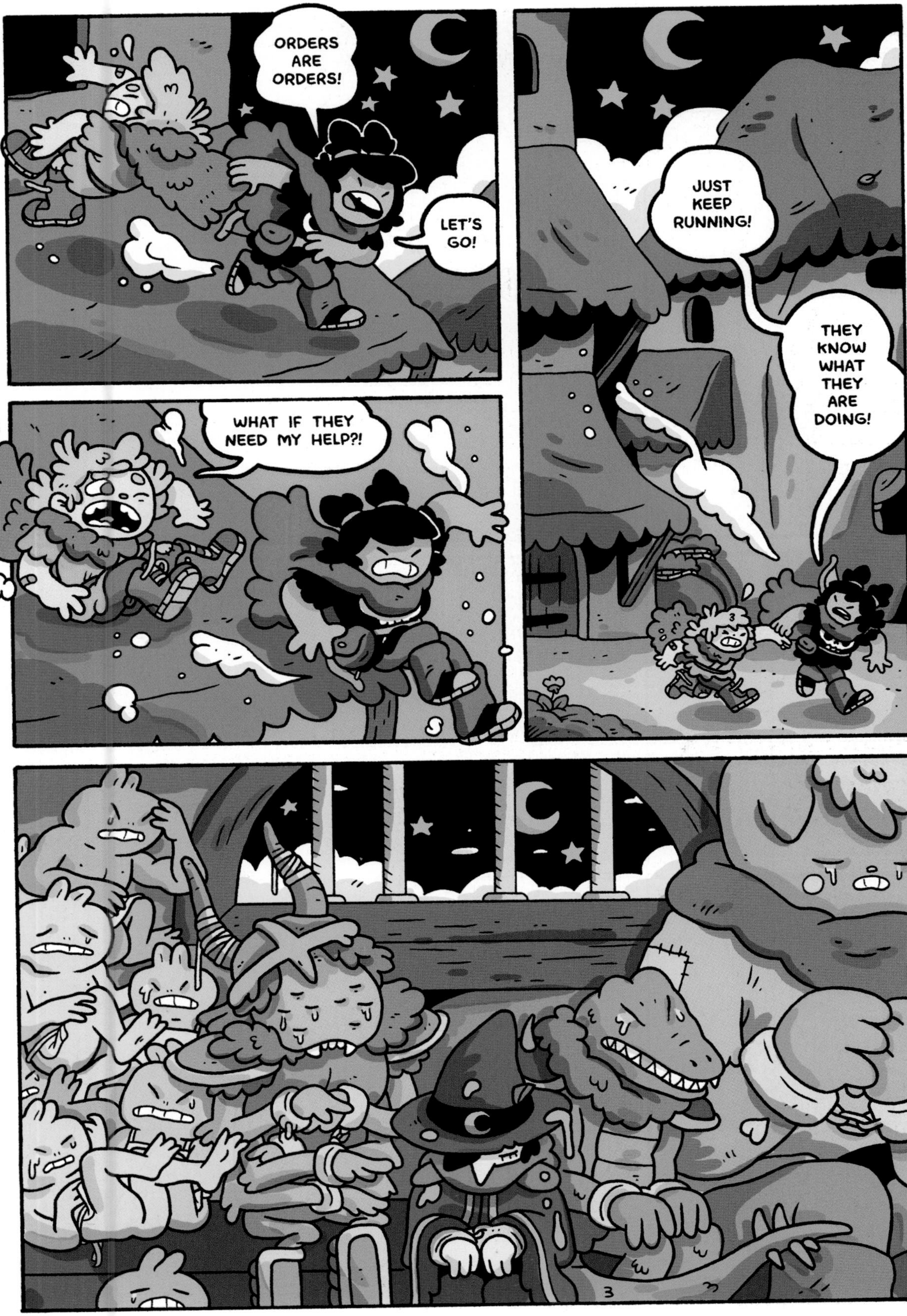
ORDERS ARE ORDERS!
LET'S GO!
WHAT IF THEY NEED MY HELP?!
JUST KEEP RUNNING!
THEY KNOW WHAT THEY ARE DOING!

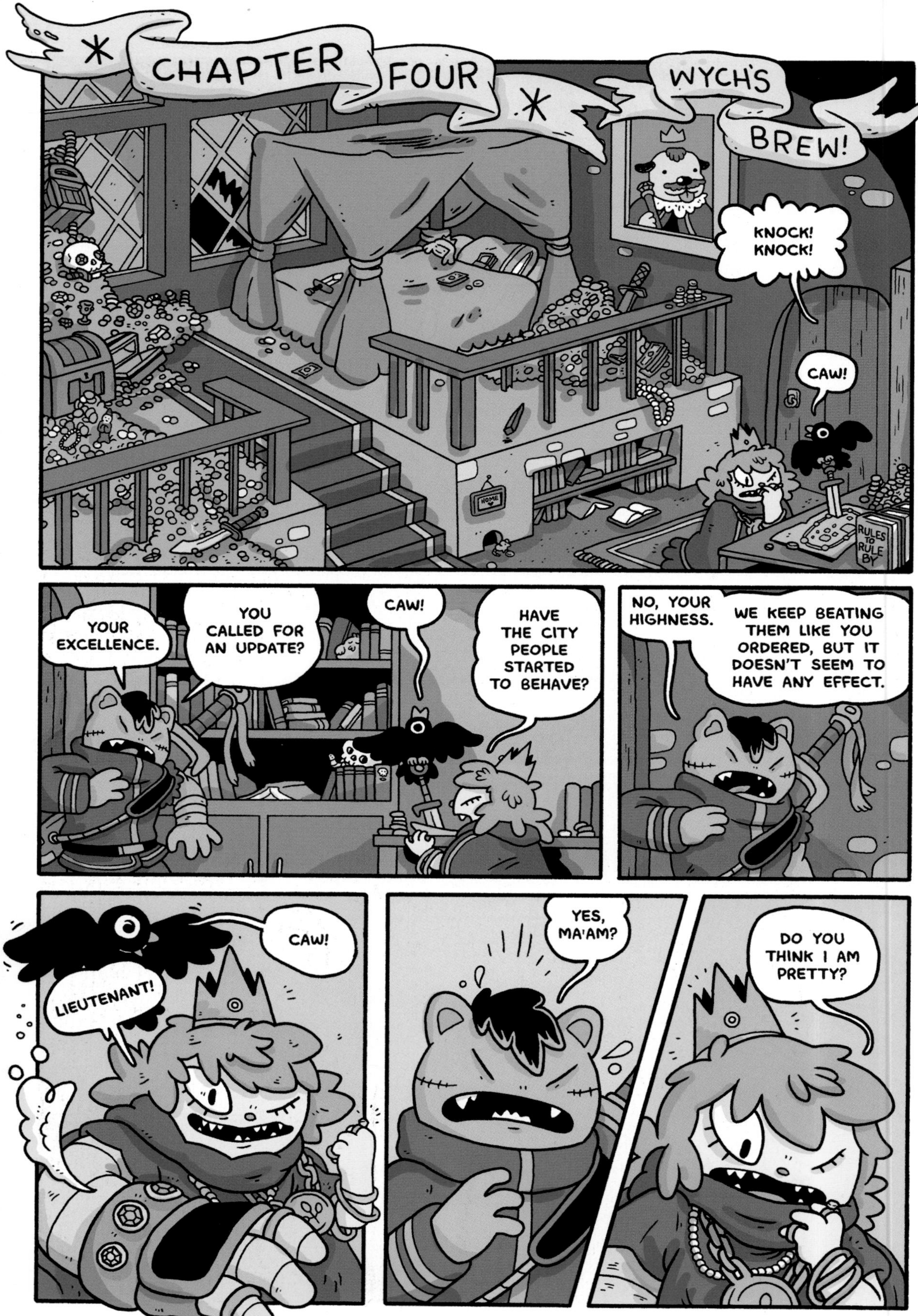
CHAPTER FOUR
WYCH'S BREW!
KNOCK! KNOCK!
CAW!
RULES TO RULE BY
HOME
YOUR EXCELLENCE.
YOU CALLED FOR AN UPDATE?
CAW!
HAVE THE CITY PEOPLE STARTED TO BEHAVE?
NO, YOUR HIGHNESS.
WE KEEP BEATING THEM LIKE YOU ORDERED, BUT IT DOESN'T SEEM TO HAVE ANY EFFECT.
CAW!
LIEUTENANT!
YES, MA'AM?
DO YOU THINK I AM PRETTY?

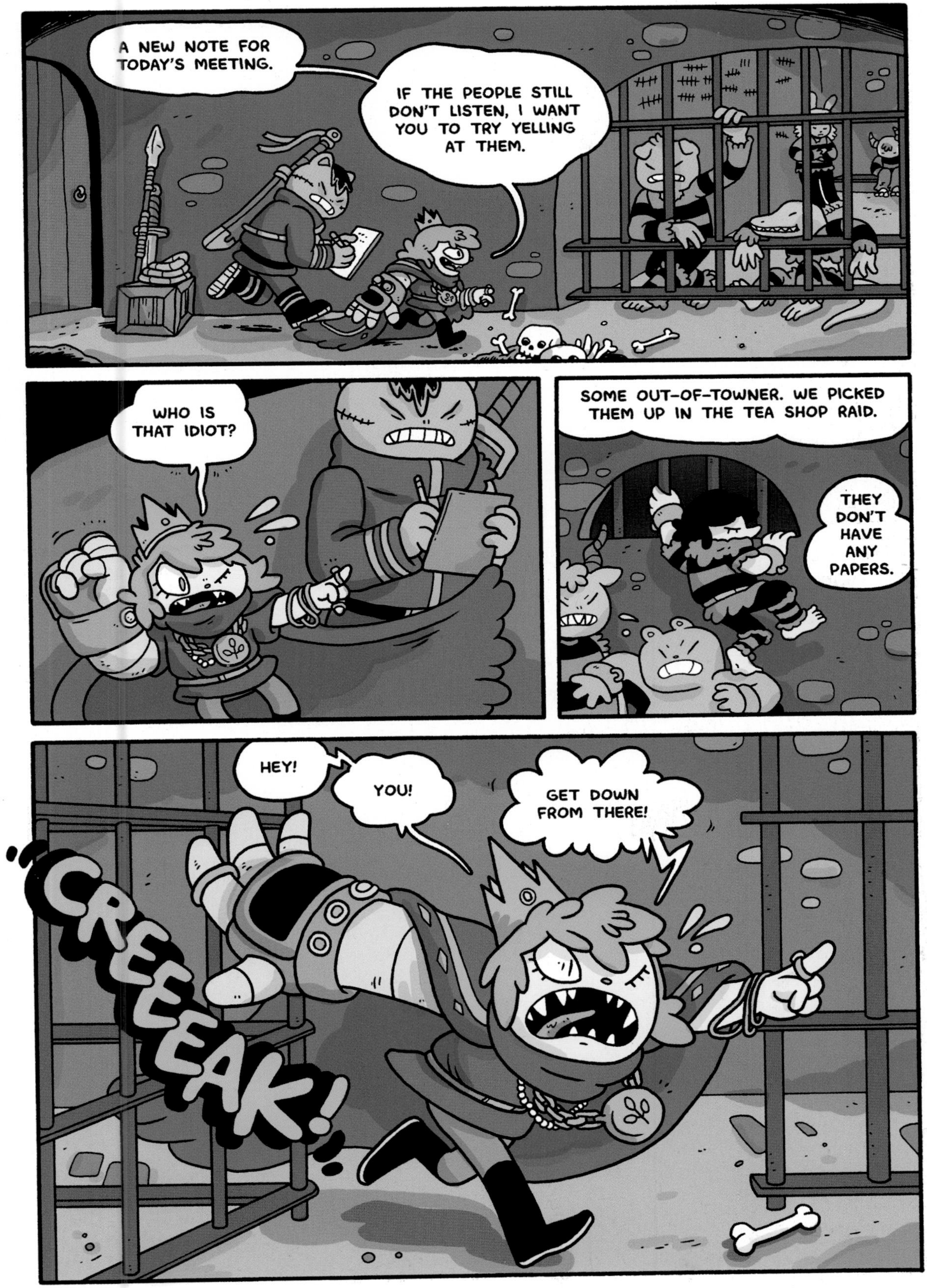
A NEW NOTE FOR TODAY'S MEETING.
IF THE PEOPLE STILL DON'T LISTEN, I WANT YOU TO TRY YELLING AT THEM.
WHO IS THAT IDIOT?
SOME OUT-OF-TOWNER. WE PICKED THEM UP IN THE TEA SHOP RAID.
THEY DON'T HAVE ANY PAPERS.
HEY!
YOU!
GET DOWN FROM THERE!
CREEEAK!

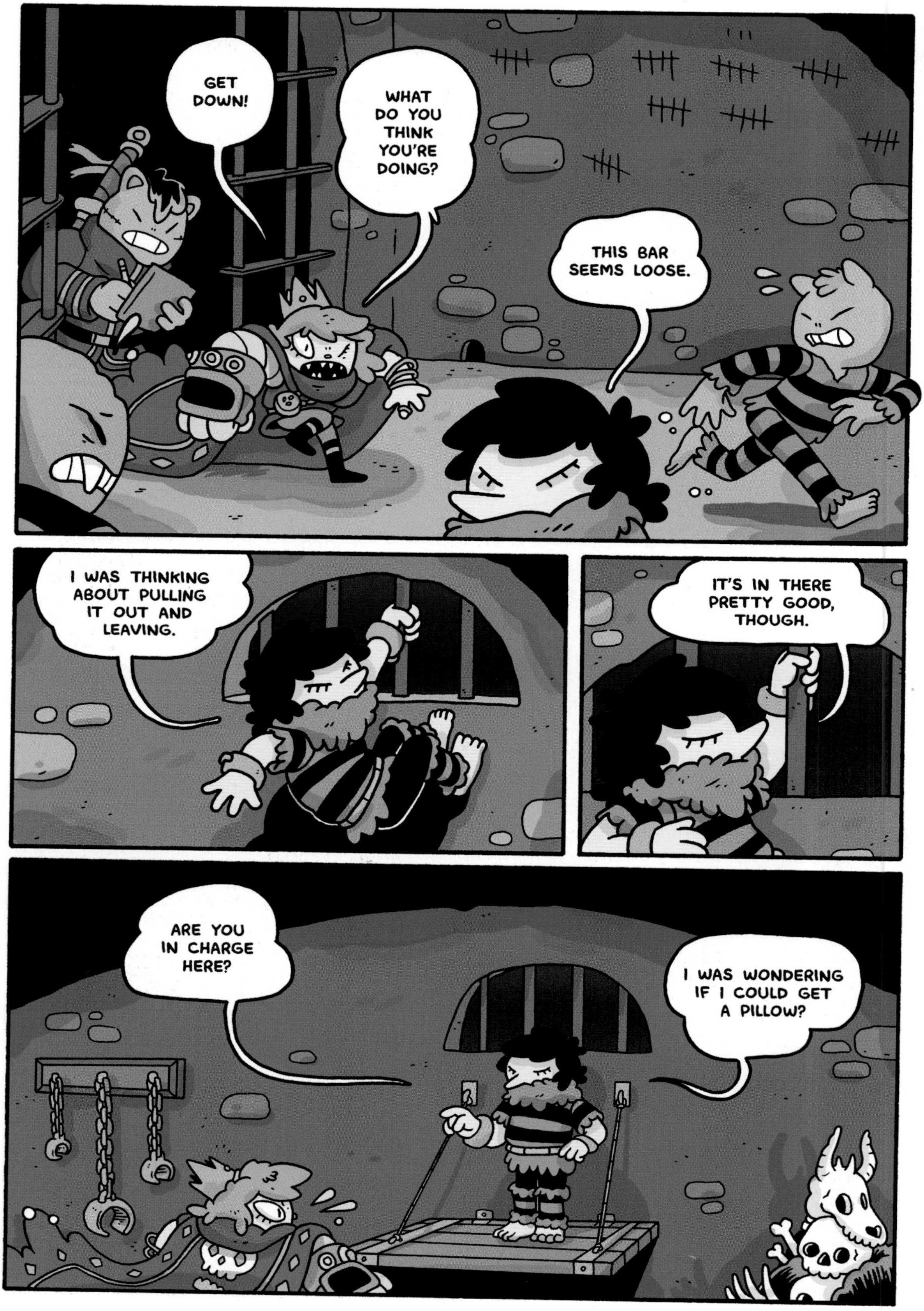
GET DOWN!
WHAT DO YOU THINK YOU'RE DOING?
THIS BAR SEEMS LOOSE.
I WAS THINKING ABOUT PULLING IT OUT AND LEAVING.
IT'S IN THERE PRETTY GOOD, THOUGH.
ARE YOU IN CHARGE HERE?
I WAS WONDERING IF I COULD GET A PILLOW?

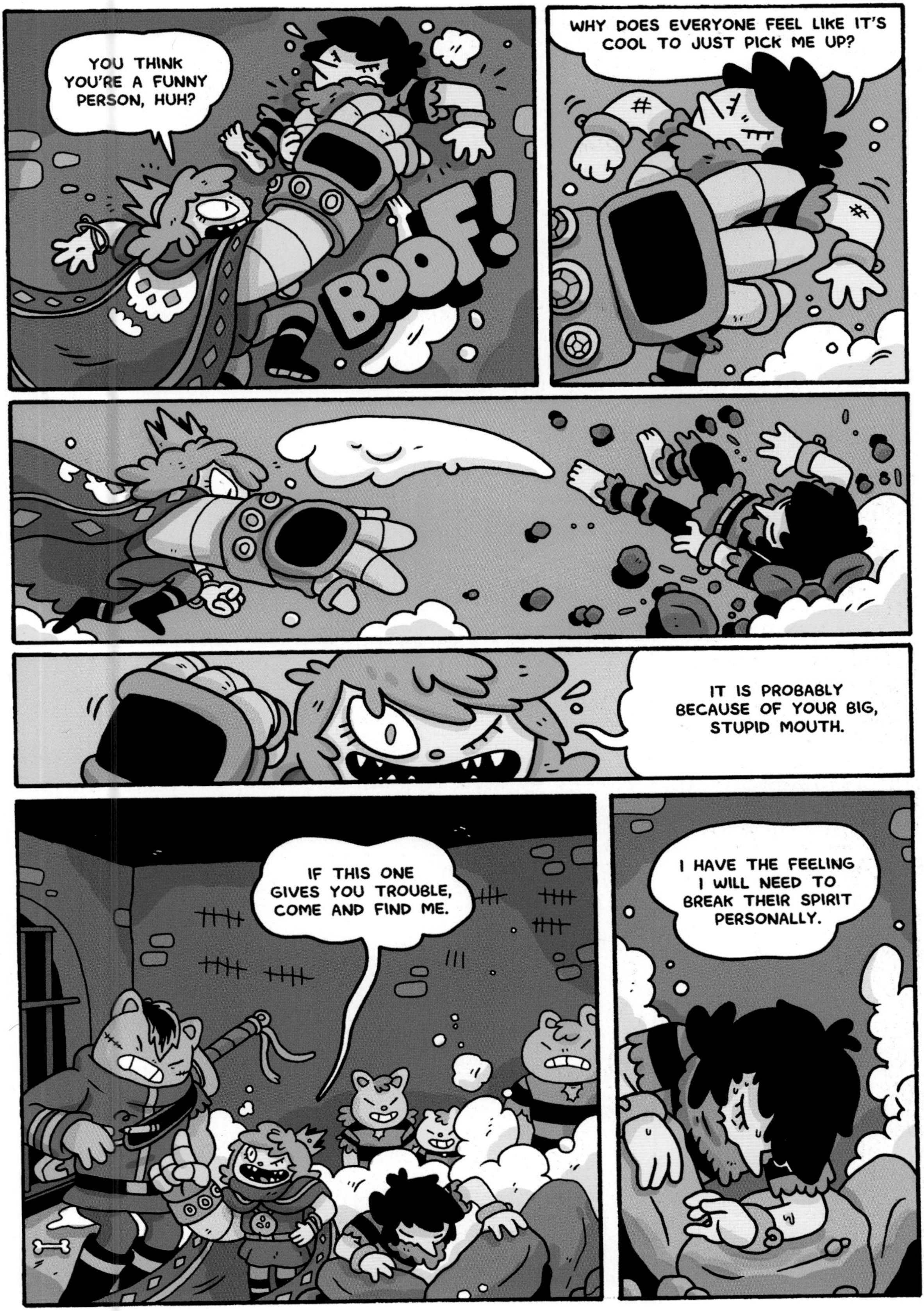
YOU THINK YOU'RE A FUNNY PERSON, HUH?
BOOF!
WHY DOES EVERYONE FEEL LIKE IT'S COOL TO JUST PICK ME UP?
IT IS PROBABLY BECAUSE OF YOUR BIG, STUPID MOUTH.
IF THIS ONE GIVES YOU TROUBLE, COME AND FIND ME.
I HAVE THE FEELING I WILL NEED TO BREAK THEIR SPIRIT PERSONALLY.

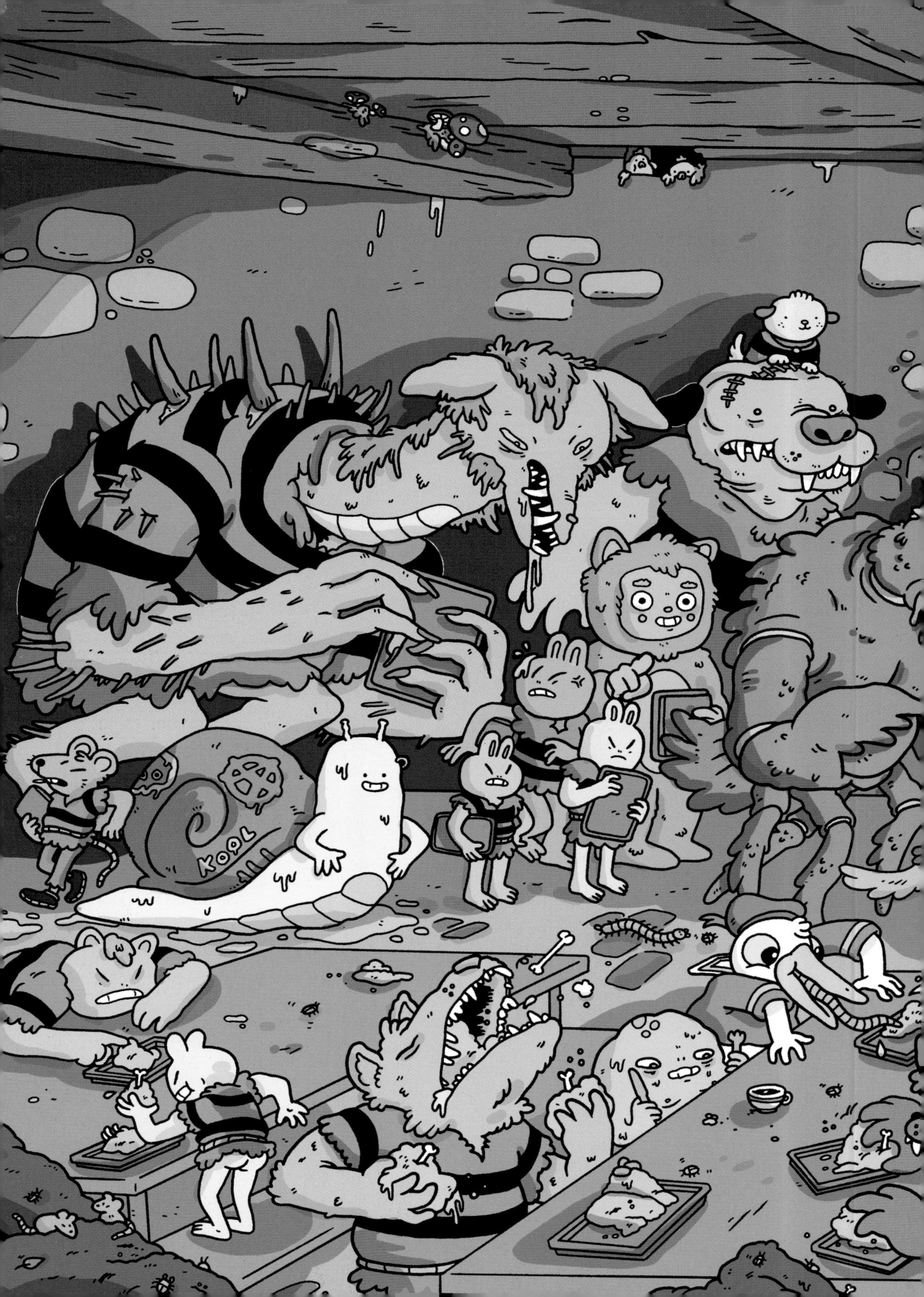
KOOL

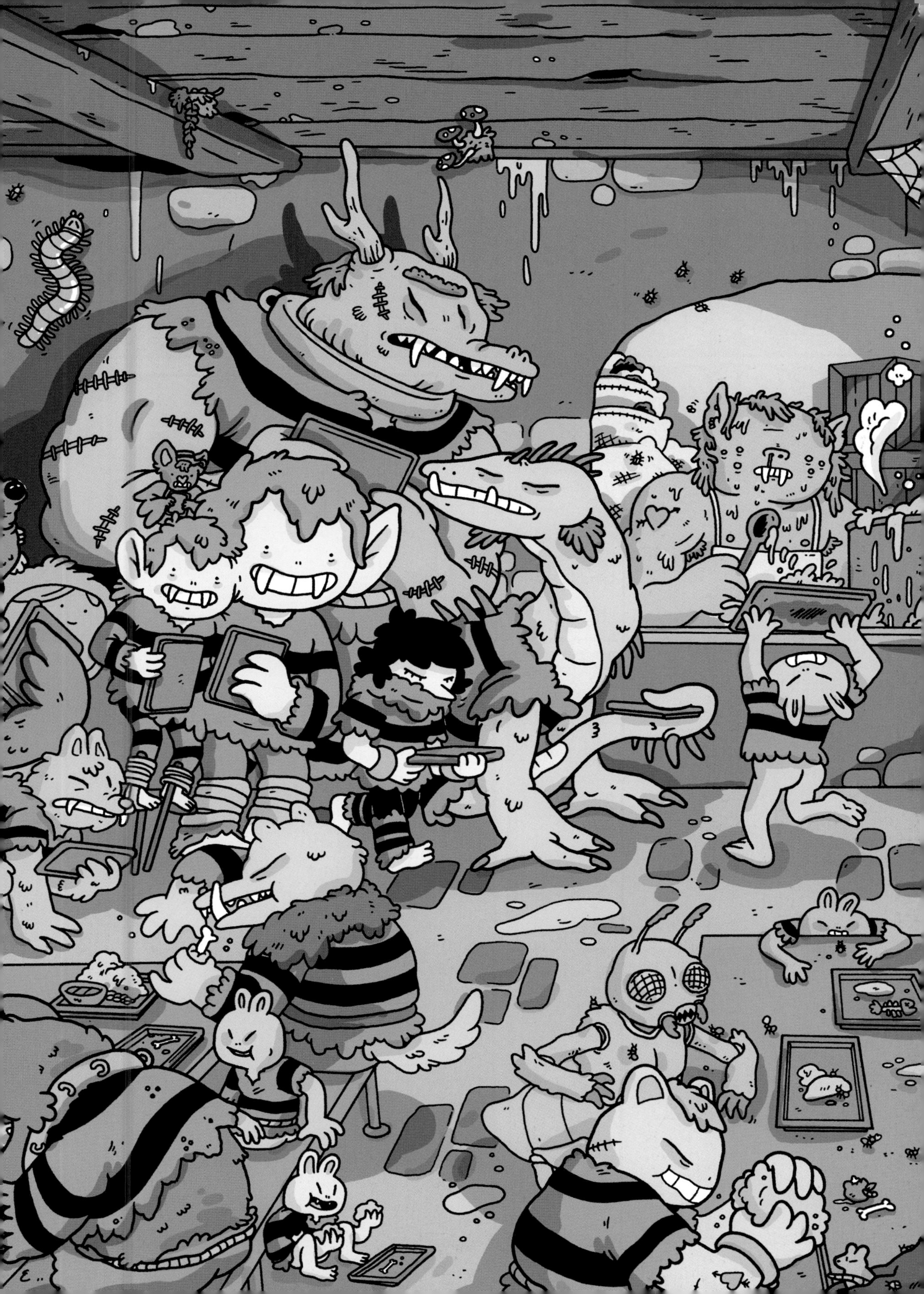

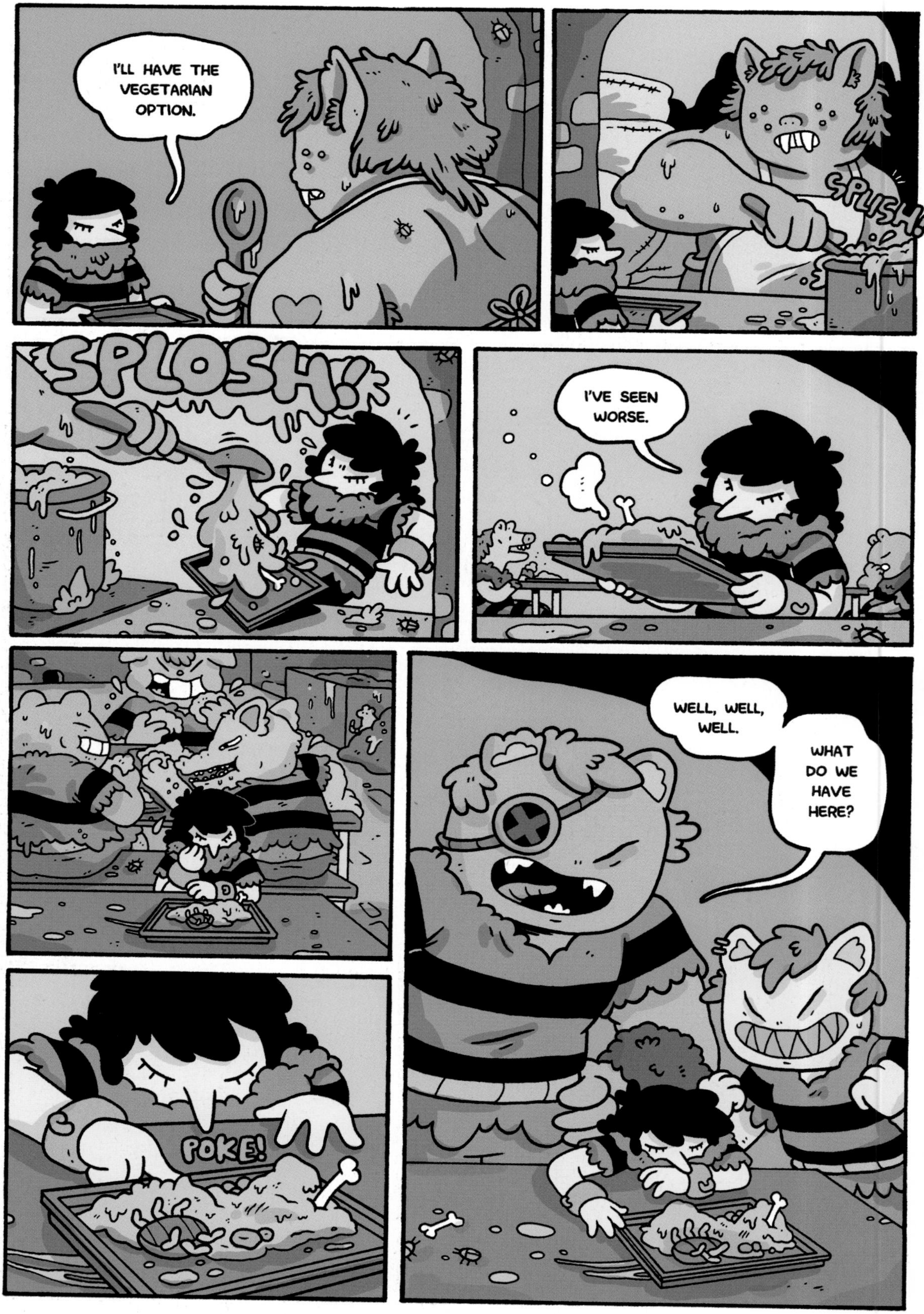
I'LL HAVE THE VEGETARIAN OPTION.
SPLISH!
SPLOSH!
I'VE SEEN WORSE.
POKE!
WELL, WELL, WELL.
WHAT DO WE HAVE HERE?

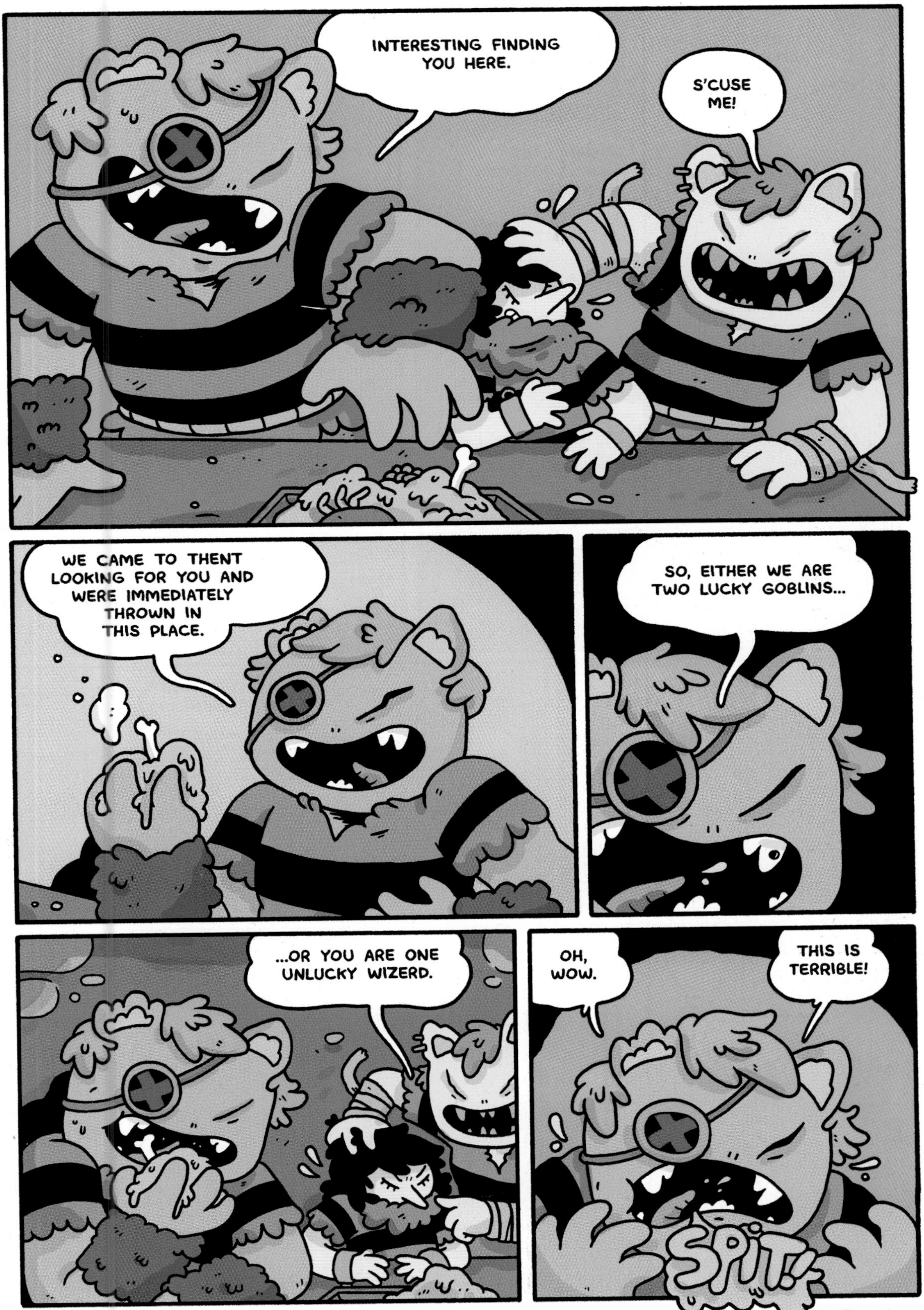
INTERESTING FINDING YOU HERE.
S'CUSE ME!
WE CAME TO THENT LOOKING FOR YOU AND WERE IMMEDIATELY THROWN IN THIS PLACE.
SO, EITHER WE ARE TWO LUCKY GOBLINS...
...OR YOU ARE ONE UNLUCKY WIZERD.
OH, WOW.
THIS IS TERRIBLE!
SPIT!

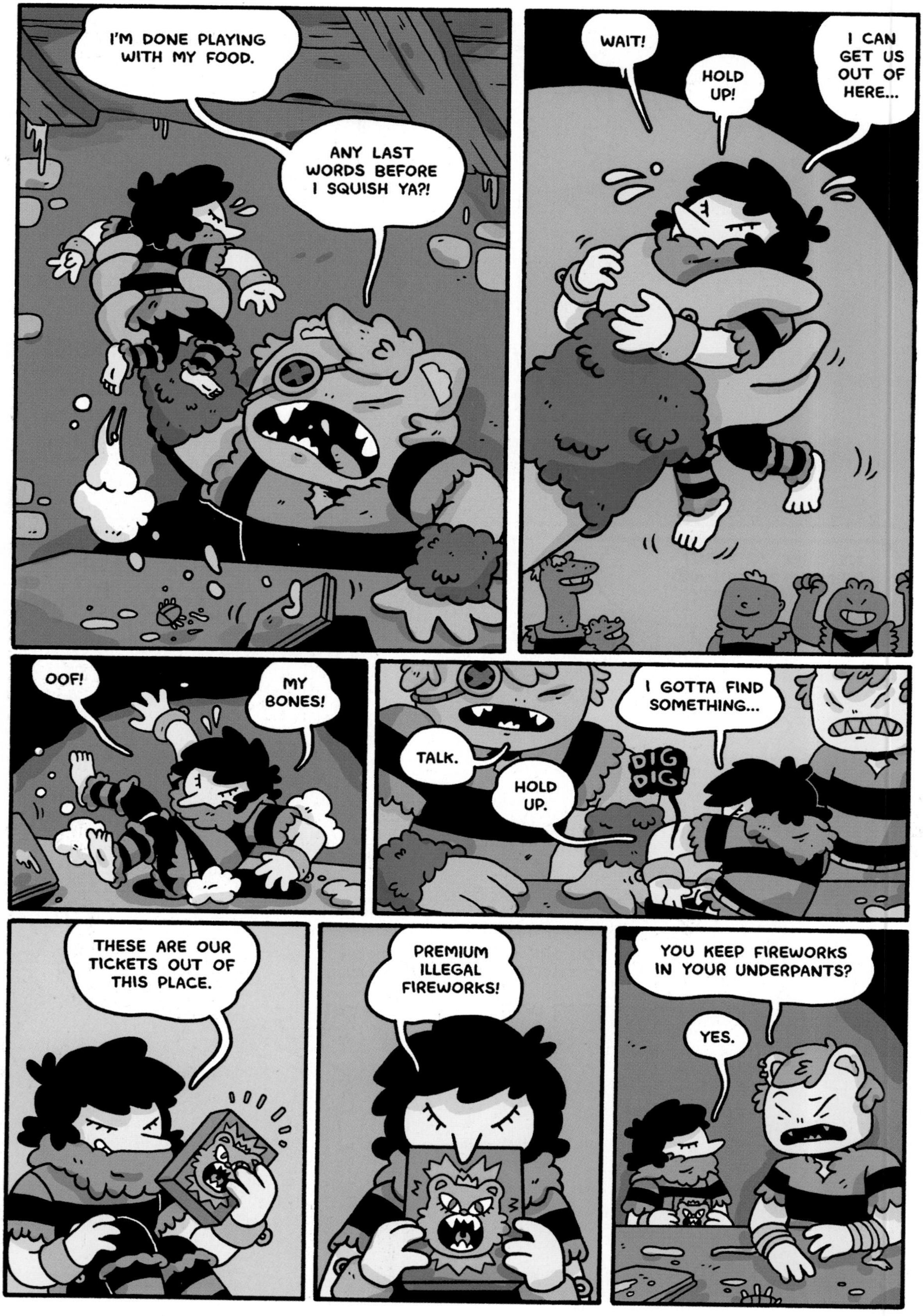
I'M DONE PLAYING WITH MY FOOD.
ANY LAST WORDS BEFORE I SQUISH YA?!
WAIT!
HOLD UP!
I CAN GET US OUT OF HERE...
OOF!
MY BONES!
TALK.
I GOTTA FIND SOMETHING...
DIG DIG!
HOLD UP.
THESE ARE OUR TICKETS OUT OF THIS PLACE.
PREMIUM ILLEGAL FIREWORKS!
YOU KEEP FIREWORKS IN YOUR UNDERPANTS?
YES.

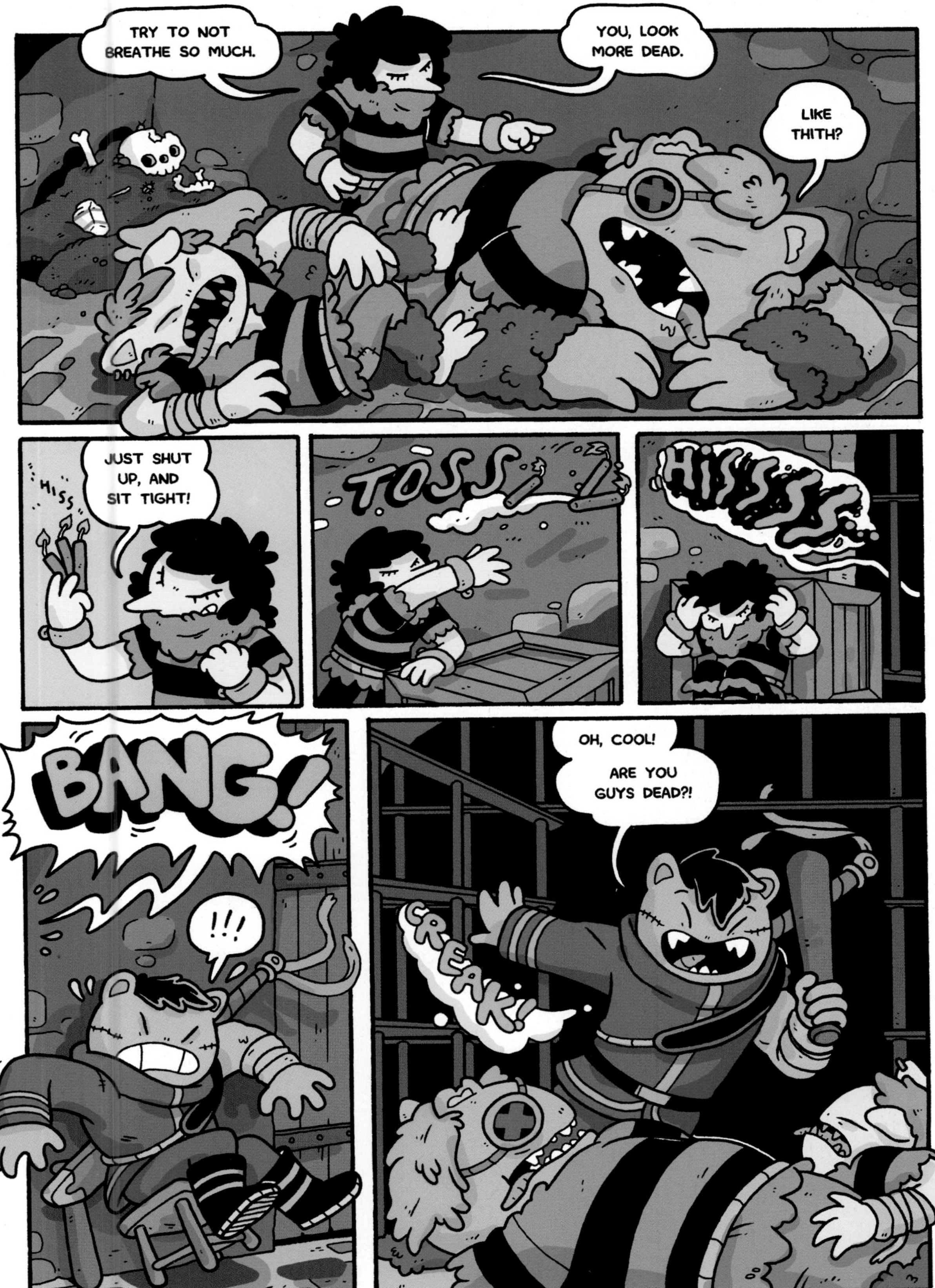

TRY TO NOT BREATHE SO MUCH.
YOU, LOOK MORE DEAD.
LIKE THITH?
HISS
JUST SHUT UP, AND SIT TIGHT!
TOSS
HISSSS
BANG!
!!!
OH, COOL!
ARE YOU GUYS DEAD?!
CREAK!

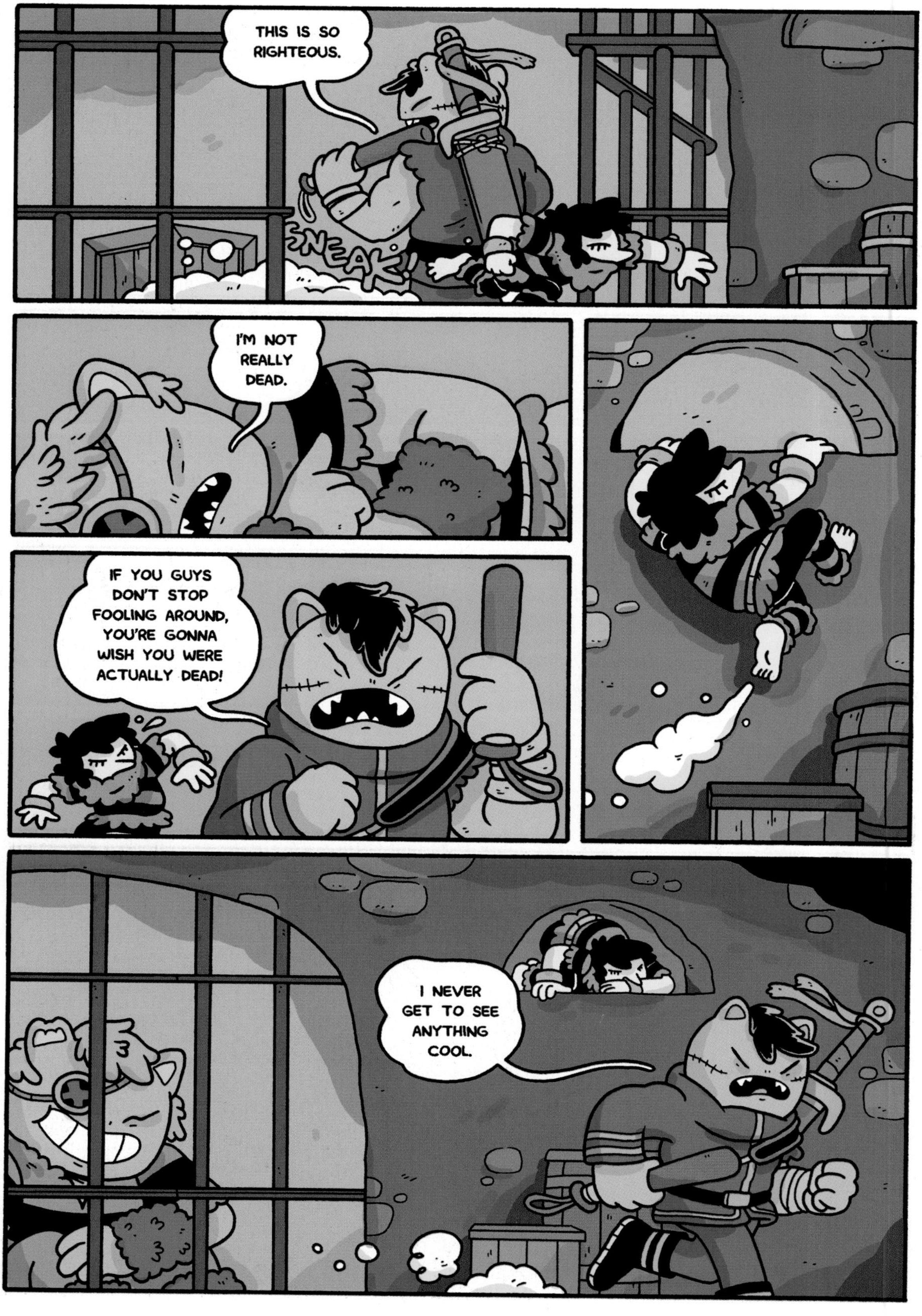
THIS IS SO RIGHTEOUS.
SNEAK!
I'M NOT REALLY DEAD.
IF YOU GUYS DON'T STOP FOOLING AROUND, YOU'RE GONNA WISH YOU WERE ACTUALLY DEAD!
I NEVER GET TO SEE ANYTHING COOL.

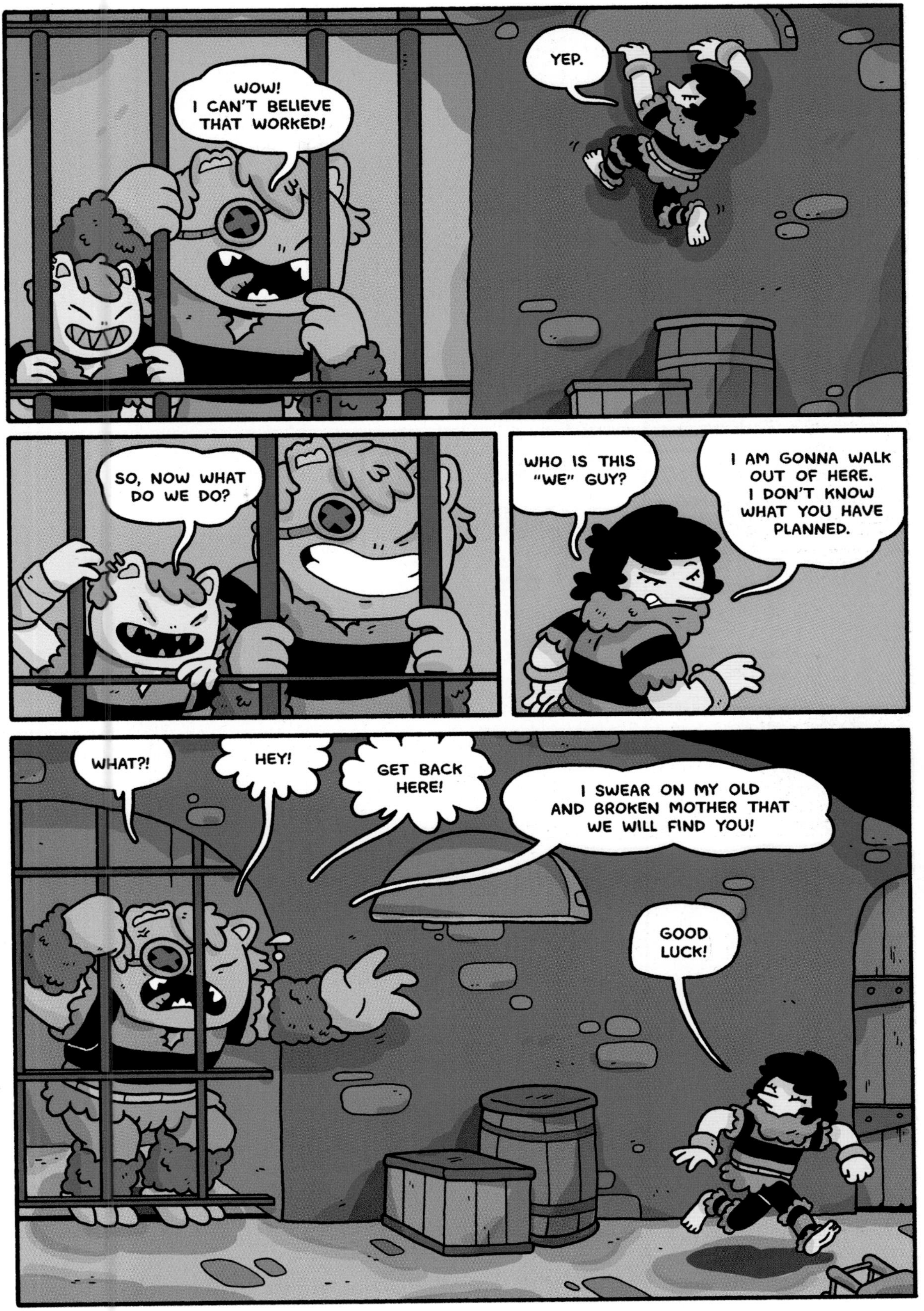
WOW! I CAN'T BELIEVE THAT WORKED!
YEP.
SO, NOW WHAT DO WE DO?
WHO IS THIS "WE" GUY?
I AM GONNA WALK OUT OF HERE. I DON'T KNOW WHAT YOU HAVE PLANNED.
WHAT?!
HEY!
GET BACK HERE!
I SWEAR ON MY OLD AND BROKEN MOTHER THAT WE WILL FIND YOU!
GOOD LUCK!

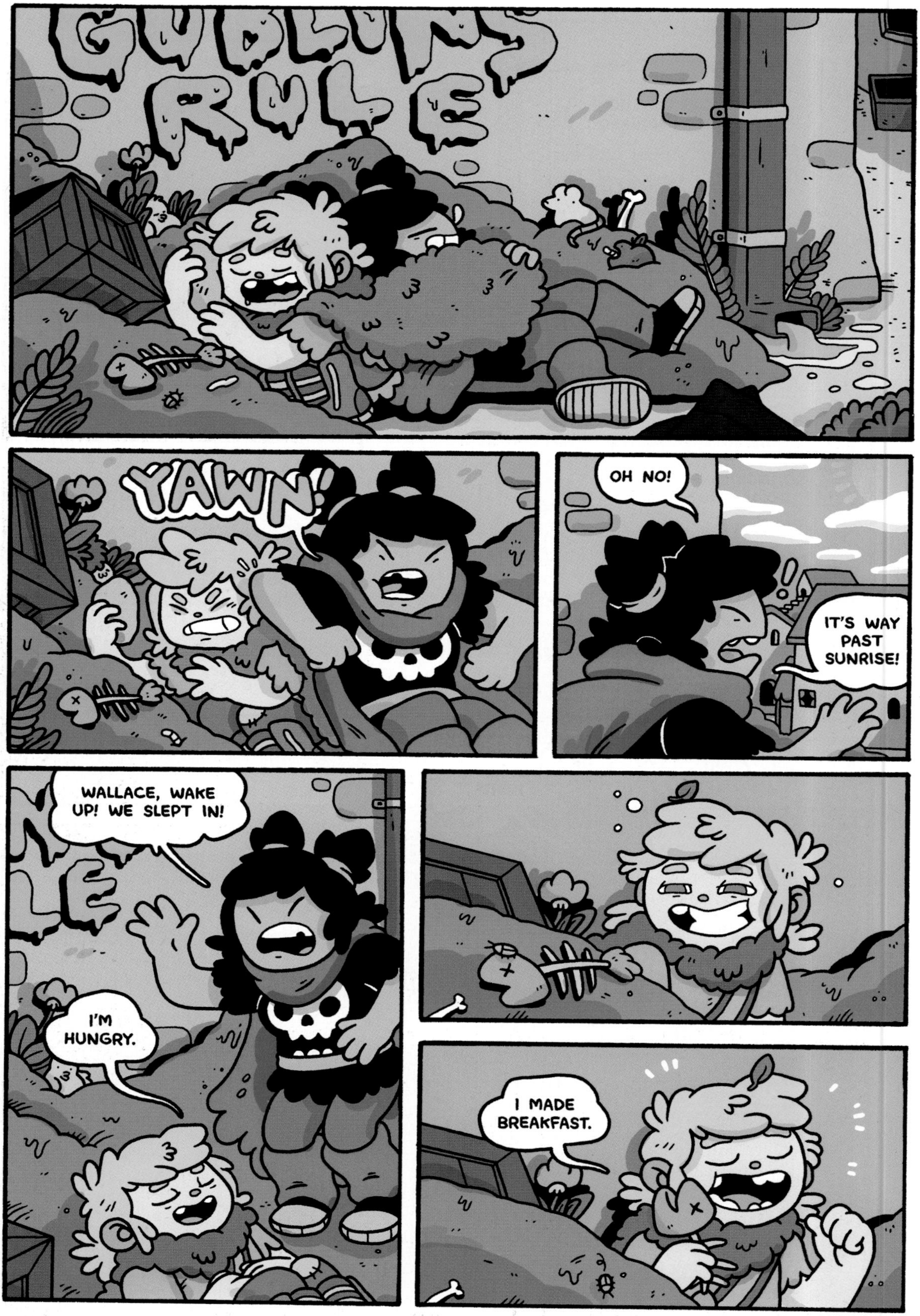
GOBLINS RULE
YAWN!
OH NO!
IT'S WAY PAST SUNRISE!
WALLACE, WAKE UP! WE SLEPT IN!
I'M HUNGRY.
I MADE BREAKFAST.

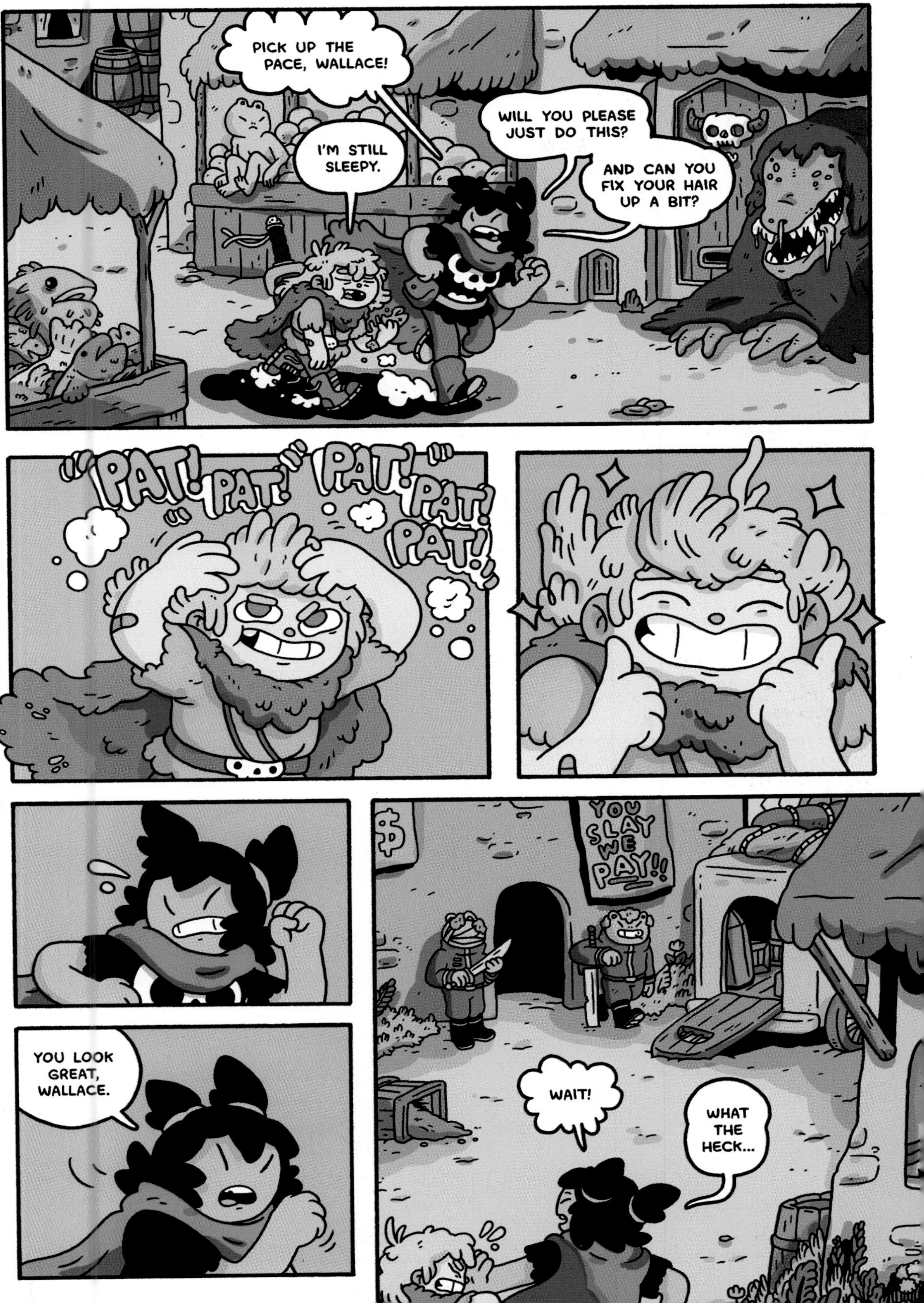

PICK UP THE PACE, WALLACE!
I'M STILL SLEEPY.
WILL YOU PLEASE JUST DO THIS?
AND CAN YOU FIX YOUR HAIR UP A BIT?
"PAT!" "PAT!" "PAT!" "PAT!" PAT!!
YOU LOOK GREAT, WALLACE.
YOU SLAY WE PAY!!
$
WAIT!
WHAT THE HECK...

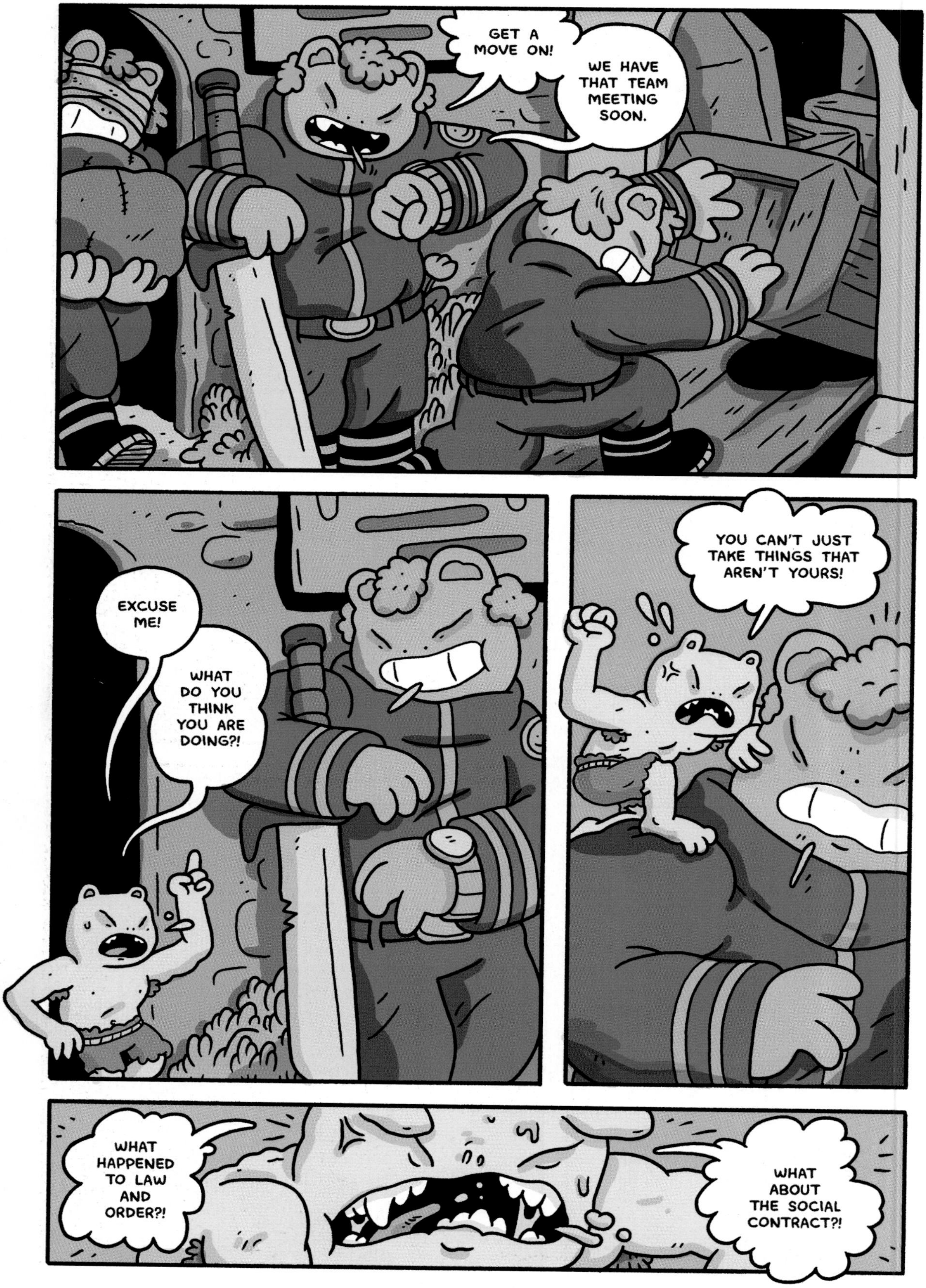
GET A MOVE ON!
WE HAVE THAT TEAM MEETING SOON.
EXCUSE ME!
WHAT DO YOU THINK YOU ARE DOING?!
YOU CAN'T JUST TAKE THINGS THAT AREN'T YOURS!
WHAT HAPPENED TO LAW AND ORDER?!
WHAT ABOUT THE SOCIAL CONTRACT?!

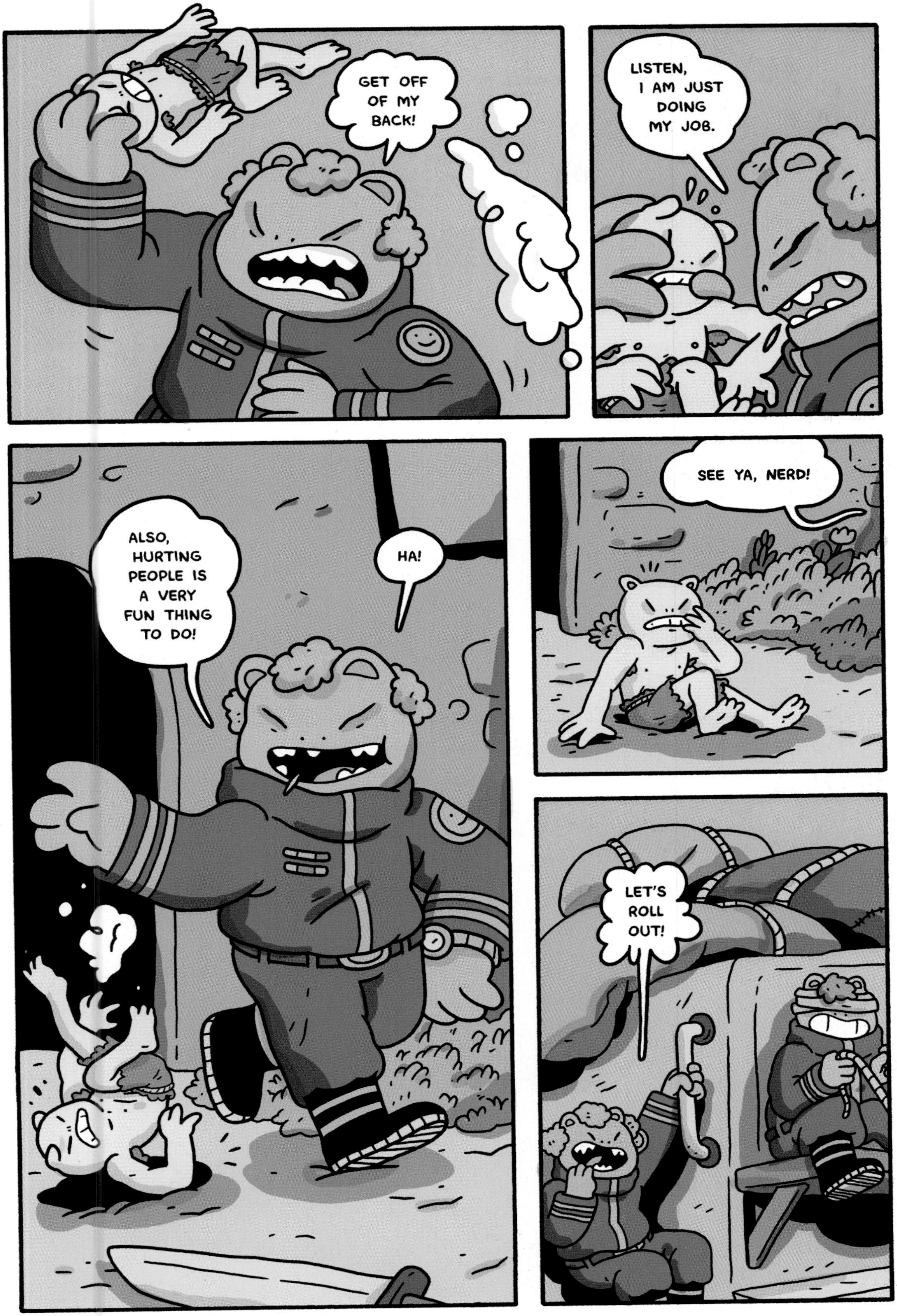
GET OFF OF MY BACK!
LISTEN, I AM JUST DOING MY JOB.
ALSO, HURTING PEOPLE IS A VERY FUN THING TO DO!
HA!
SEE YA, NERD!
LET'S ROLL OUT!

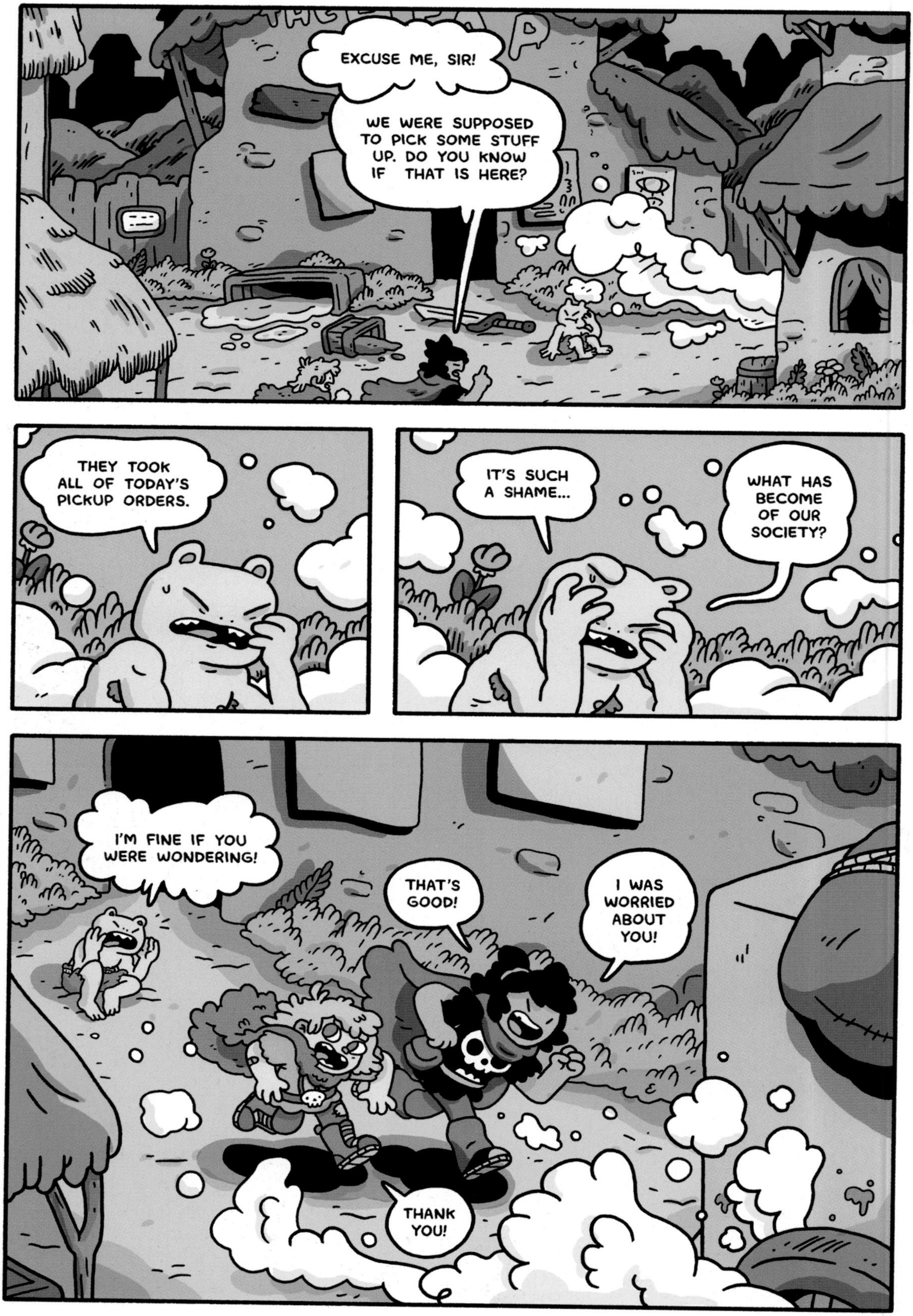
EXCUSE ME, SIR!
WE WERE SUPPOSED TO PICK SOME STUFF UP. DO YOU KNOW IF THAT IS HERE?
THEY TOOK ALL OF TODAY'S PICKUP ORDERS.
IT'S SUCH A SHAME...
WHAT HAS BECOME OF OUR SOCIETY?
I'M FINE IF YOU WERE WONDERING!
THAT'S GOOD!
I WAS WORRIED ABOUT YOU!
THANK YOU!

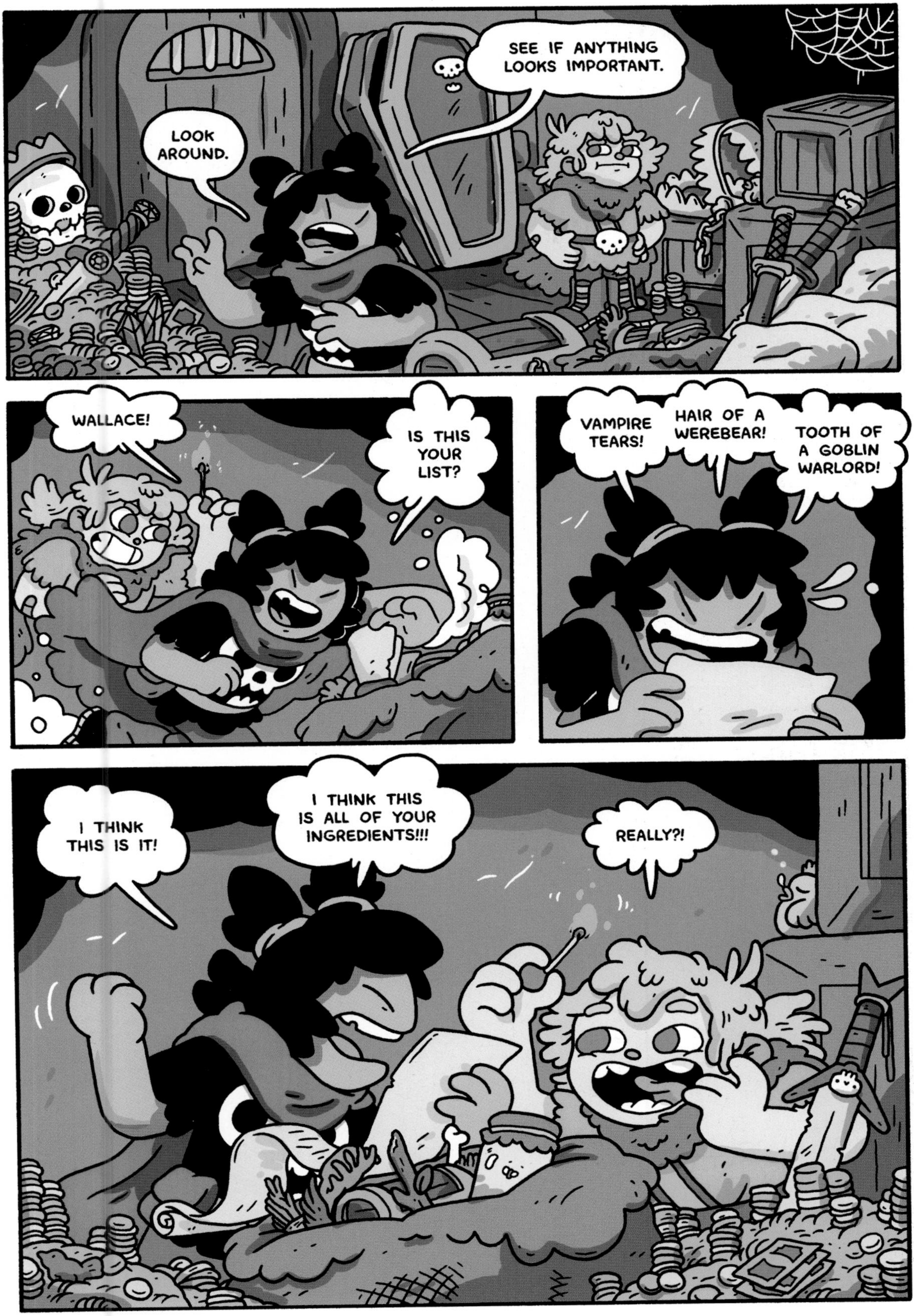
LOOK AROUND.
SEE IF ANYTHING LOOKS IMPORTANT.
WALLACE!
IS THIS YOUR LIST?
VAMPIRE TEARS!
HAIR OF A WEREBEAR!
TOOTH OF A GOBLIN WARLORD!
I THINK THIS IS IT!
I THINK THIS IS ALL OF YOUR INGREDIENTS!!!
REALLY?!

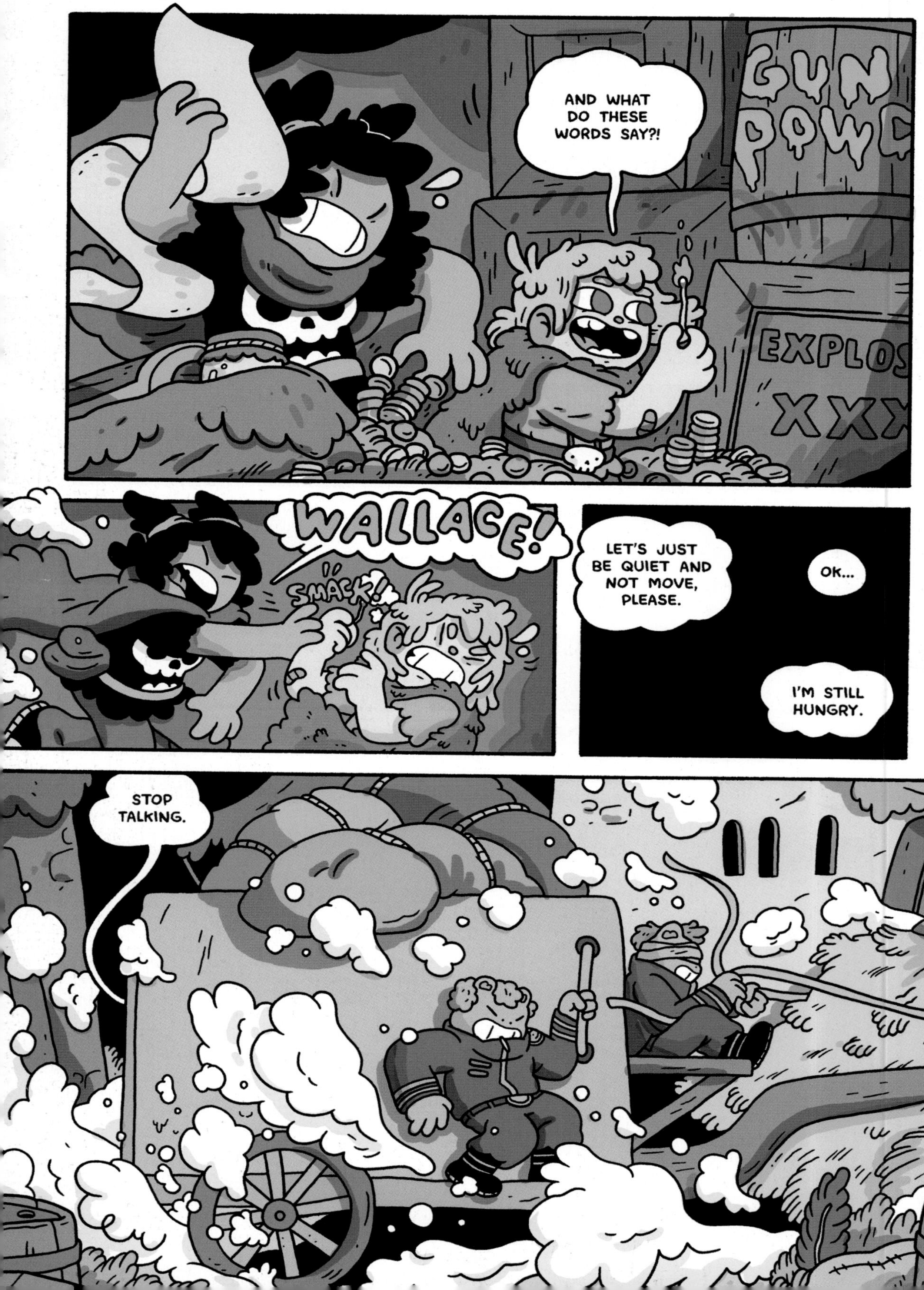
GUN POWD
AND WHAT DO THESE WORDS SAY?!
EXPLOS XXX
WALLACE!
SMACK!
LET'S JUST BE QUIET AND NOT MOVE, PLEASE.
OK...
I'M STILL HUNGRY.
STOP TALKING.

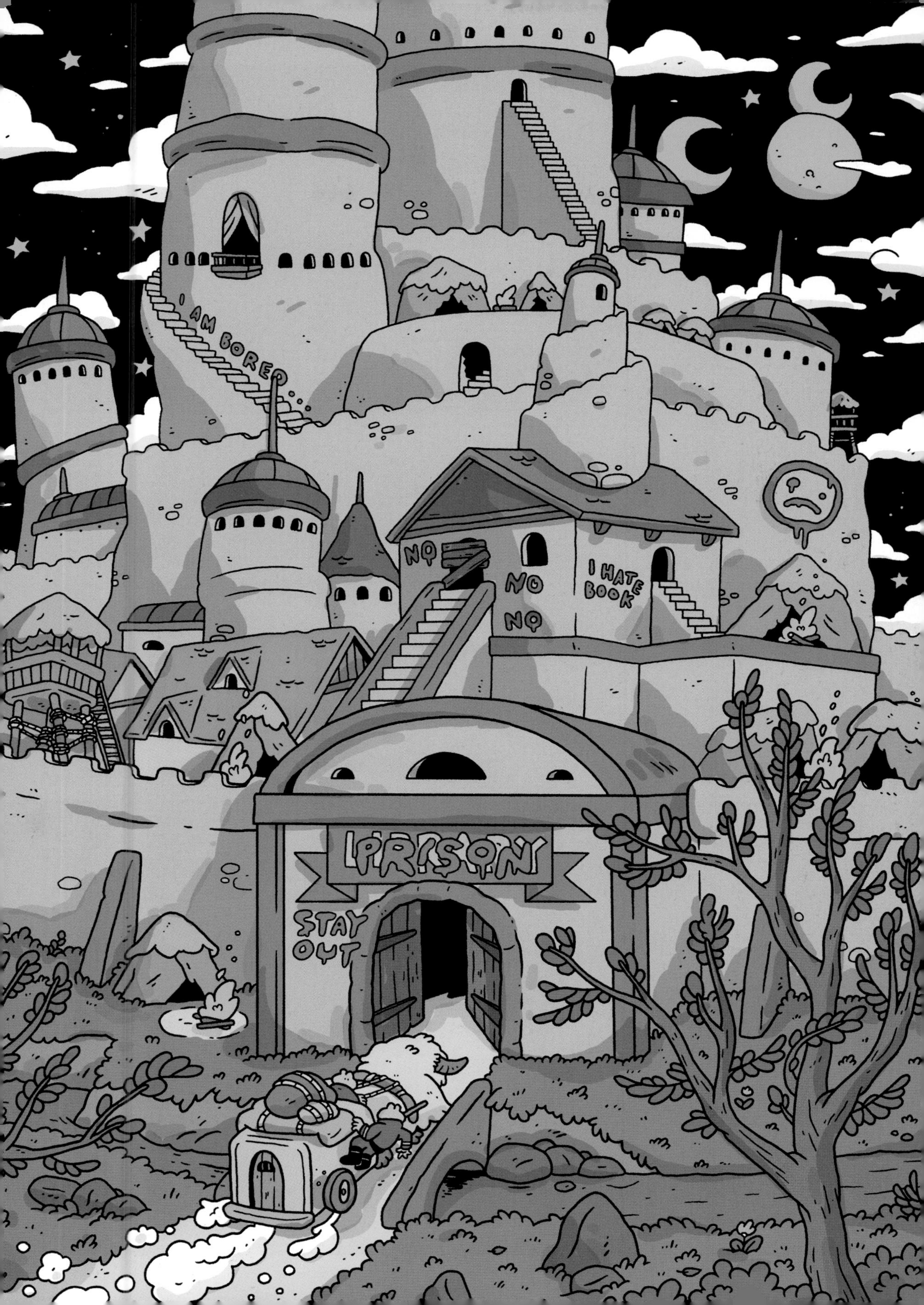

I AM BORED
NO
NO
NO
I HATE BOOK
PRISON
STAY OUT

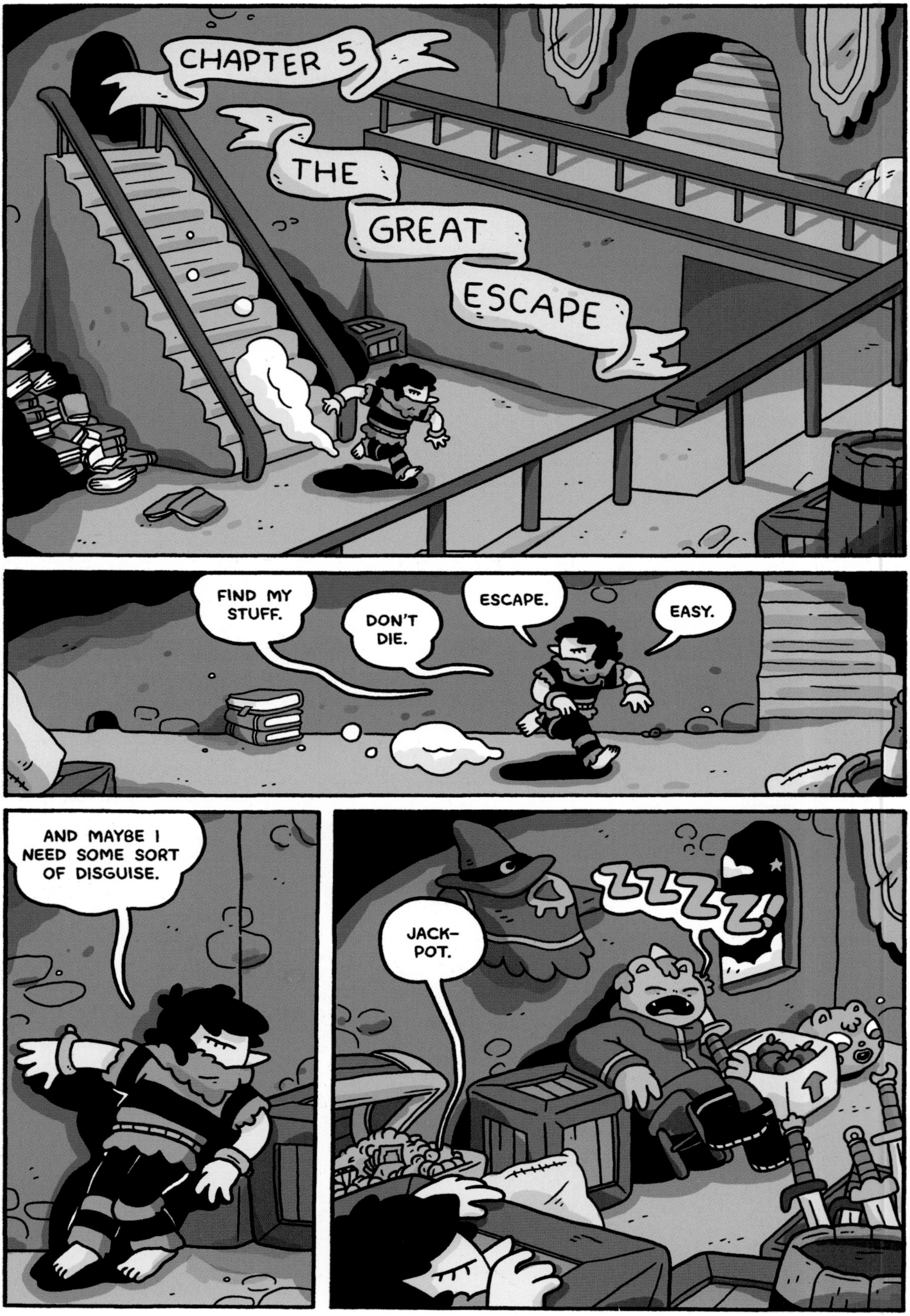
CHAPTER 5
THE GREAT ESCAPE
FIND MY STUFF.
DON'T DIE.
ESCAPE.
EASY.
AND MAYBE I NEED SOME SORT OF DISGUISE.
JACK-POT.
ZZZZZ!

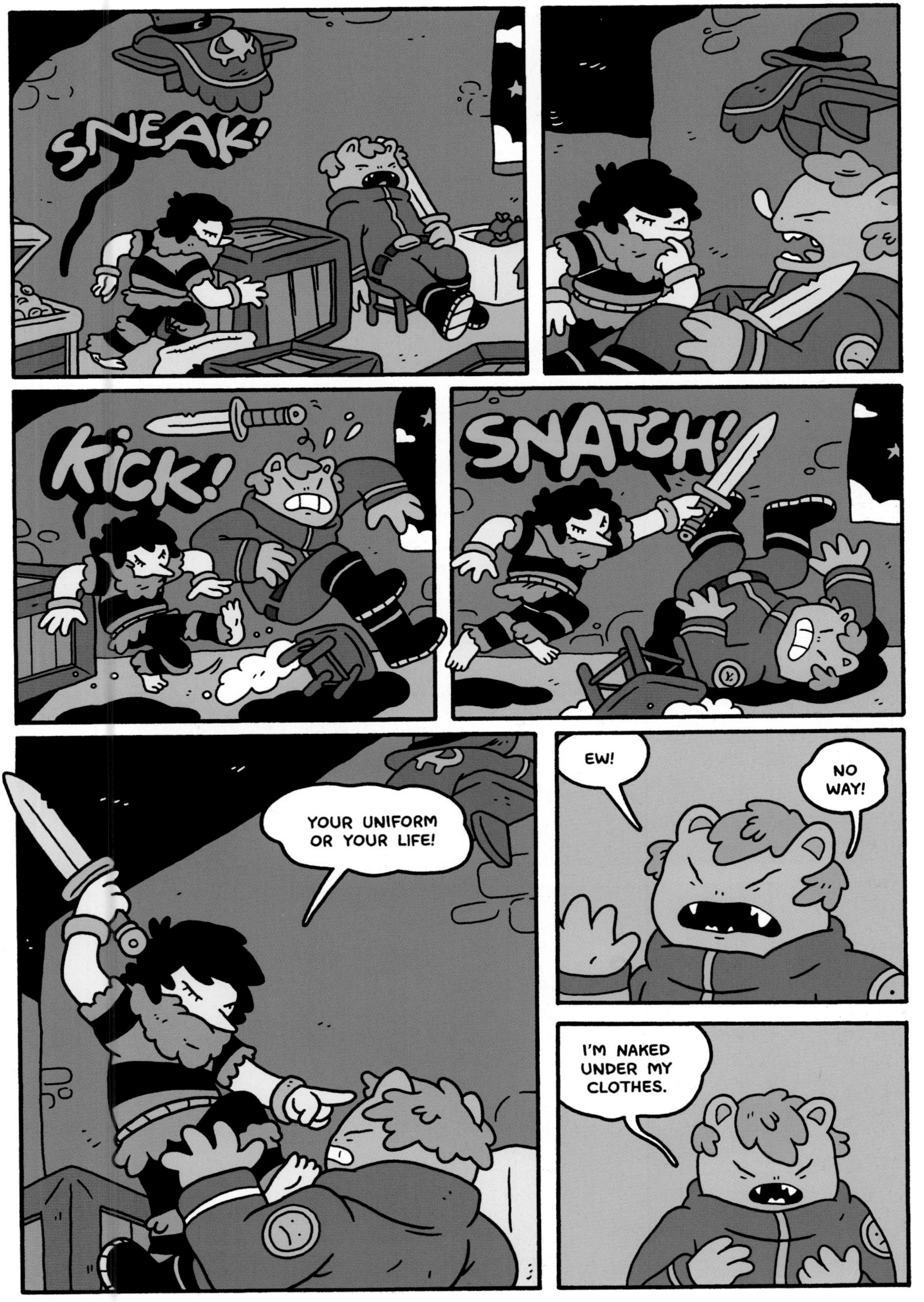
SNEAK!
KICK!
SNATCH!
YOUR UNIFORM OR YOUR LIFE!
EW!
NO WAY!
I'M NAKED UNDER MY CLOTHES.

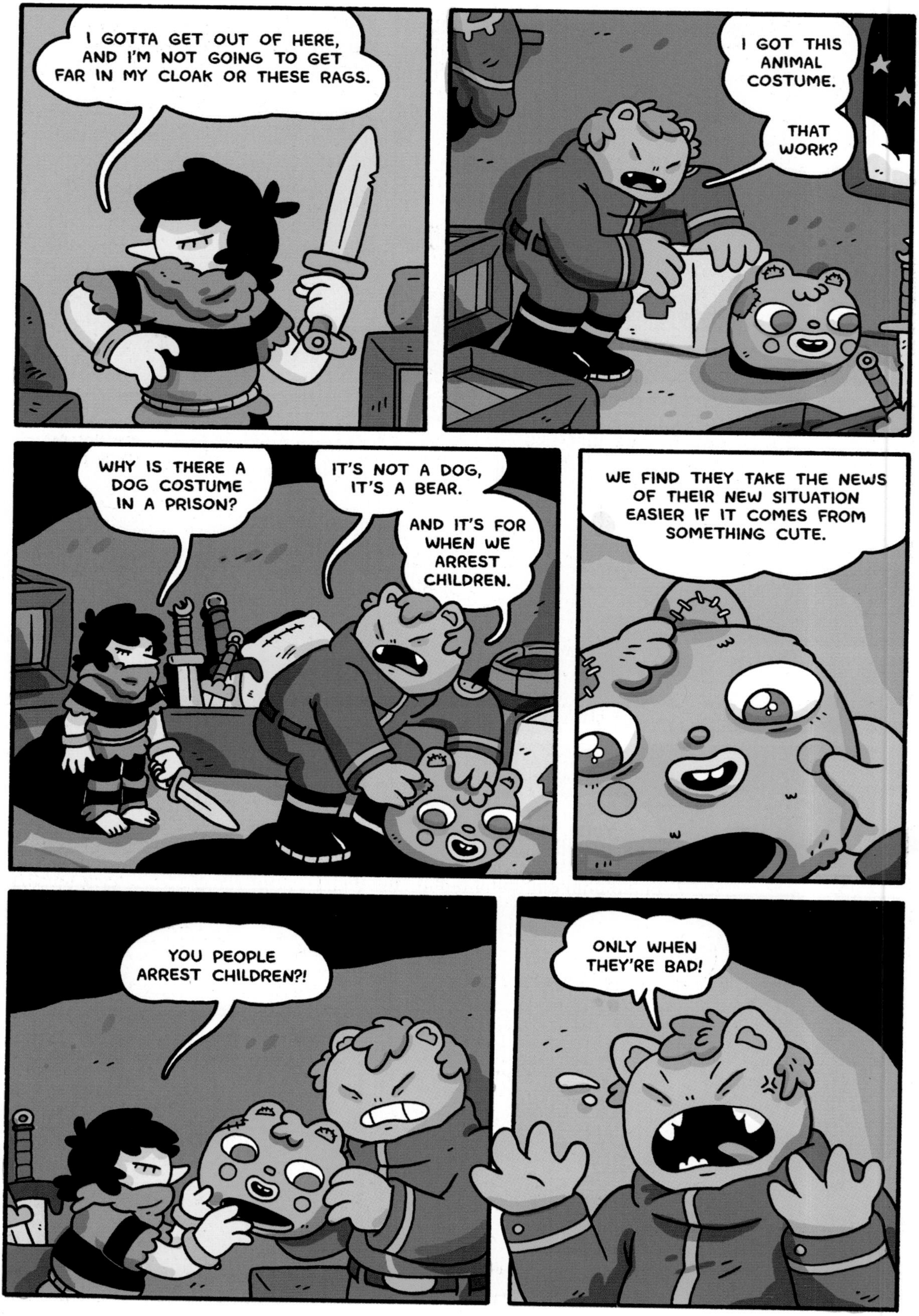
I GOTTA GET OUT OF HERE, AND I'M NOT GOING TO GET FAR IN MY CLOAK OR THESE RAGS.
I GOT THIS ANIMAL COSTUME.
THAT WORK?
WHY IS THERE A DOG COSTUME IN A PRISON?
IT'S NOT A DOG, IT'S A BEAR.
AND IT'S FOR WHEN WE ARREST CHILDREN.
WE FIND THEY TAKE THE NEWS OF THEIR NEW SITUATION EASIER IF IT COMES FROM SOMETHING CUTE.
YOU PEOPLE ARREST CHILDREN?!
ONLY WHEN THEY'RE BAD!

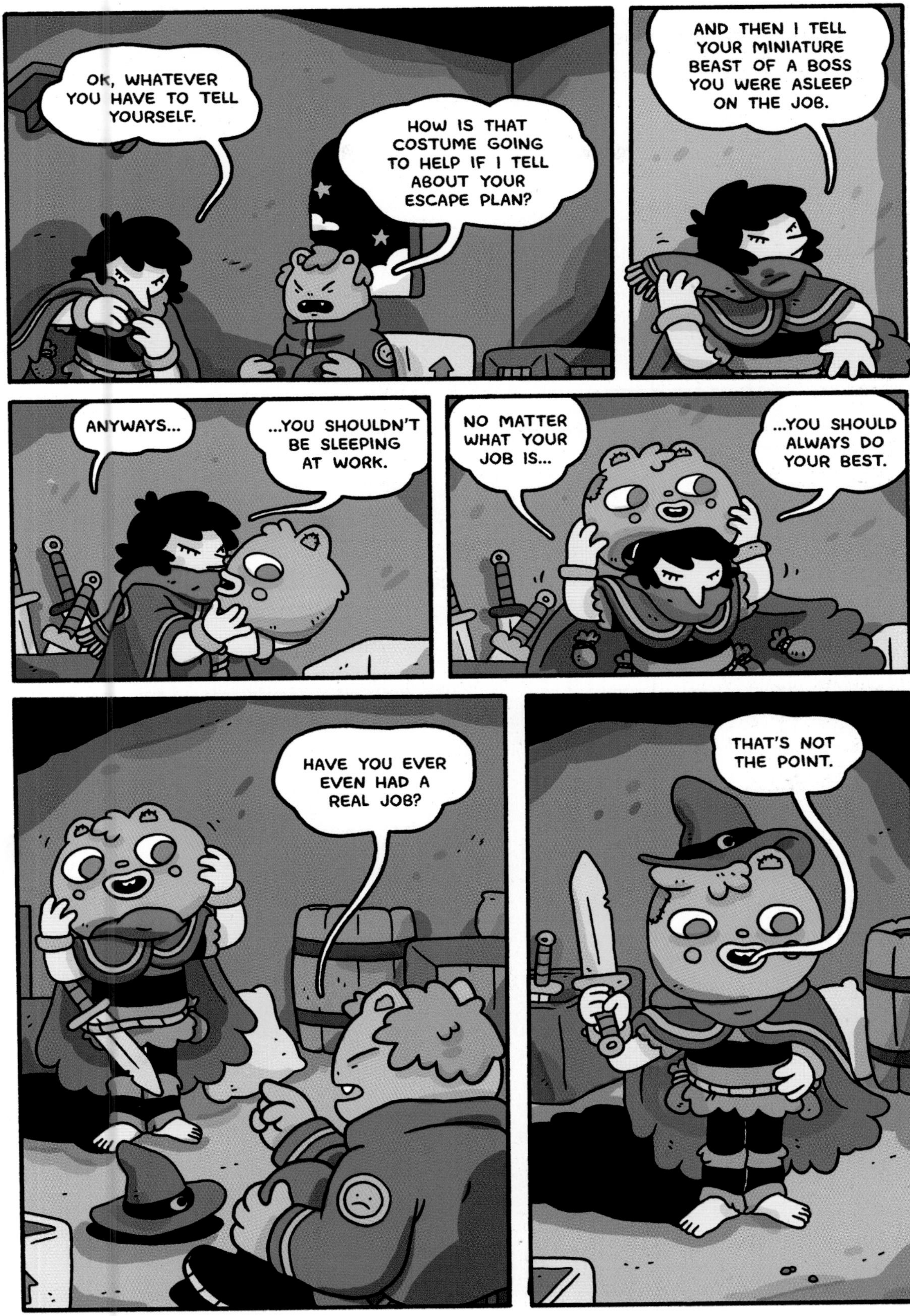
OK, WHATEVER YOU HAVE TO TELL YOURSELF.
HOW IS THAT COSTUME GOING TO HELP IF I TELL ABOUT YOUR ESCAPE PLAN?
AND THEN I TELL YOUR MINIATURE BEAST OF A BOSS YOU WERE ASLEEP ON THE JOB.
ANYWAYS...
...YOU SHOULDN'T BE SLEEPING AT WORK.
NO MATTER WHAT YOUR JOB IS...
...YOU SHOULD ALWAYS DO YOUR BEST.
HAVE YOU EVER EVEN HAD A REAL JOB?
THAT'S NOT THE POINT.

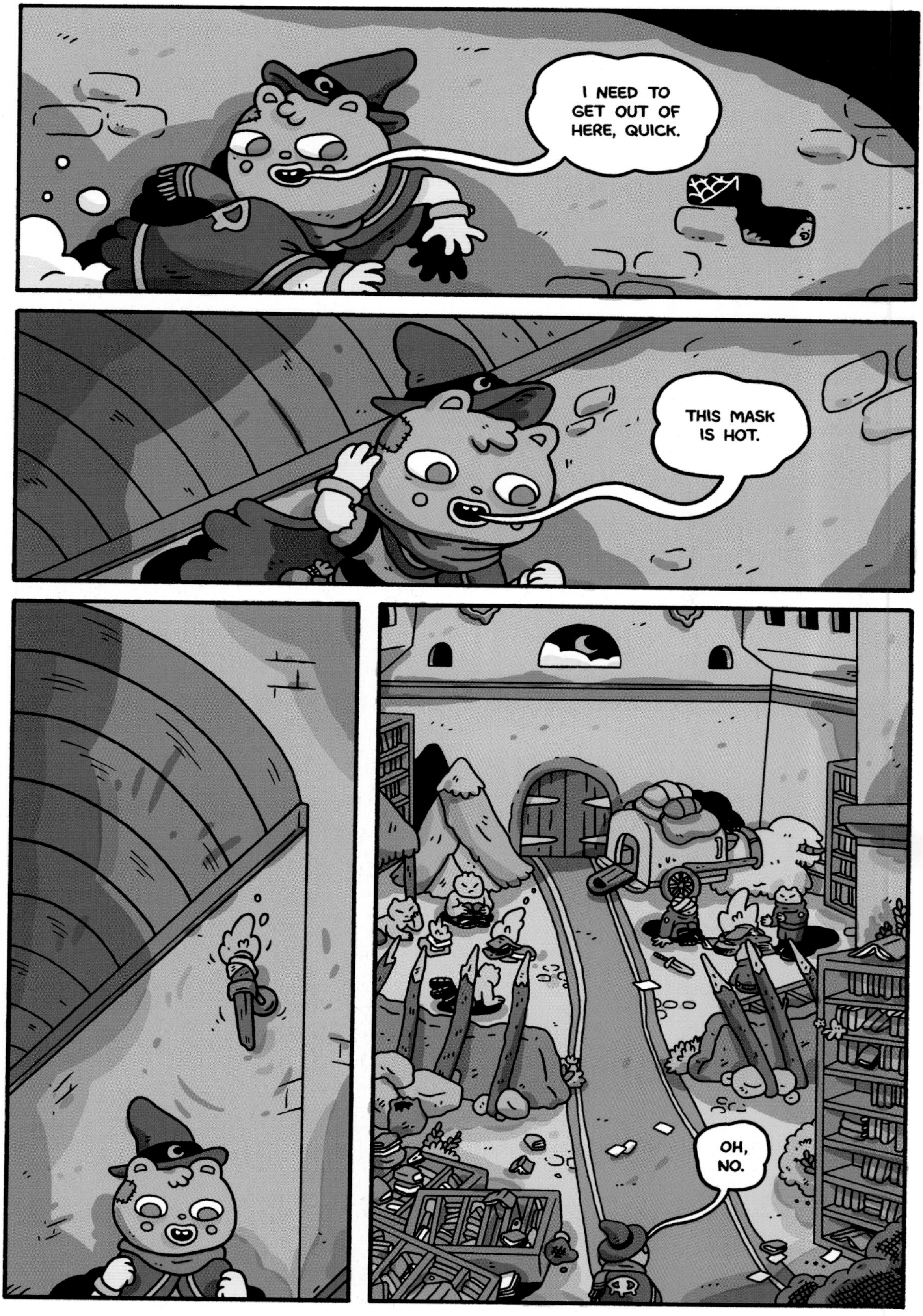
I NEED TO GET OUT OF HERE, QUICK.
THIS MASK IS HOT.
OH, NO.

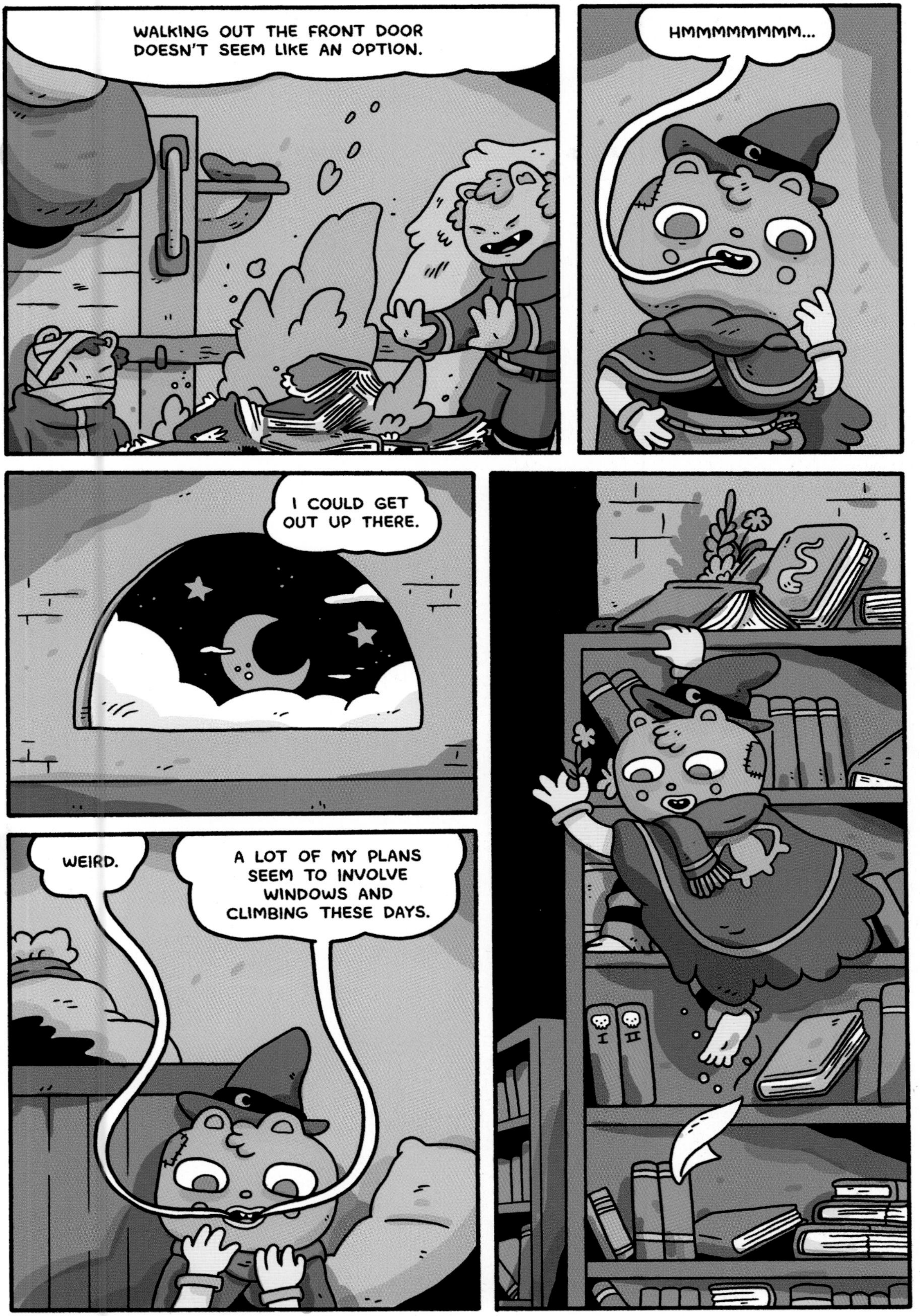
WALKING OUT THE FRONT DOOR DOESN'T SEEM LIKE AN OPTION.
HMMMMMMMM...
I COULD GET OUT UP THERE.
WEIRD.
A LOT OF MY PLANS SEEM TO INVOLVE WINDOWS AND CLIMBING THESE DAYS.

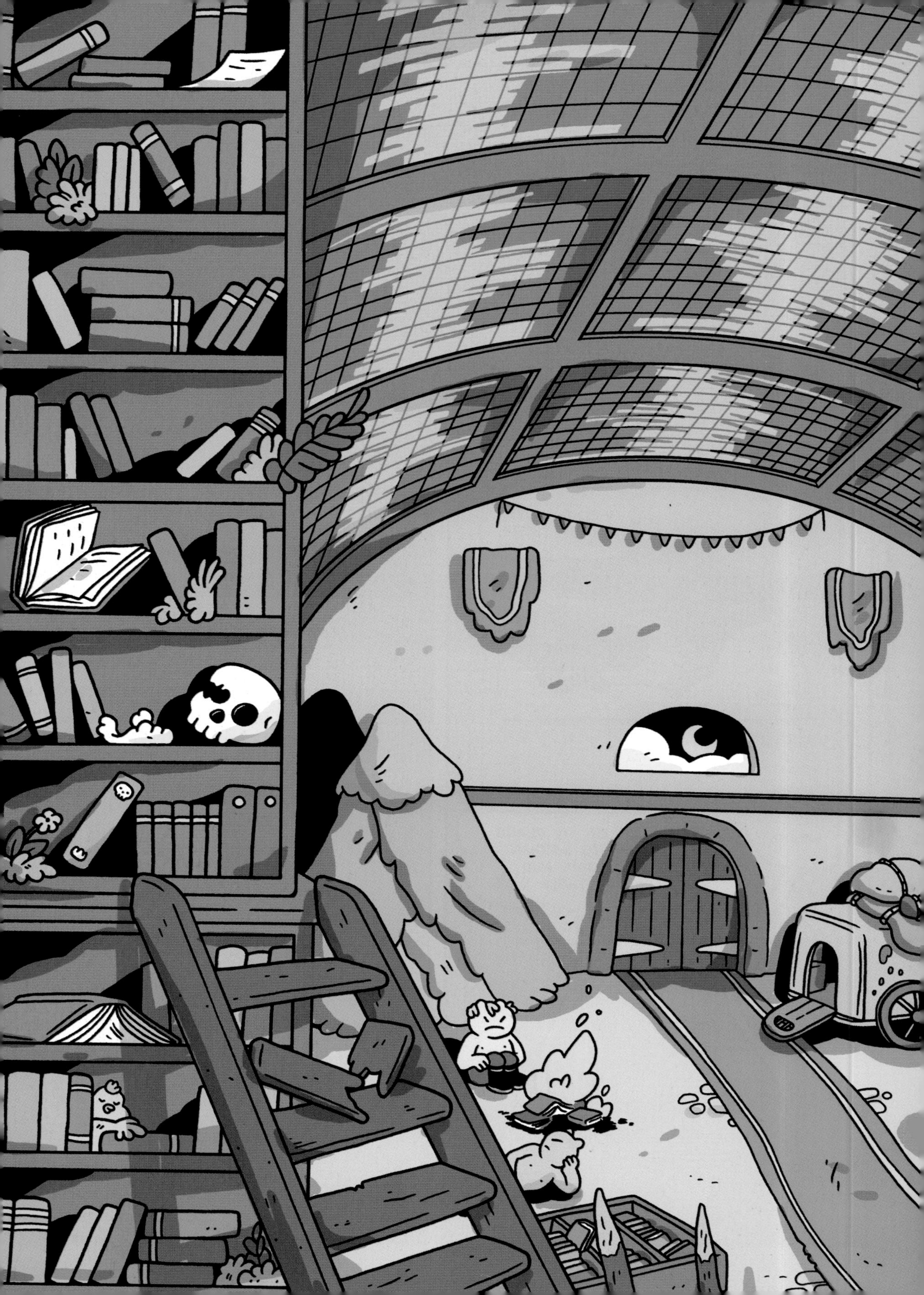

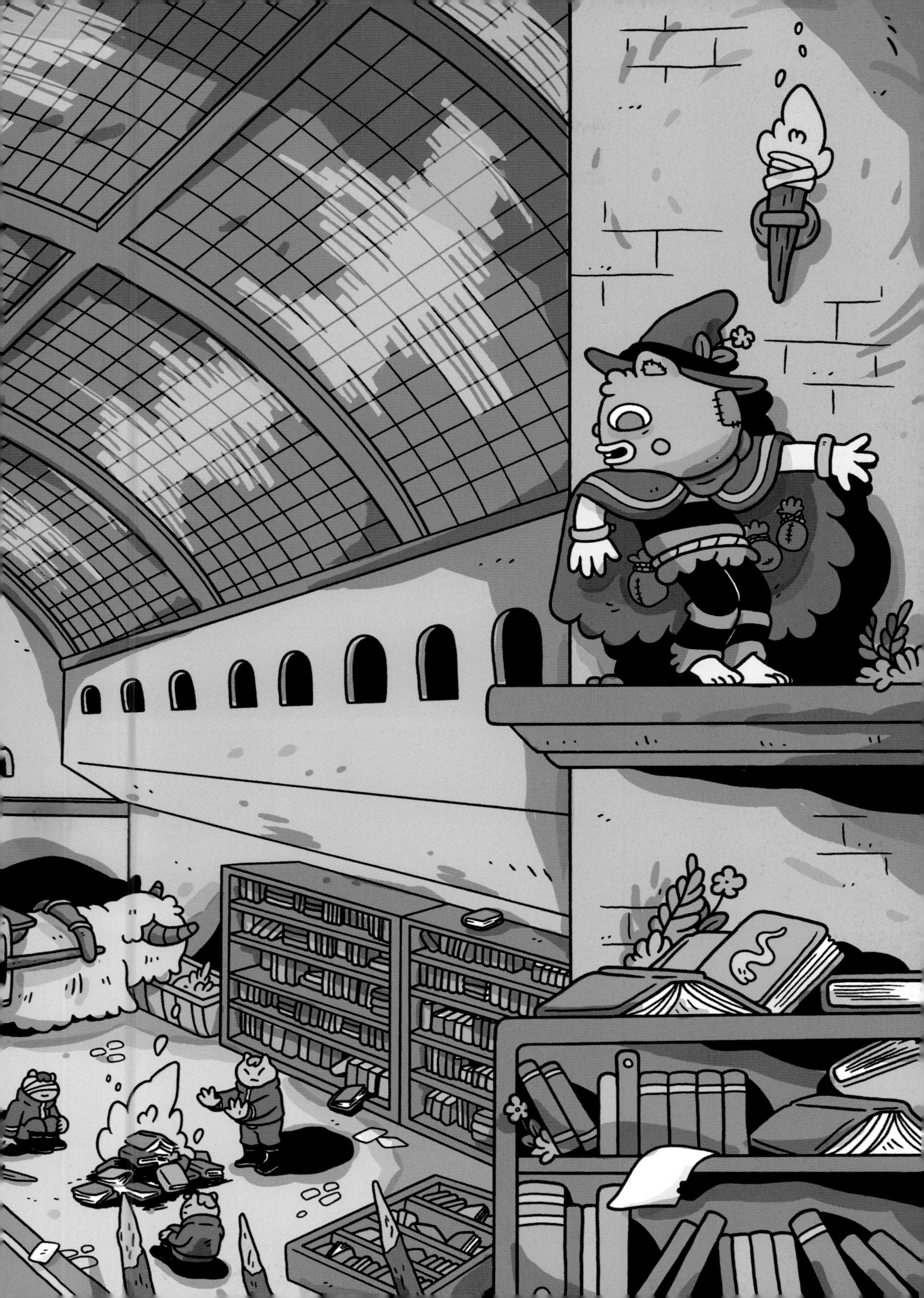

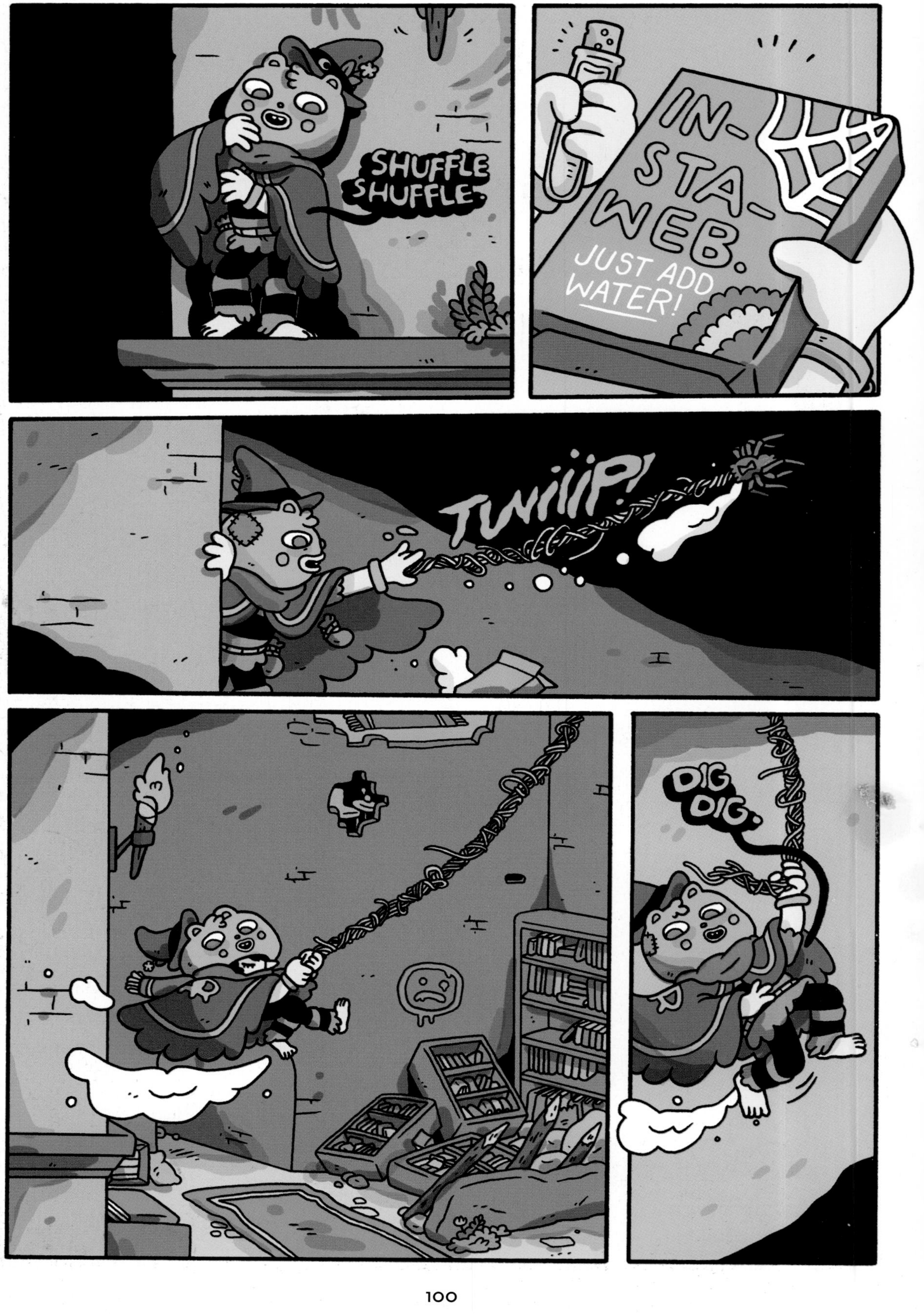
SHUFFLE SHUFFLE
IN-STA-WEB.
JUST ADD WATER!
TWIIIP!
DIG DIG

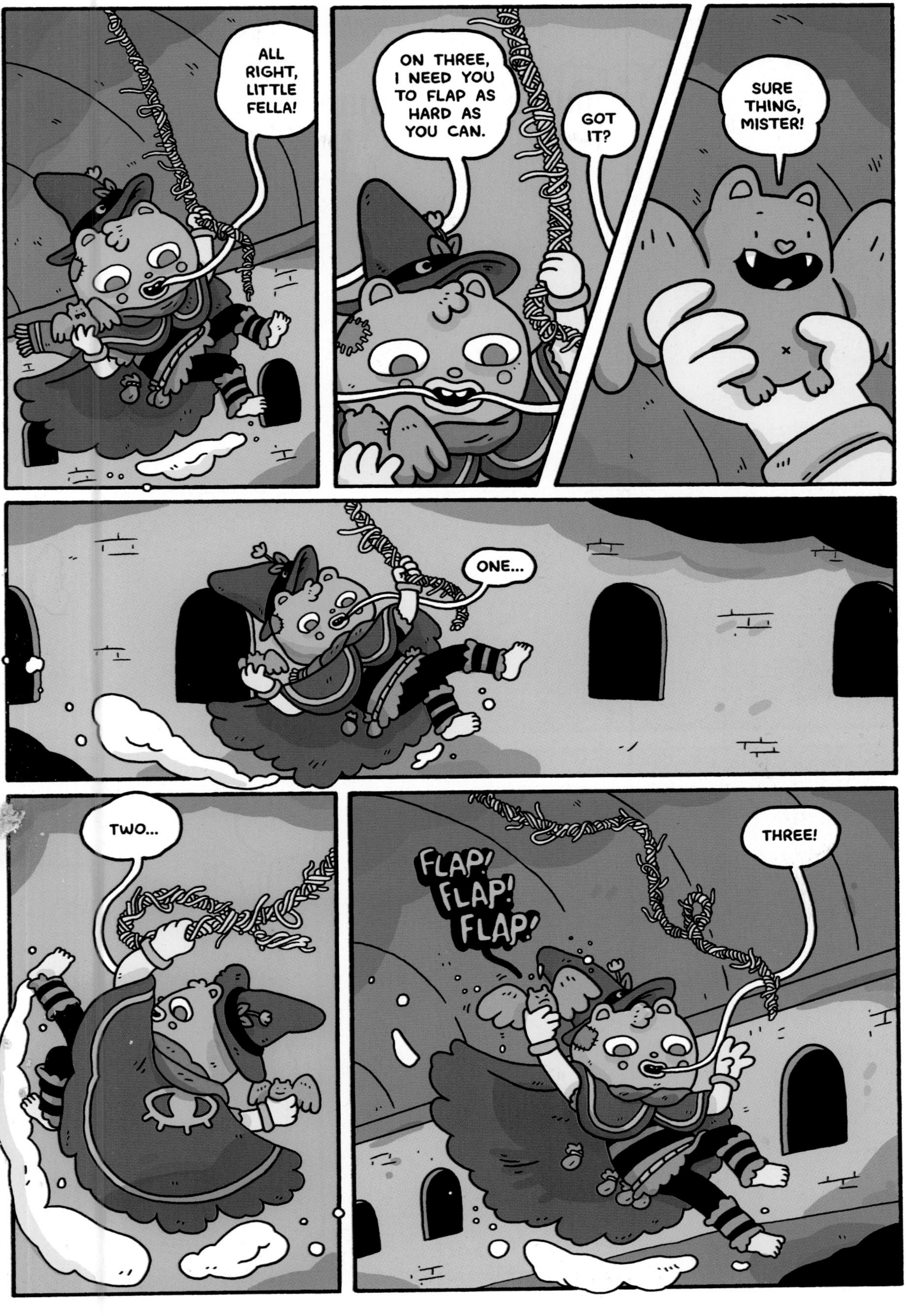
ALL RIGHT, LITTLE FELLA!
ON THREE, I NEED YOU TO FLAP AS HARD AS YOU CAN.
GOT IT?
SURE THING, MISTER!
ONE...
TWO...
FLAP! FLAP! FLAP!
THREE!

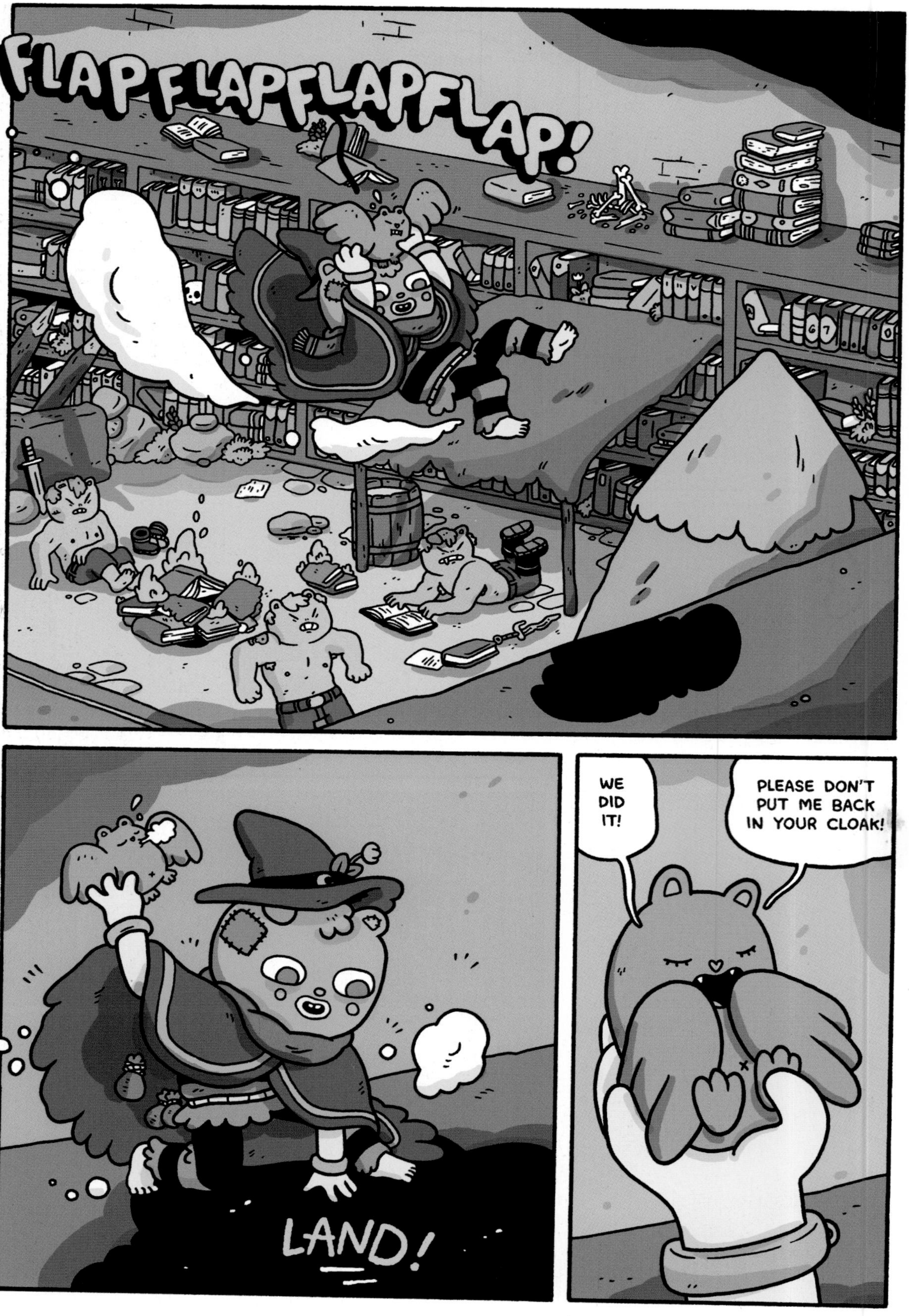
FLAPFLAPFLAPFLAP!
LAND!
WE DID IT!
PLEASE DON'T PUT ME BACK IN YOUR CLOAK!

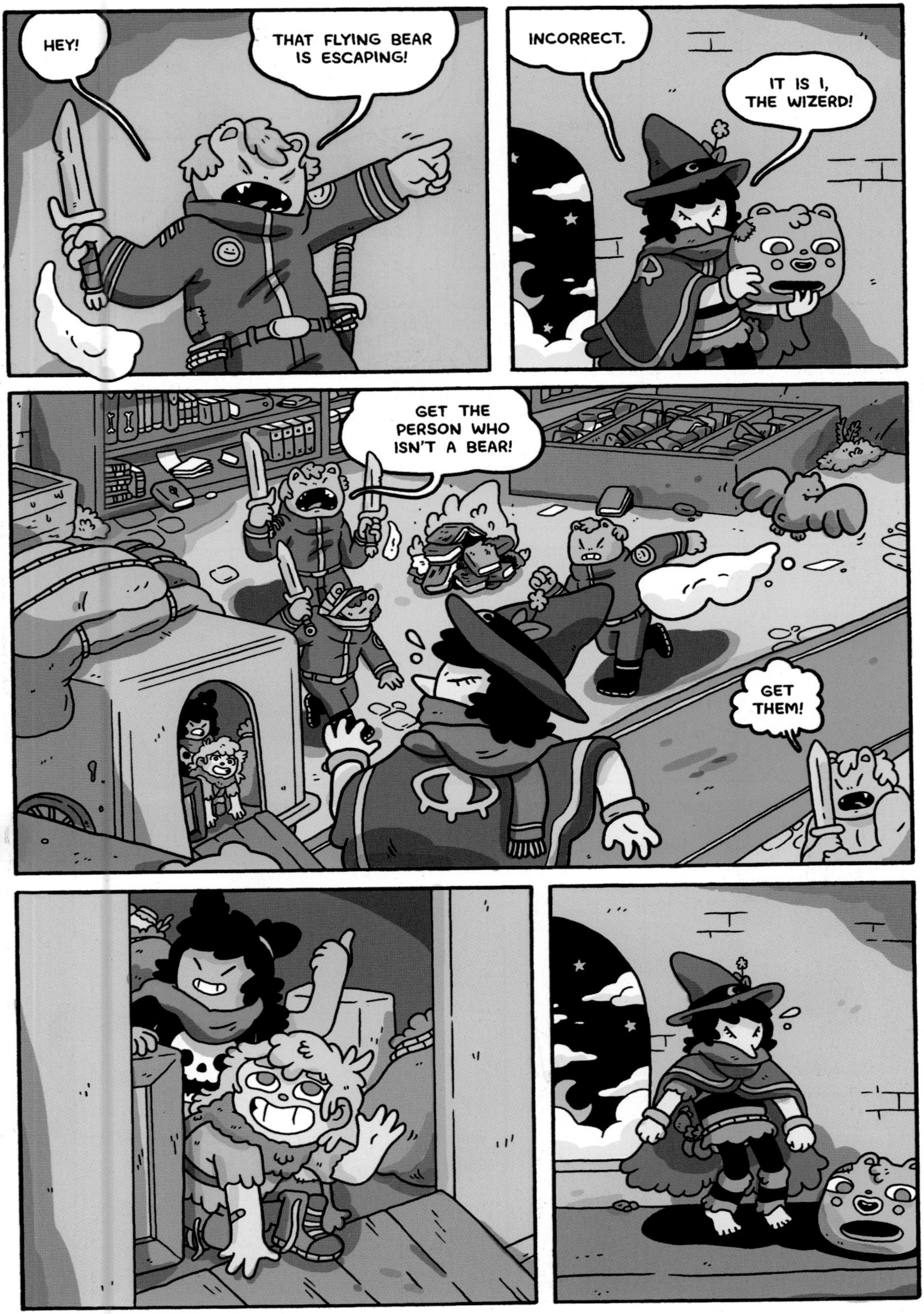
HEY!
THAT FLYING BEAR IS ESCAPING!
INCORRECT.
IT IS I, THE WIZERD!
GET THE PERSON WHO ISN'T A BEAR!
GET THEM!

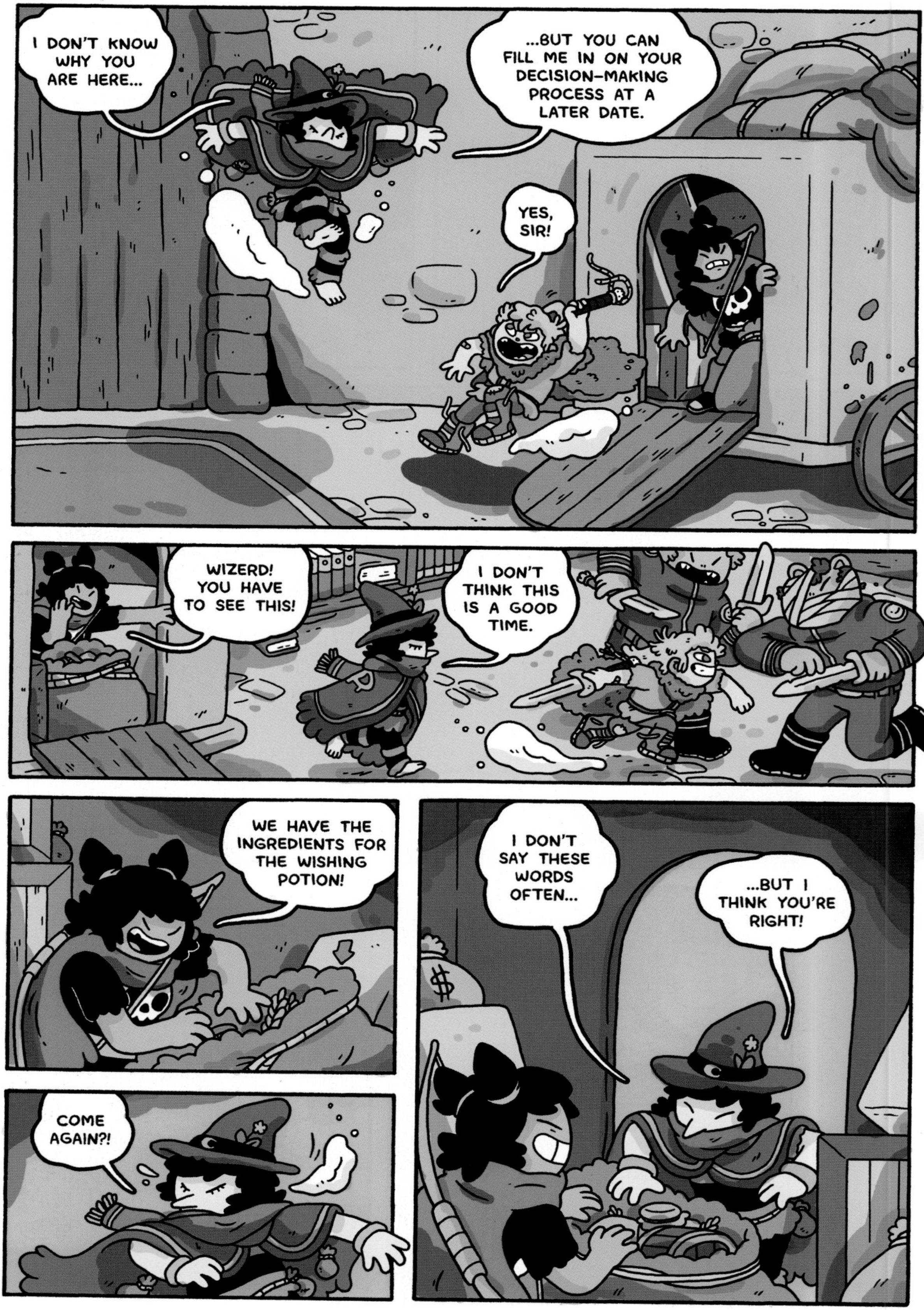
I DON'T KNOW WHY YOU ARE HERE...
...BUT YOU CAN FILL ME IN ON YOUR DECISION-MAKING PROCESS AT A LATER DATE.
YES, SIR!
WIZERD! YOU HAVE TO SEE THIS!
I DON'T THINK THIS IS A GOOD TIME.
WE HAVE THE INGREDIENTS FOR THE WISHING POTION!
COME AGAIN?!
I DON'T SAY THESE WORDS OFTEN...
...BUT I THINK YOU'RE RIGHT!

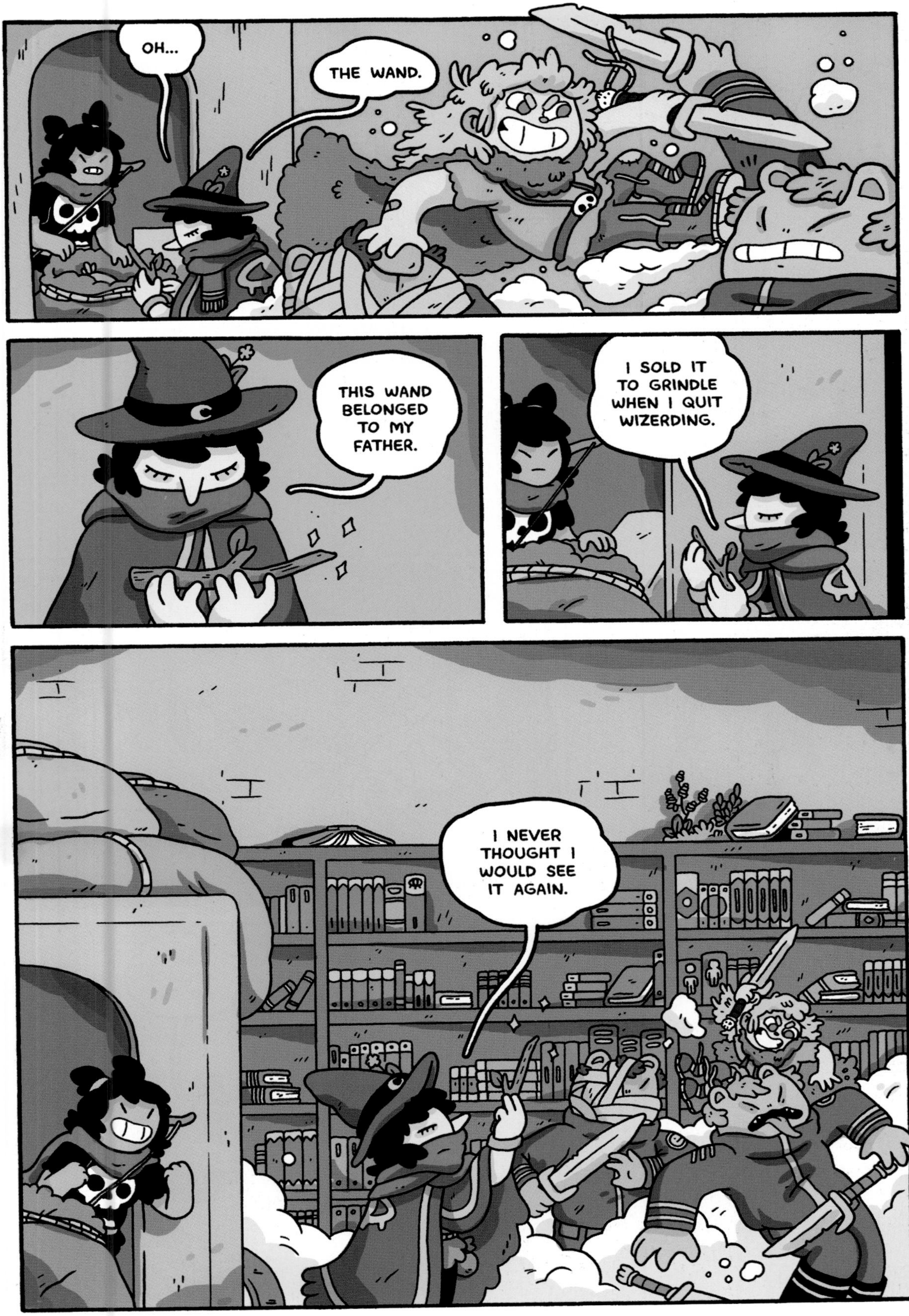
OH...
THE WAND.
THIS WAND BELONGED TO MY FATHER.
I SOLD IT TO GRINDLE WHEN I QUIT WIZERDING.
I NEVER THOUGHT I WOULD SEE IT AGAIN.

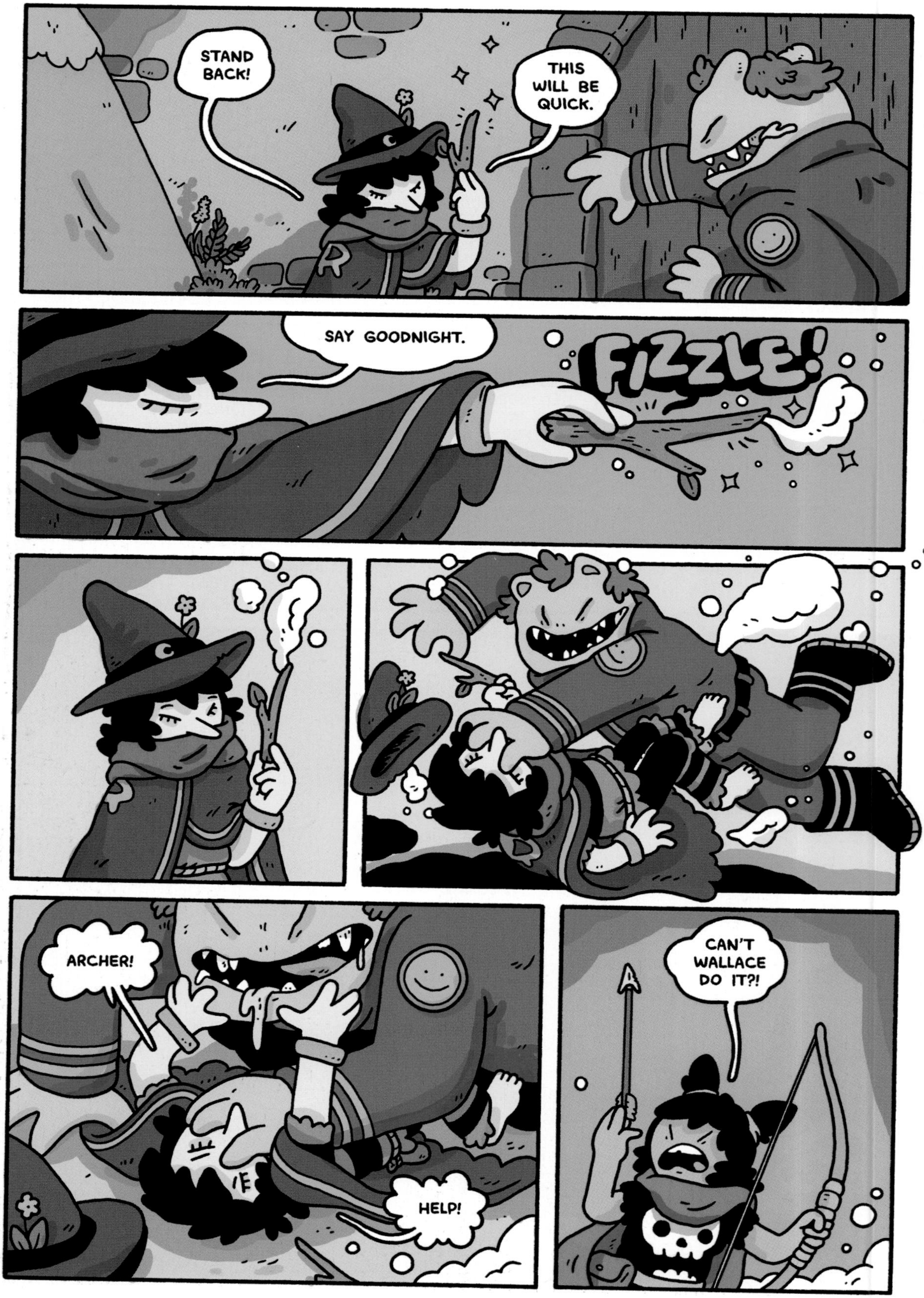
STAND BACK!
THIS WILL BE QUICK.
SAY GOODNIGHT.
FIZZLE!
ARCHER!
HELP!
CAN'T WALLACE DO IT?!

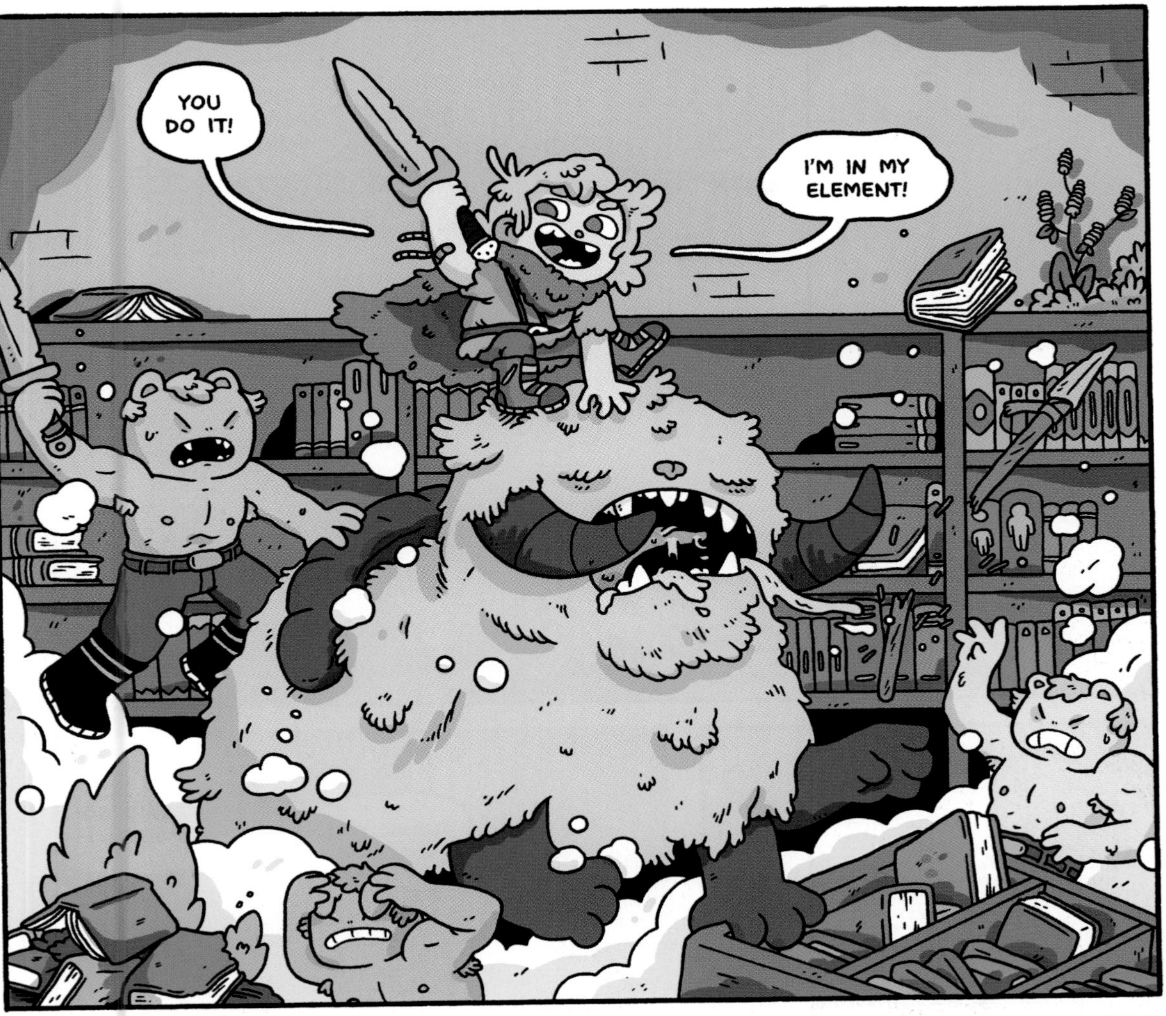
YOU DO IT!
I'M IN MY ELEMENT!

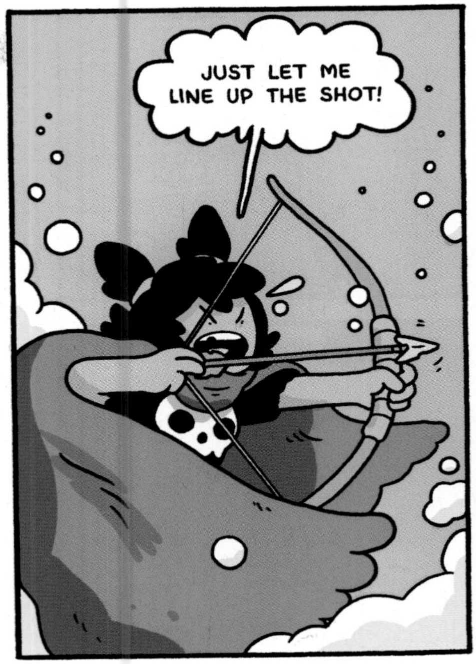
JUST LET ME LINE UP THE SHOT!

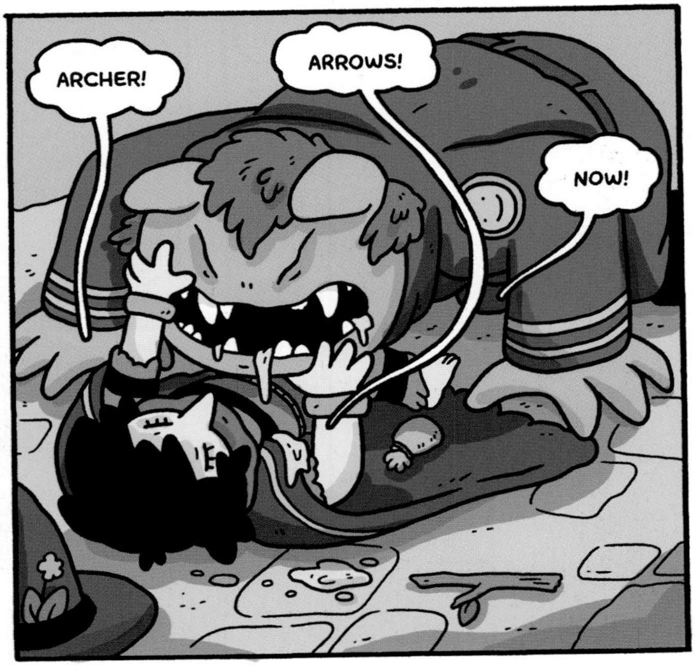
ARCHER!
ARROWS!
NOW!

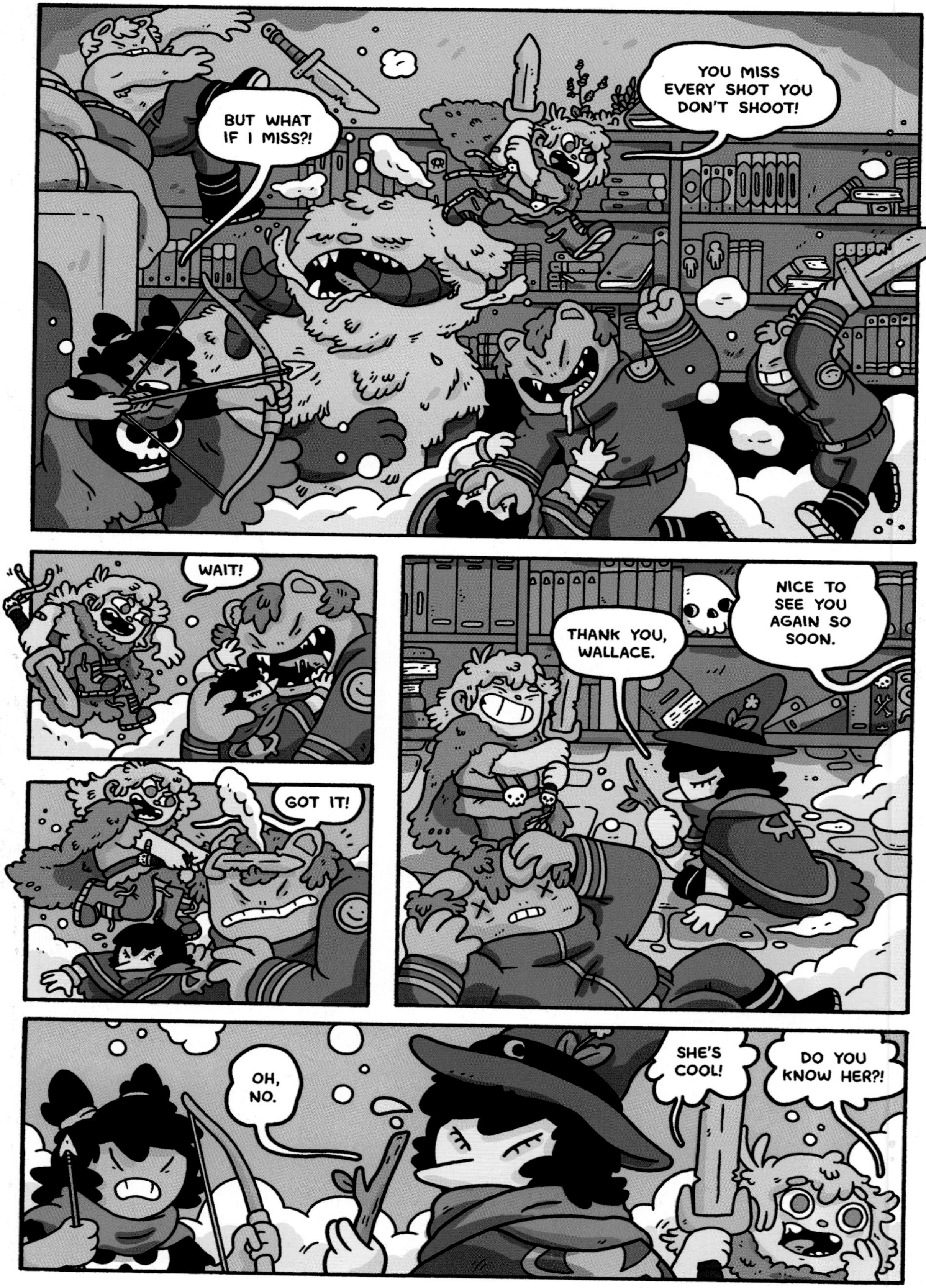
BUT WHAT IF I MISS?!
YOU MISS EVERY SHOT YOU DON'T SHOOT!
WAIT!
GOT IT!
THANK YOU, WALLACE.
NICE TO SEE YOU AGAIN SO SOON.
OH, NO.
SHE'S COOL!
DO YOU KNOW HER?!

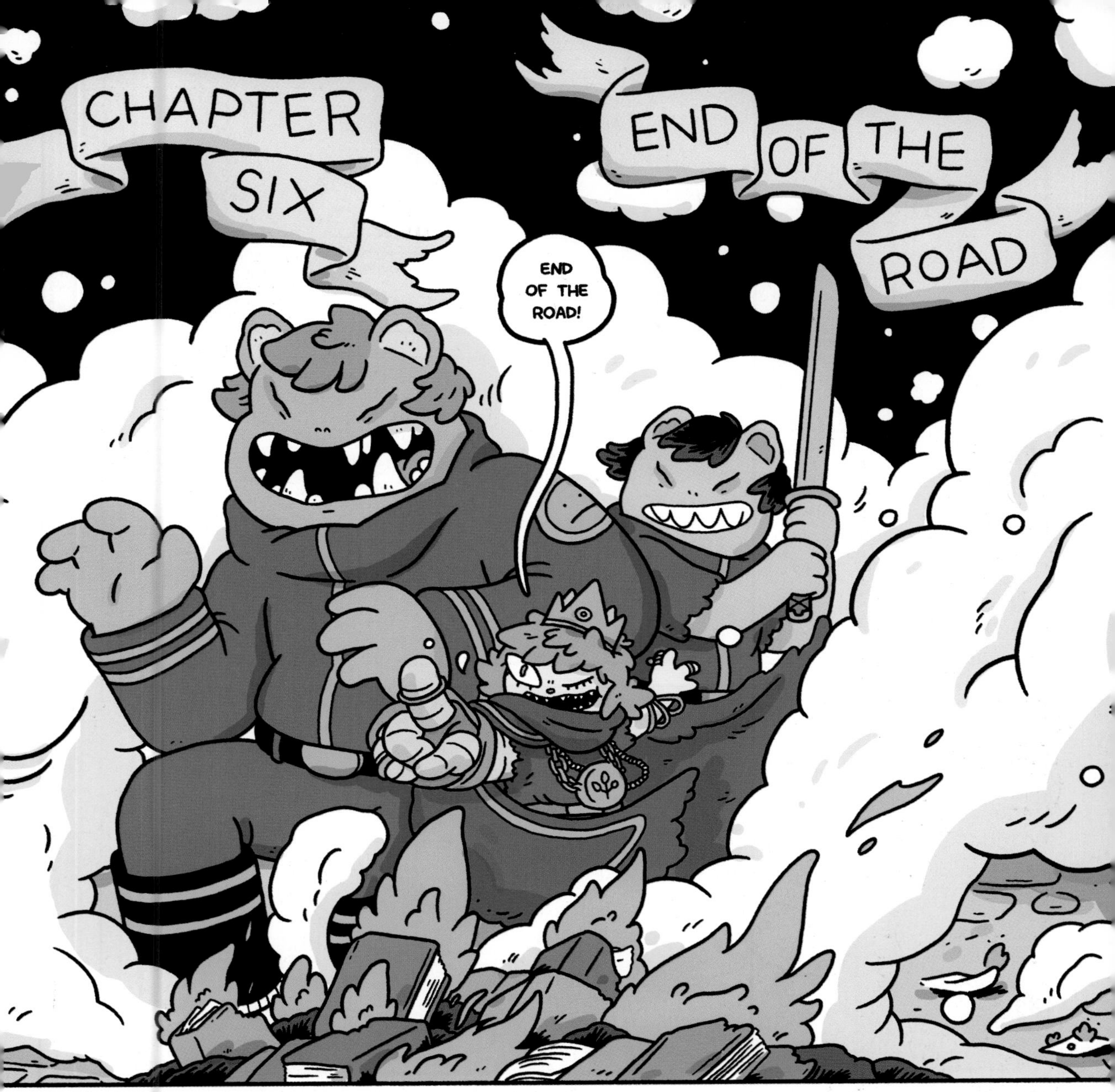
CHAPTER SIX
END OF THE ROAD
END OF THE ROAD!

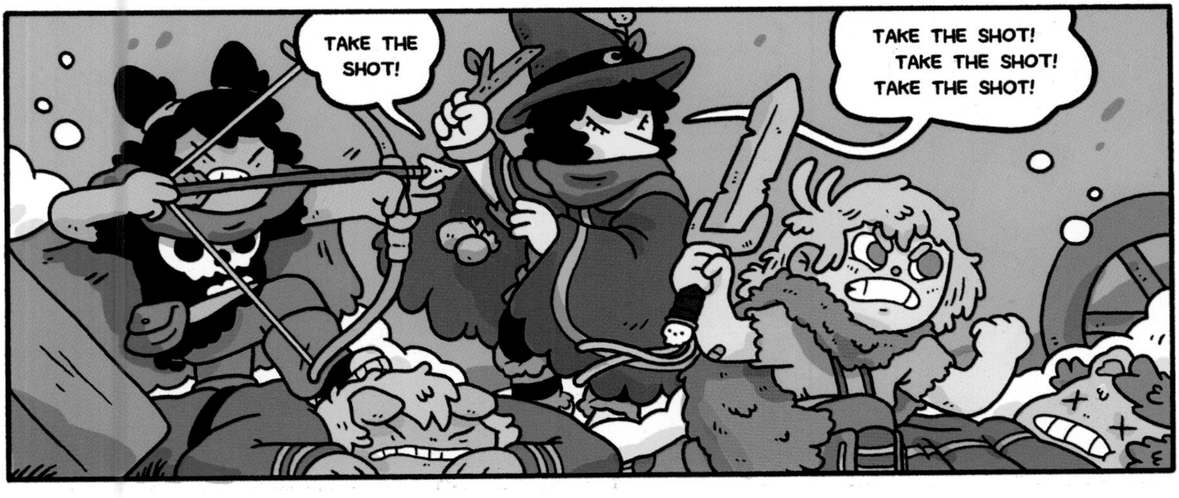
TAKE THE SHOT!
TAKE THE SHOT! TAKE THE SHOT! TAKE THE SHOT!

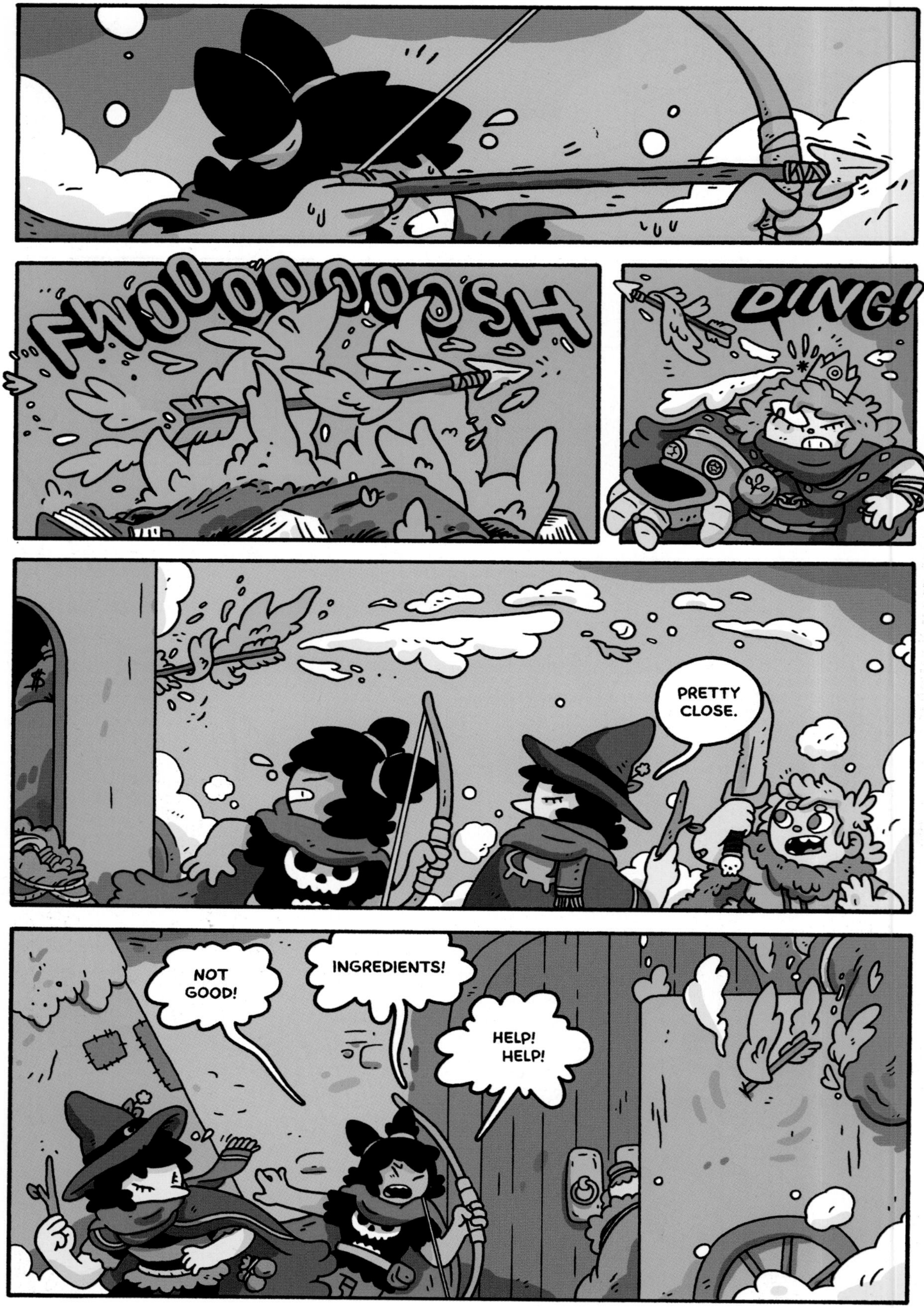
FWOOOOOOOSH
DING!
PRETTY CLOSE.
NOT GOOD!
INGREDIENTS!
HELP! HELP!

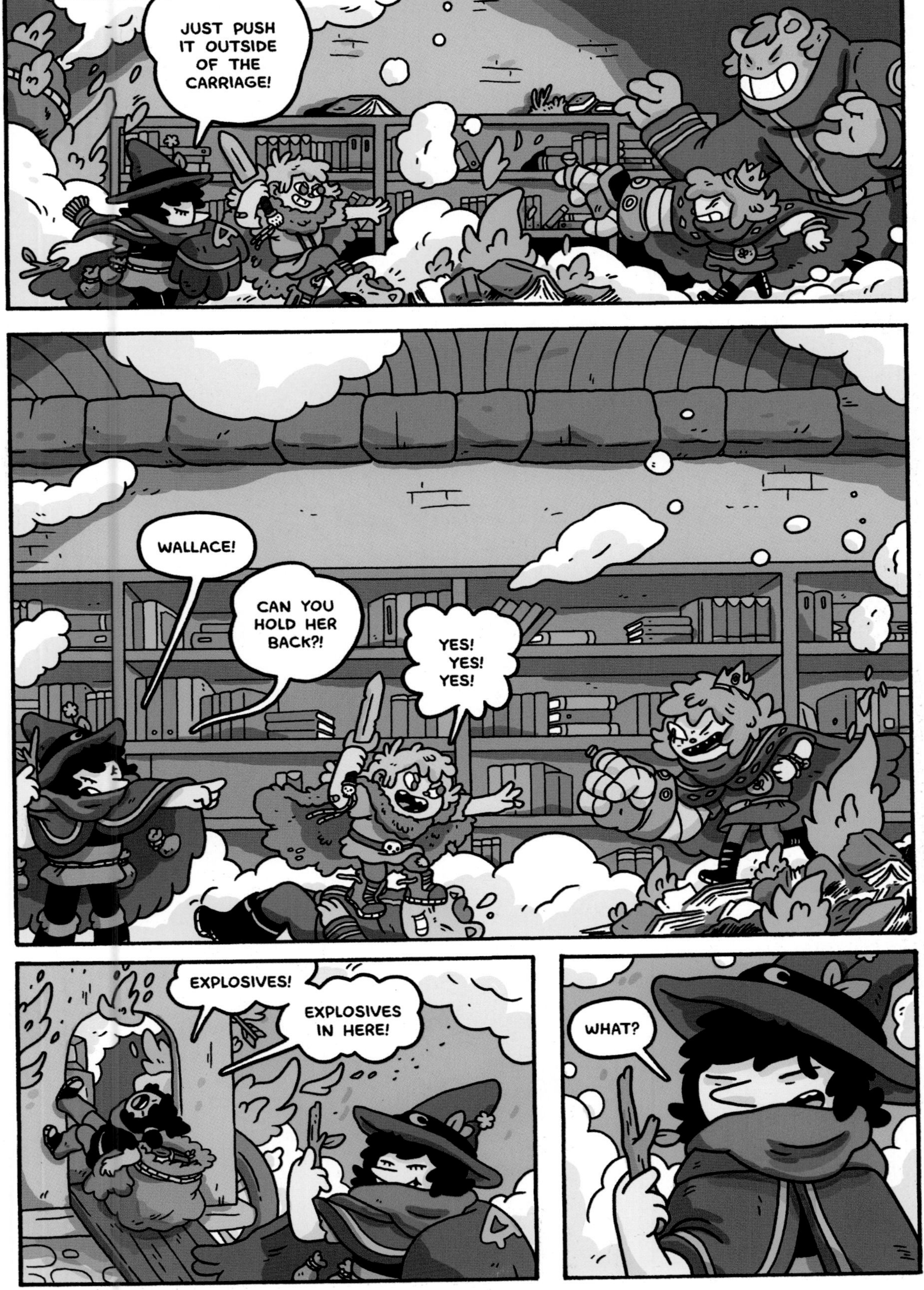
JUST PUSH IT OUTSIDE OF THE CARRIAGE!
WALLACE!
CAN YOU HOLD HER BACK?!
YES! YES! YES!
EXPLOSIVES!
EXPLOSIVES IN HERE!
WHAT?

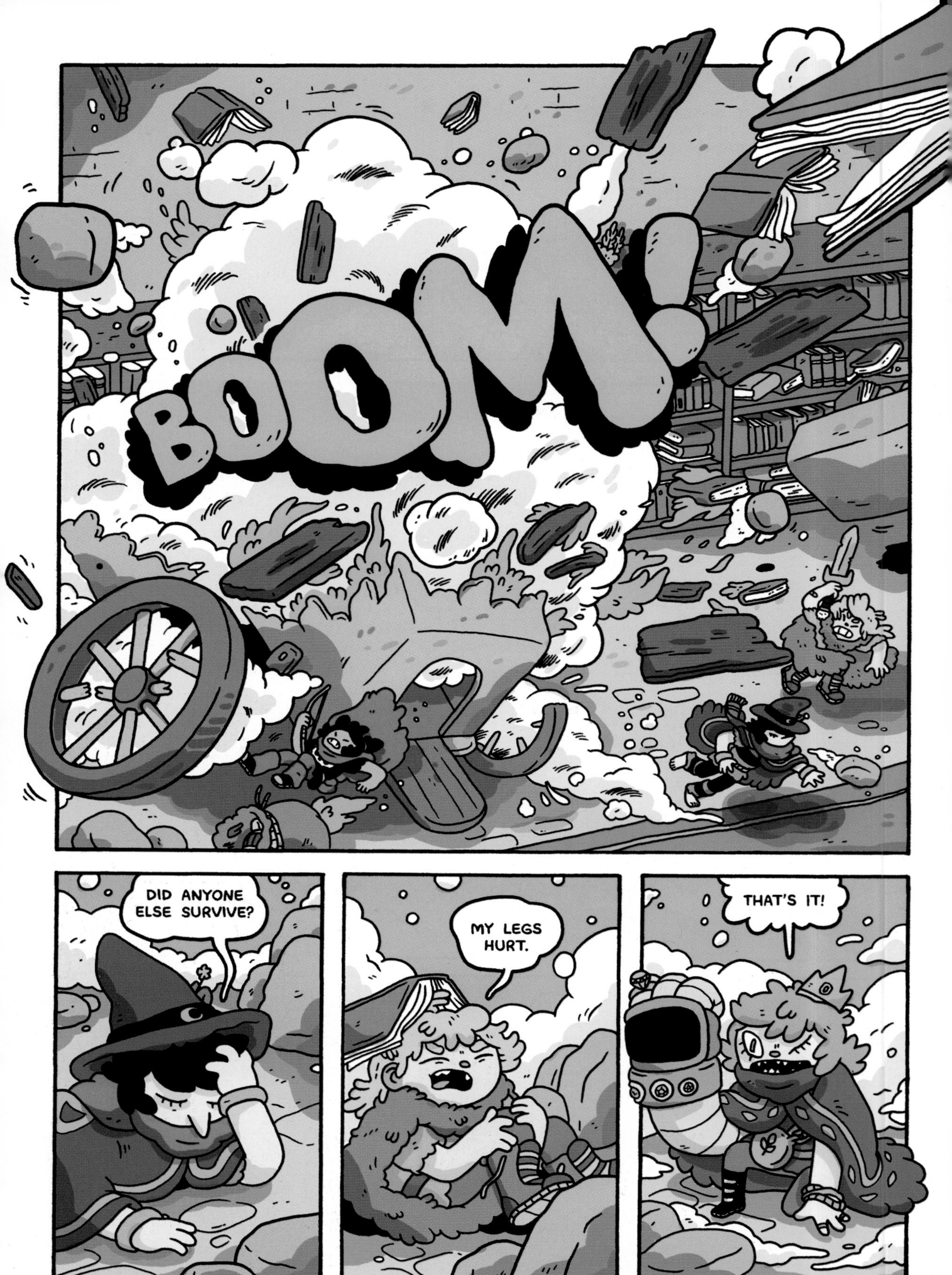
BOOM!
DID ANYONE ELSE SURVIVE?
MY LEGS HURT.
THAT'S IT!

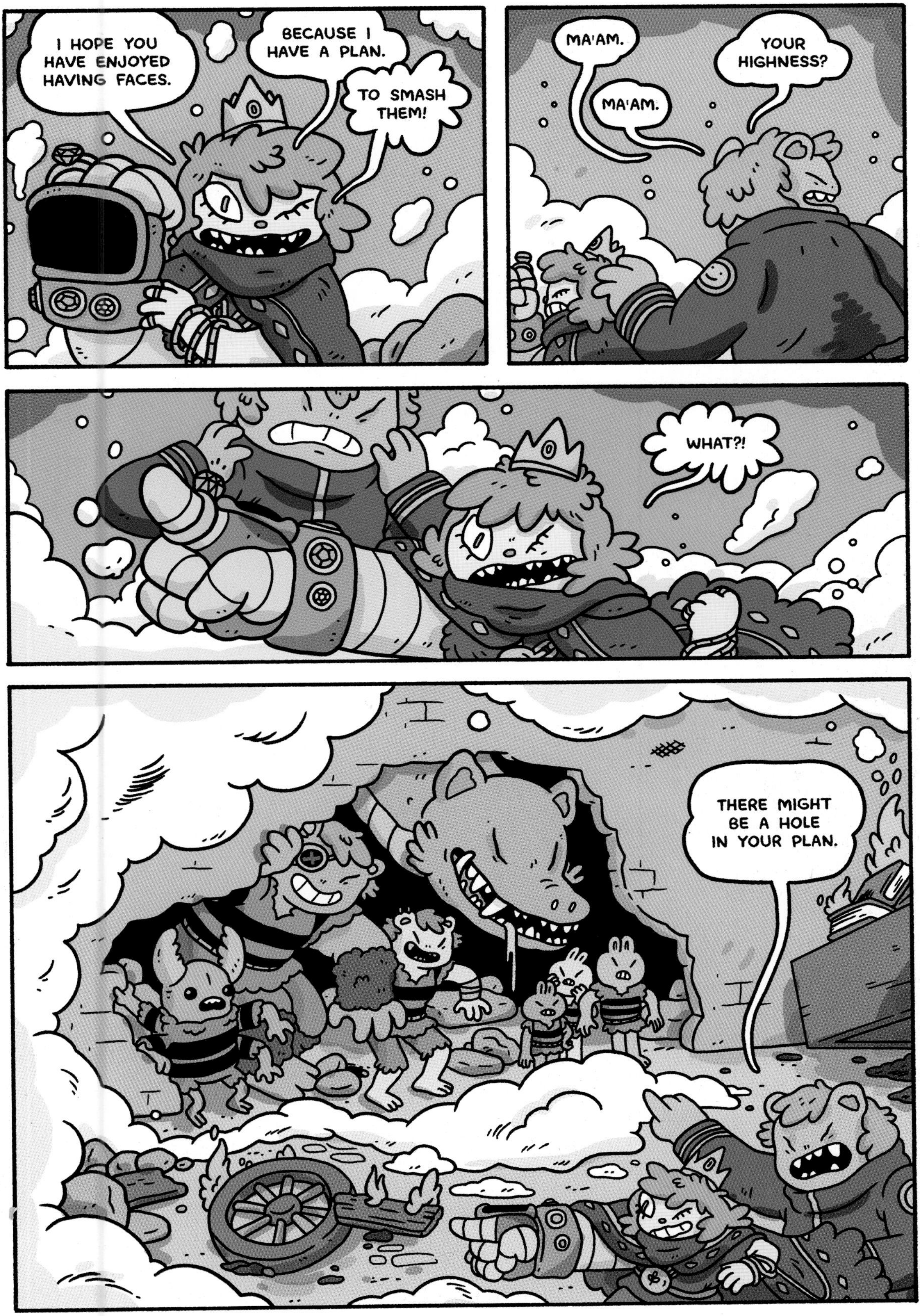
I HOPE YOU HAVE ENJOYED HAVING FACES.
BECAUSE I HAVE A PLAN.
TO SMASH THEM!
MA'AM.
MA'AM.
YOUR HIGHNESS?
WHAT?!
THERE MIGHT BE A HOLE IN YOUR PLAN.

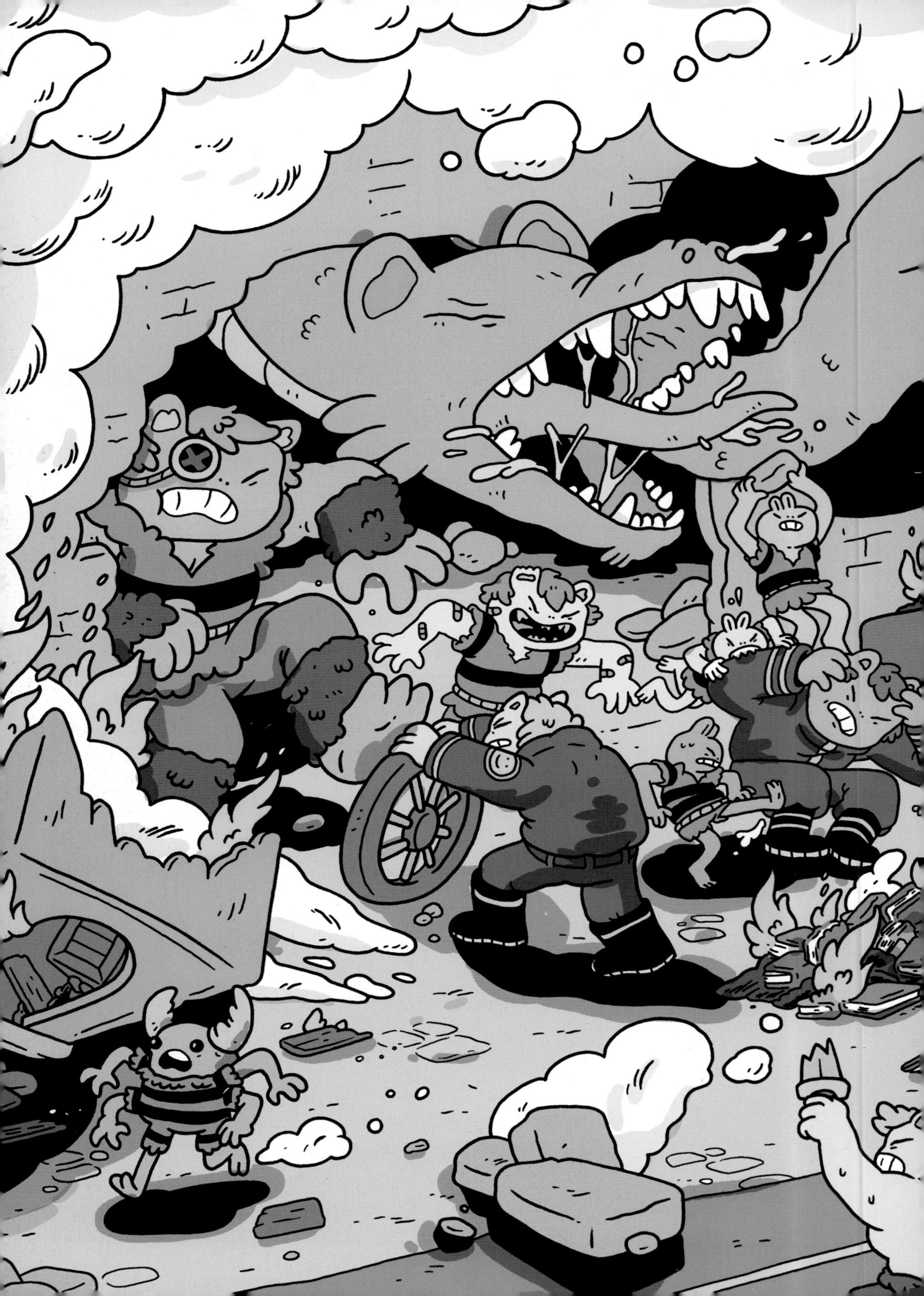

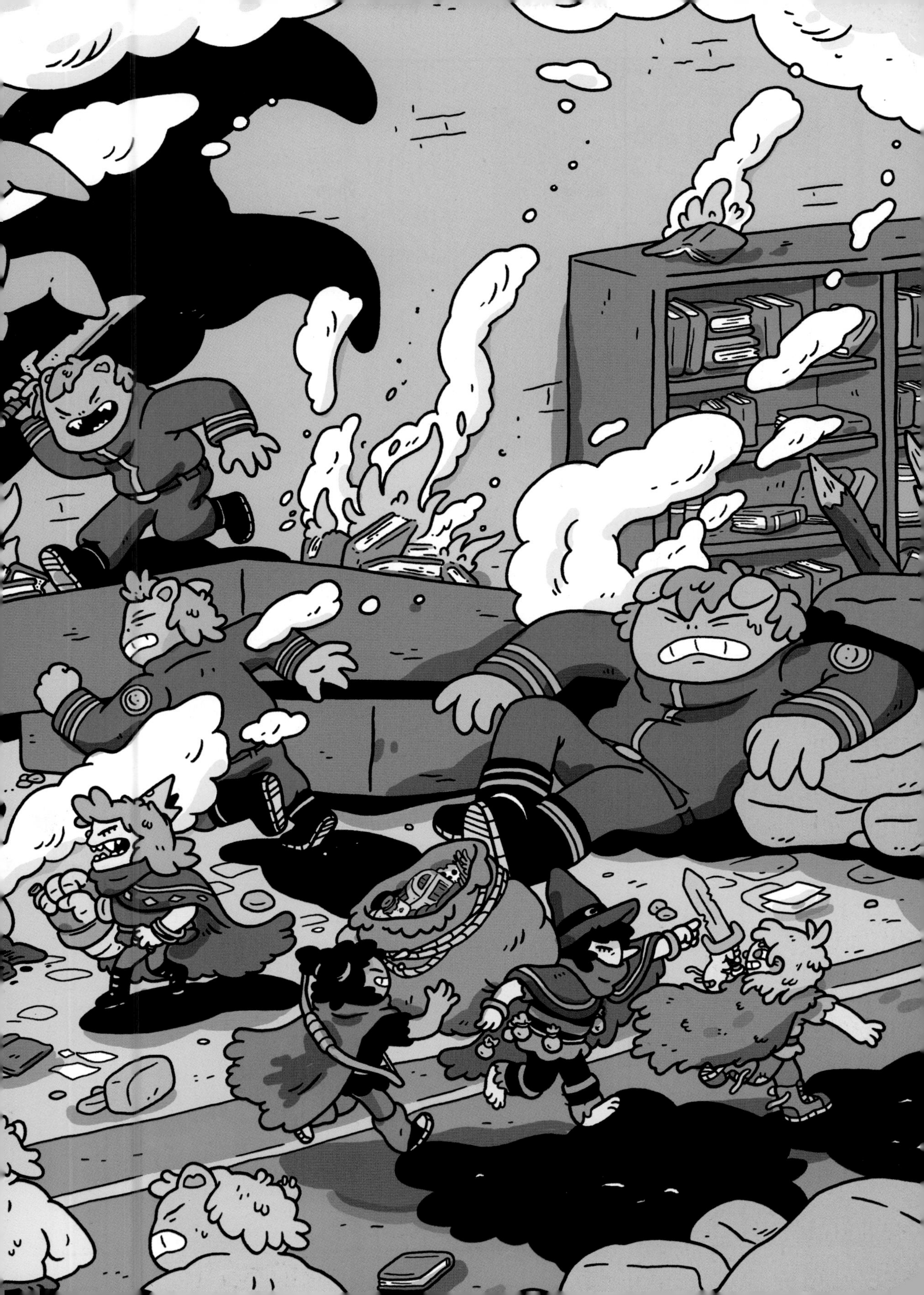

ISN'T THIS THE WRONG DIRECTION?

SURE.

BUT WE ALSO DON'T WANT TO DIE IN THERE.

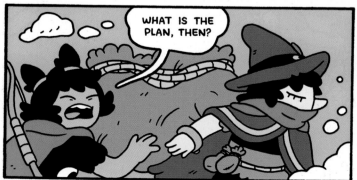

WHAT IS THE PLAN, THEN?

DON'T DIE.

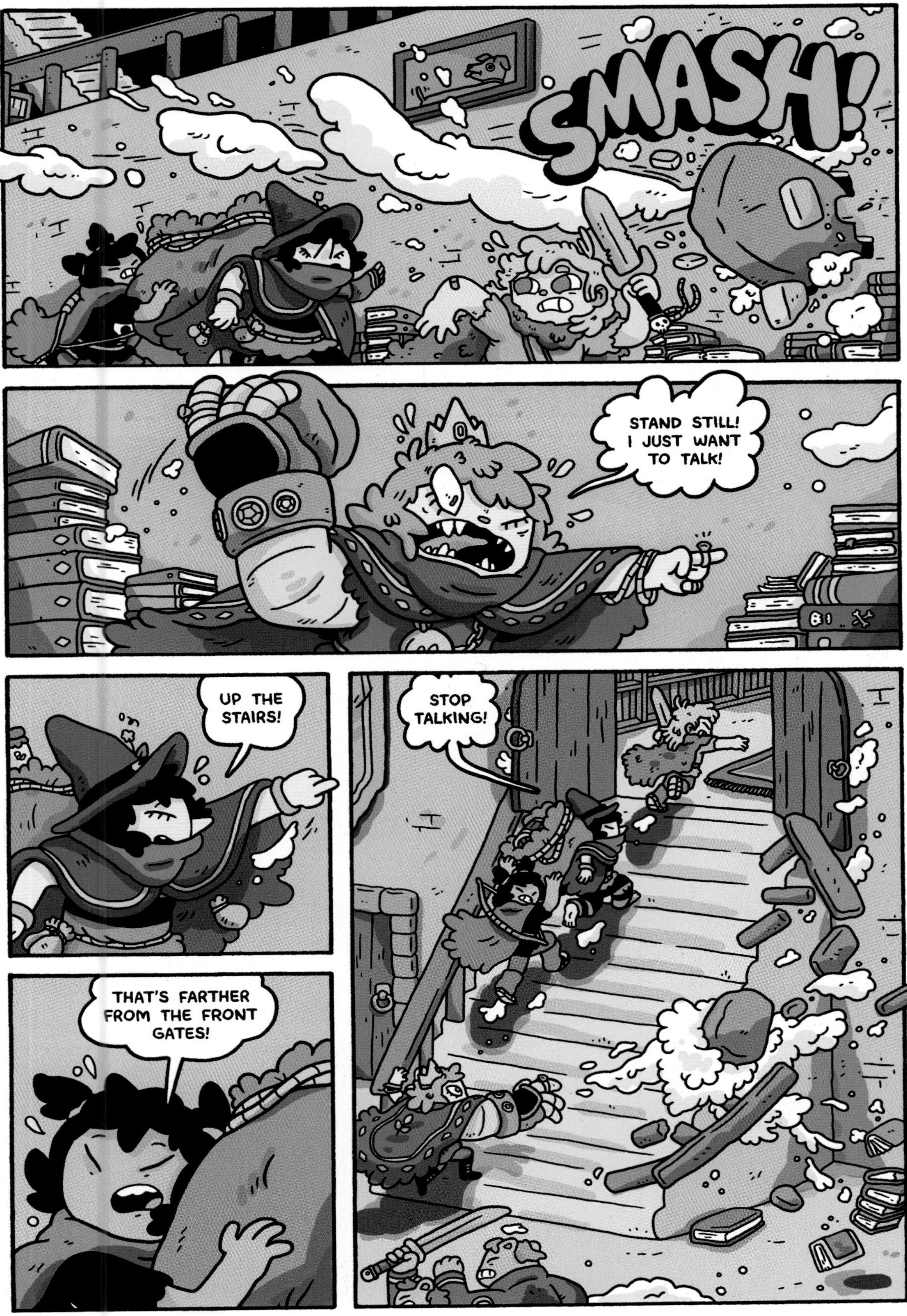
SMASH!
STAND STILL! I JUST WANT TO TALK!
UP THE STAIRS!
STOP TALKING!
THAT'S FARTHER FROM THE FRONT GATES!

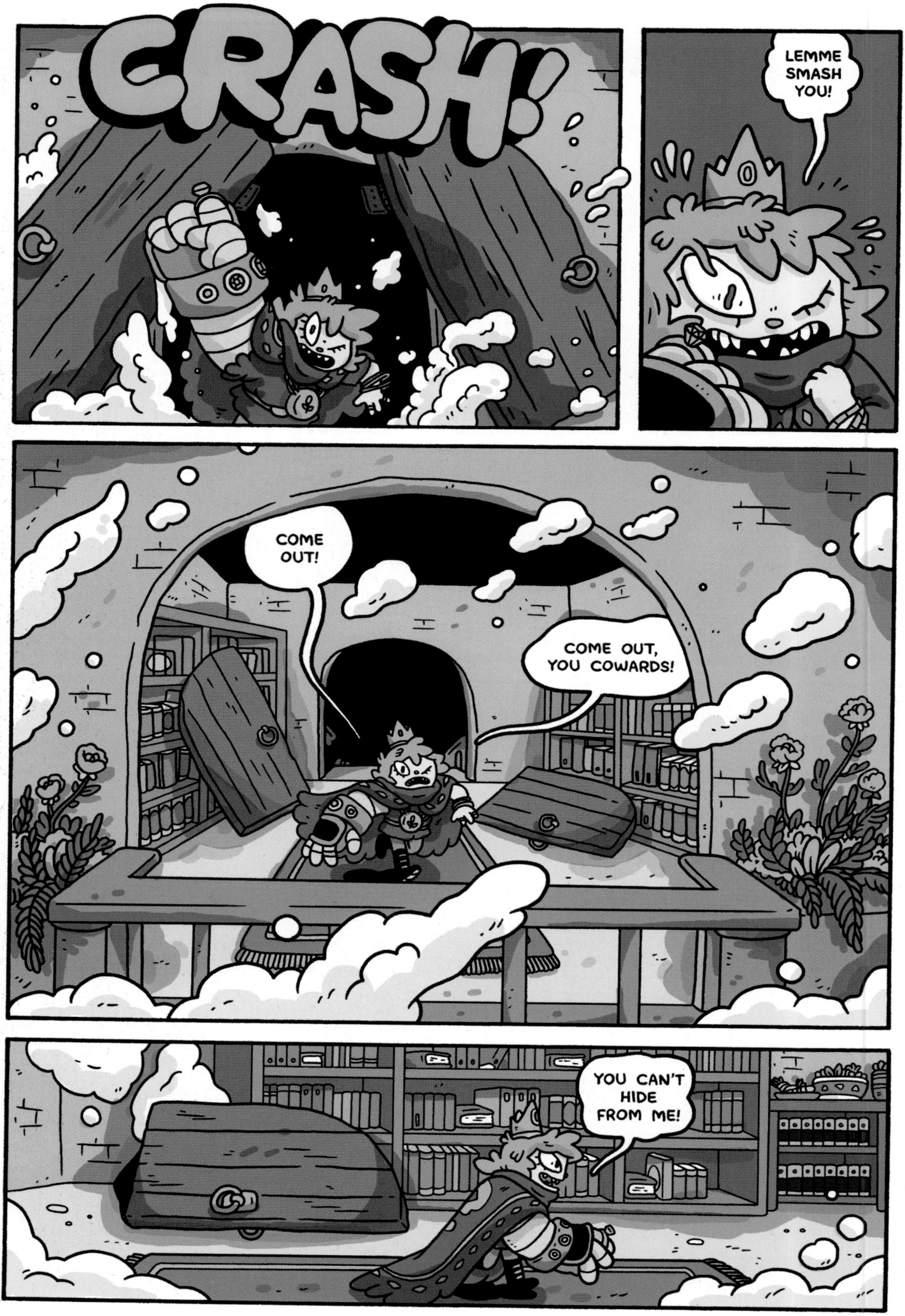
CRASH!
LEMME SMASH YOU!
COME OUT!
COME OUT, YOU COWARDS!
YOU CAN'T HIDE FROM ME!

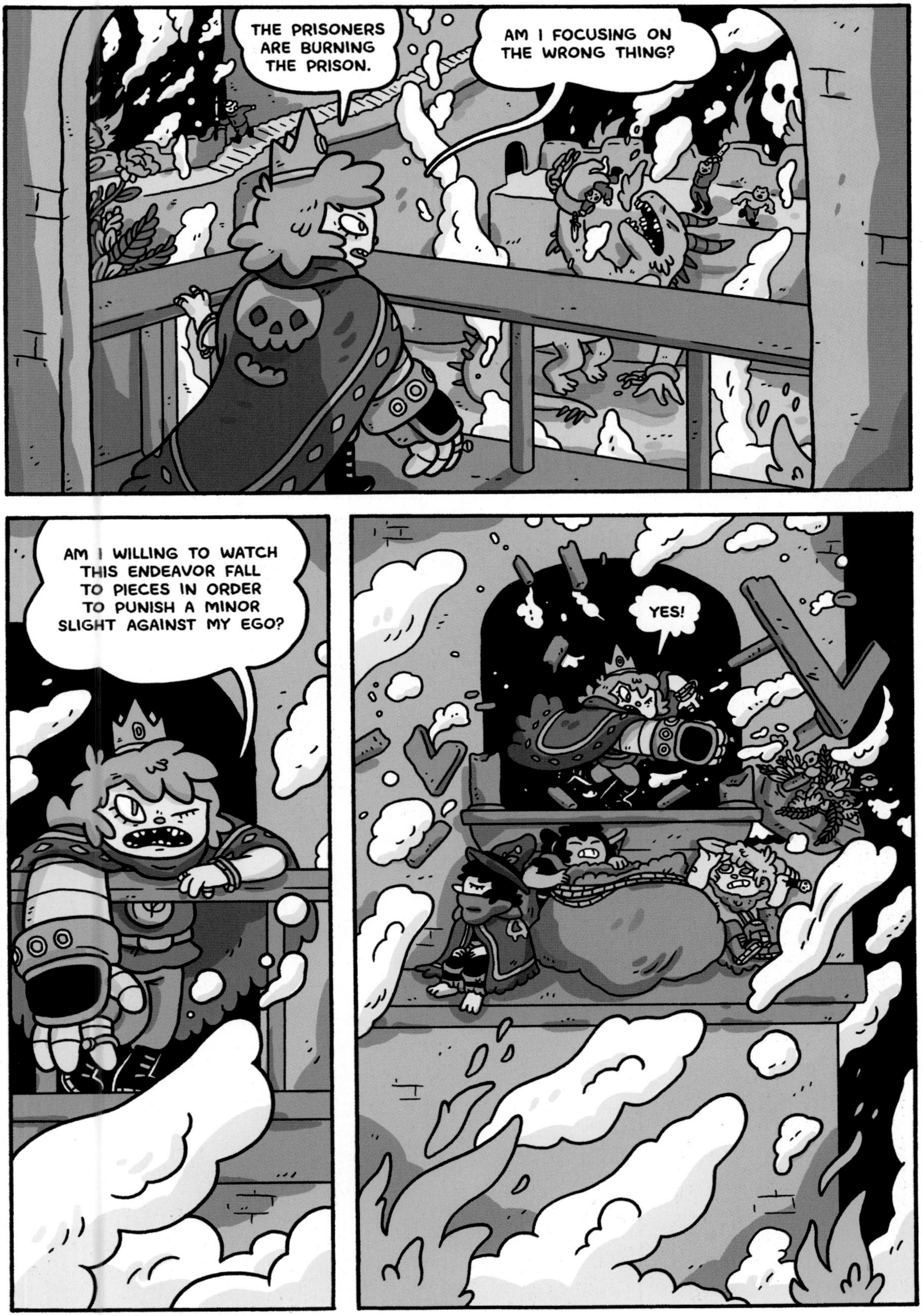
THE PRISONERS ARE BURNING THE PRISON.
AM I FOCUSING ON THE WRONG THING?
AM I WILLING TO WATCH THIS ENDEAVOR FALL TO PIECES IN ORDER TO PUNISH A MINOR SLIGHT AGAINST MY EGO?
YES!

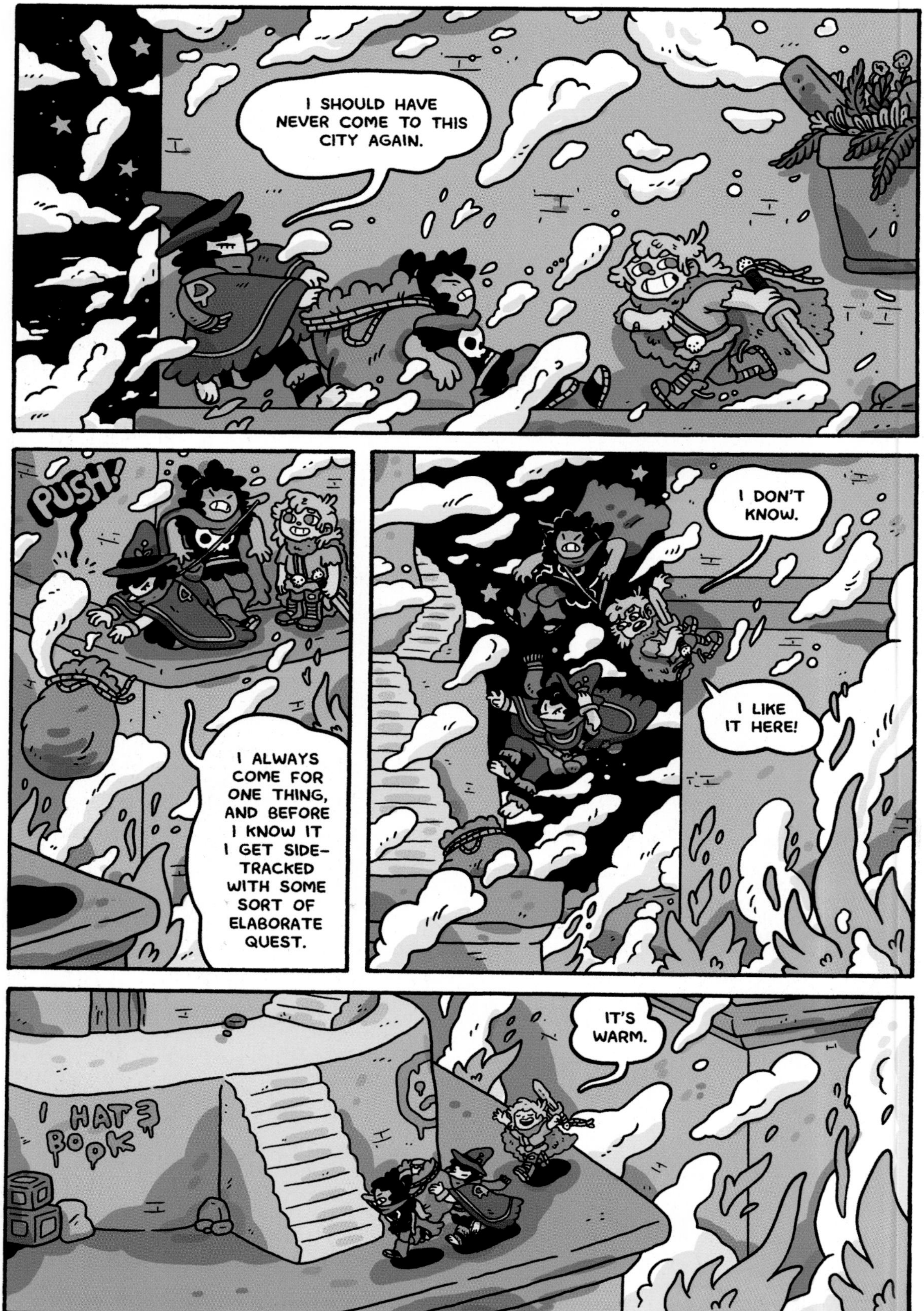
I SHOULD HAVE NEVER COME TO THIS CITY AGAIN.
PUSH!
I ALWAYS COME FOR ONE THING, AND BEFORE I KNOW IT I GET SIDE-TRACKED WITH SOME SORT OF ELABORATE QUEST.
I DON'T KNOW.
I LIKE IT HERE!
IT'S WARM.
I HAT3 BOOK

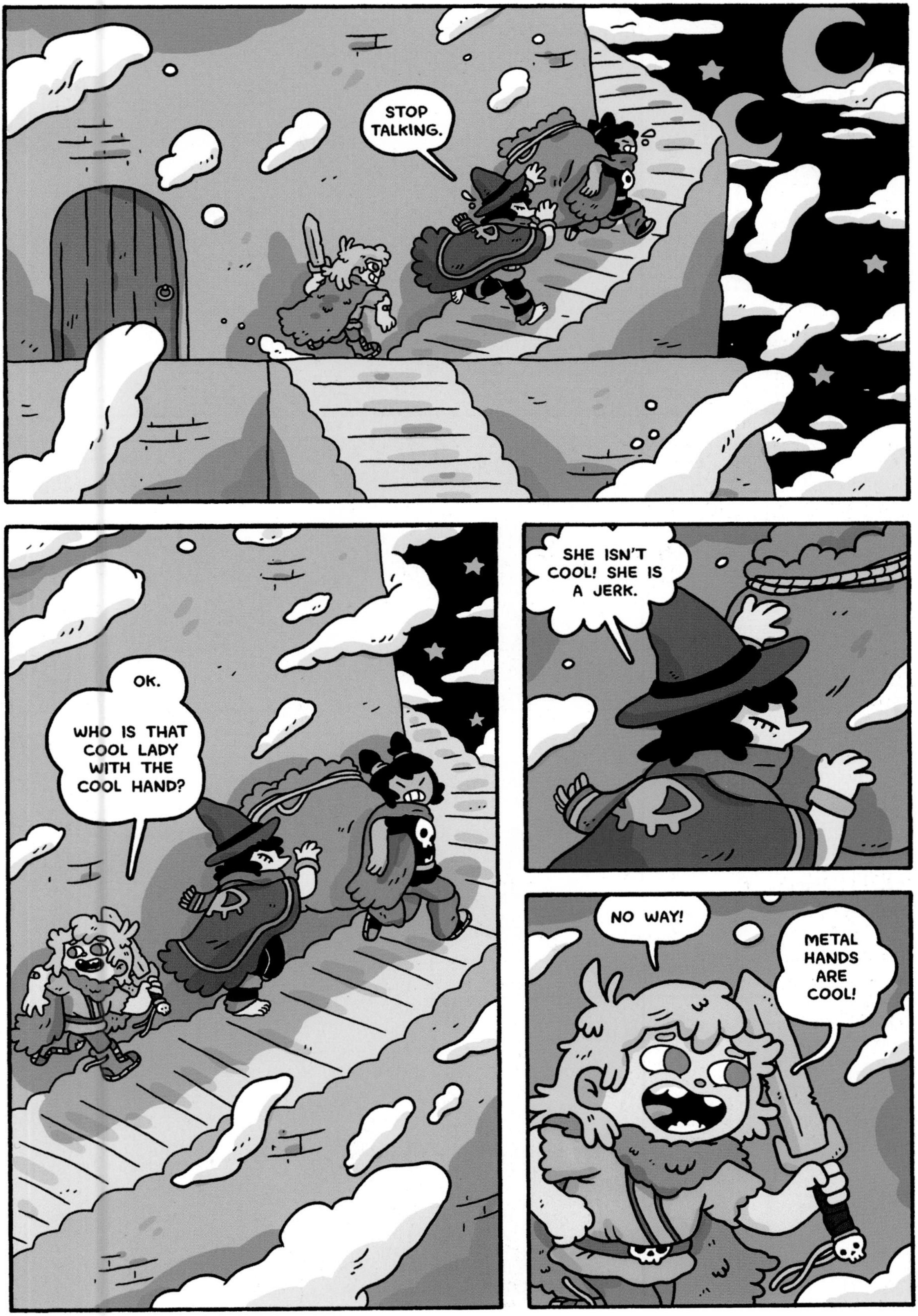
STOP TALKING.
OK.
WHO IS THAT COOL LADY WITH THE COOL HAND?
SHE ISN'T COOL! SHE IS A JERK.
NO WAY!
METAL HANDS ARE COOL!

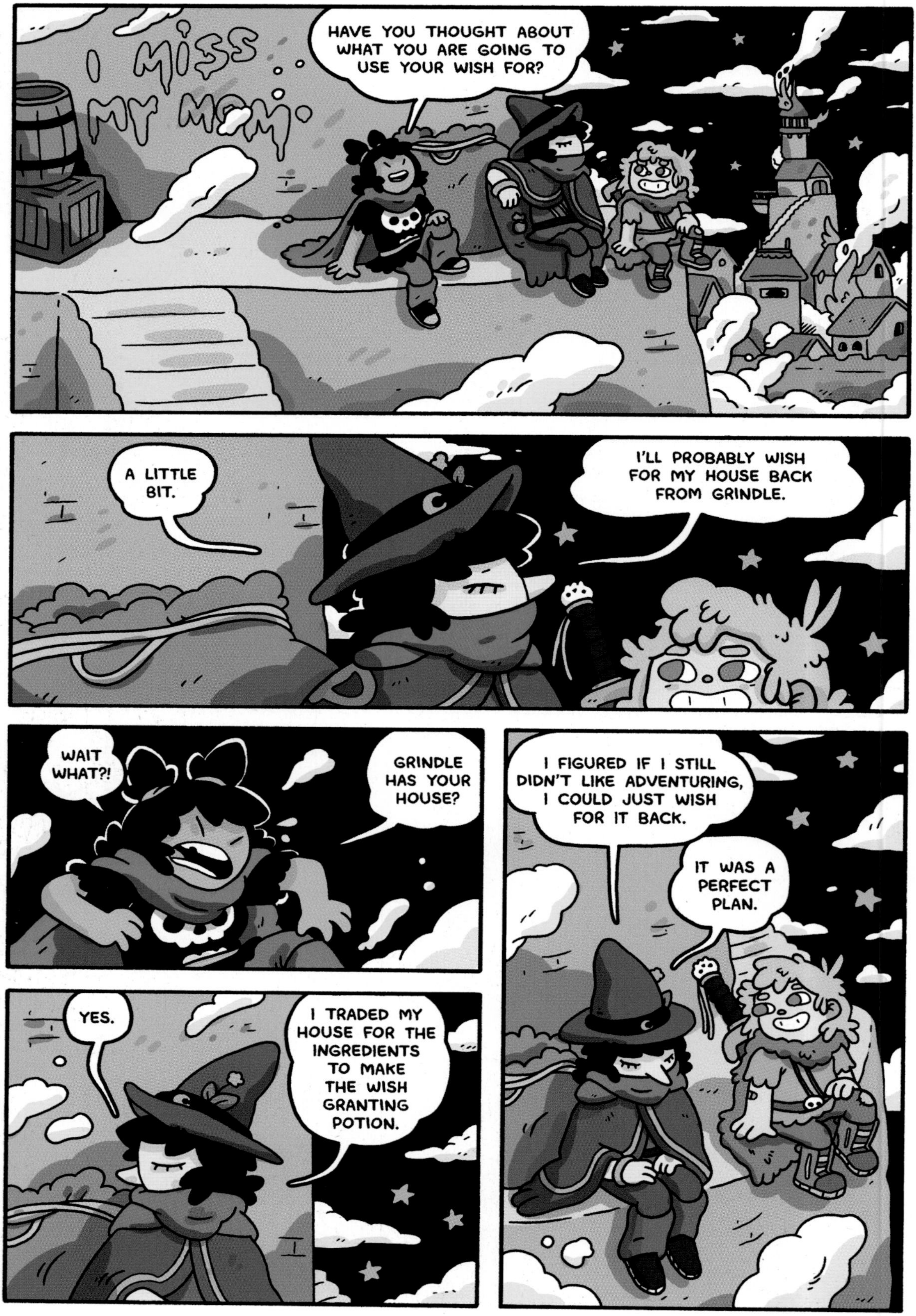
I MISS MY MOM
HAVE YOU THOUGHT ABOUT WHAT YOU ARE GOING TO USE YOUR WISH FOR?
A LITTLE BIT.
I'LL PROBABLY WISH FOR MY HOUSE BACK FROM GRINDLE.
WAIT WHAT?!
GRINDLE HAS YOUR HOUSE?
YES.
I TRADED MY HOUSE FOR THE INGREDIENTS TO MAKE THE WISH GRANTING POTION.
I FIGURED IF I STILL DIDN'T LIKE ADVENTURING, I COULD JUST WISH FOR IT BACK.
IT WAS A PERFECT PLAN.

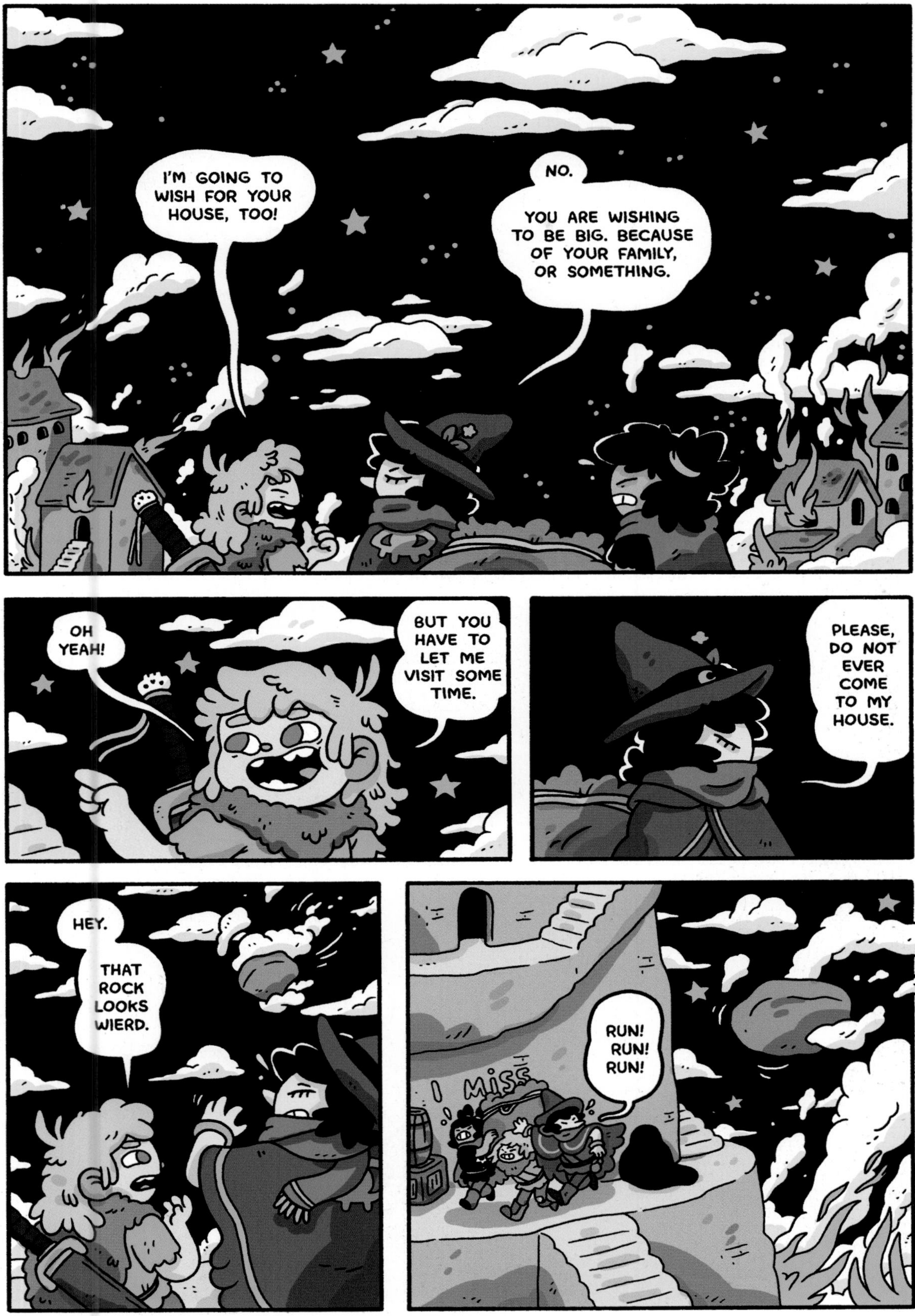

I'M GOING TO WISH FOR YOUR HOUSE, TOO!
NO.
YOU ARE WISHING TO BE BIG. BECAUSE OF YOUR FAMILY, OR SOMETHING.
OH YEAH!
BUT YOU HAVE TO LET ME VISIT SOME TIME.
PLEASE, DO NOT EVER COME TO MY HOUSE.
HEY.
THAT ROCK LOOKS WIERD.
I MISS
RUN! RUN! RUN!

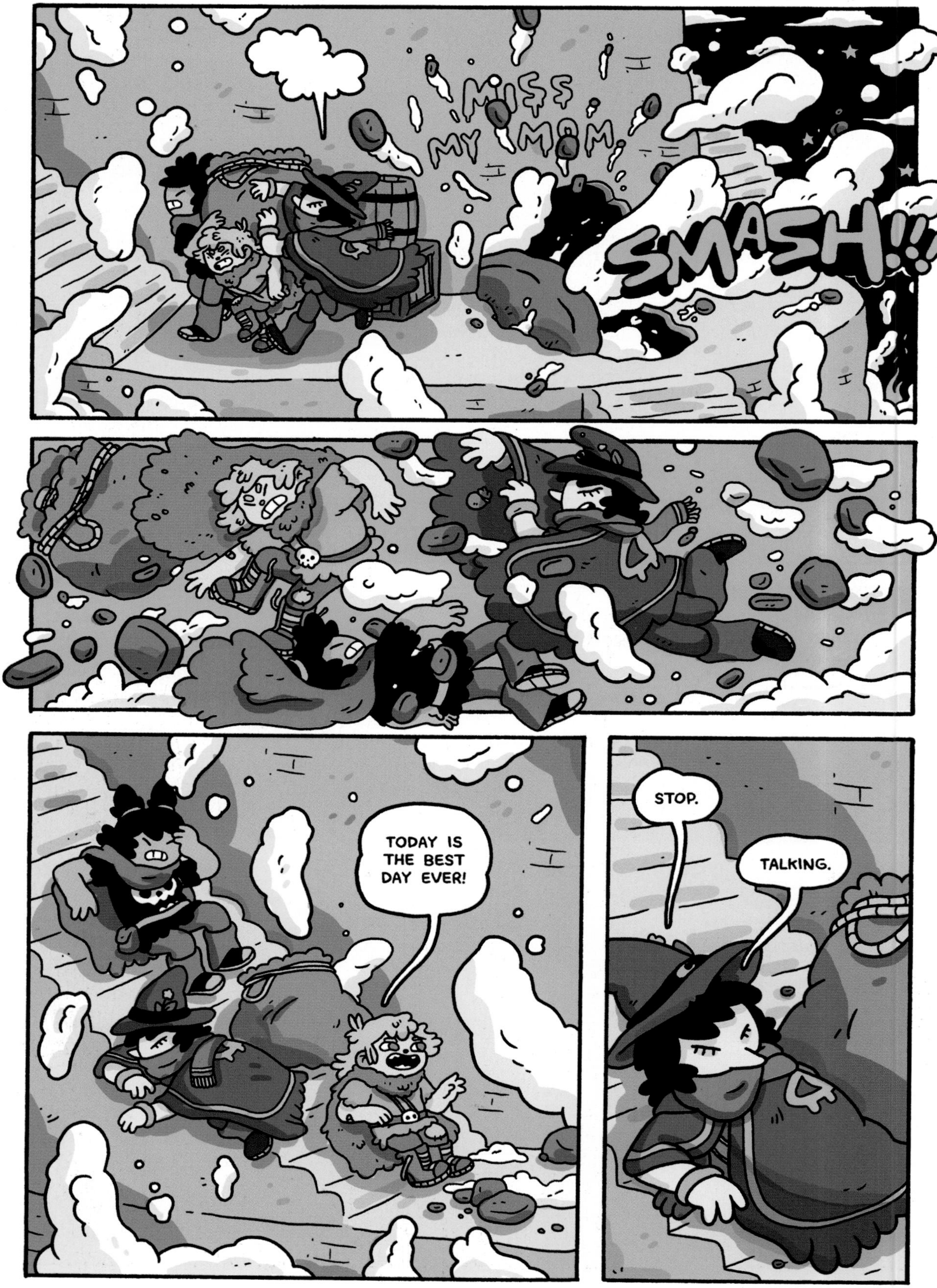
I MISS MY MOM
SMASH!!!
TODAY IS THE BEST DAY EVER!
STOP.
TALKING.

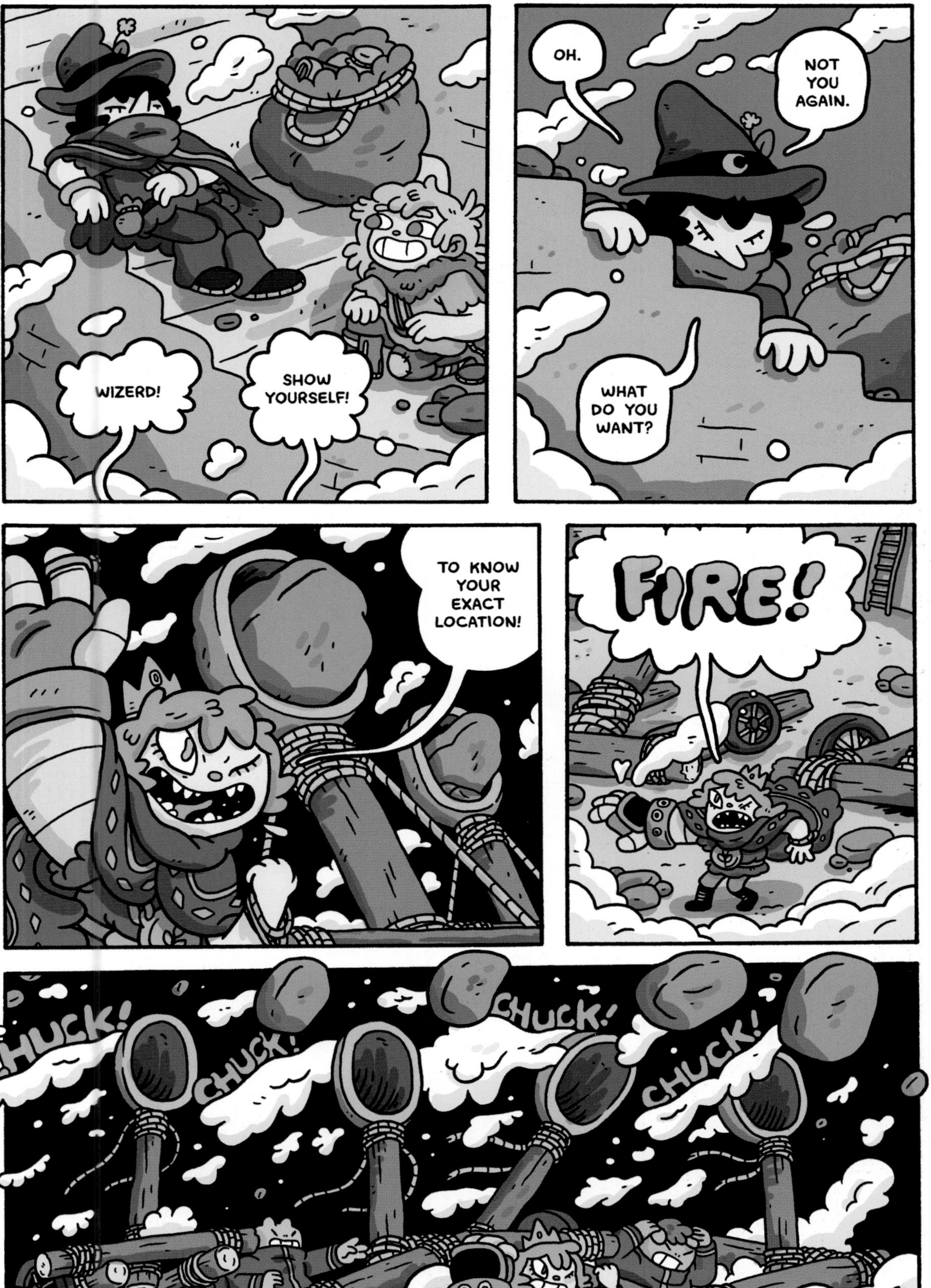
WIZERD!
SHOW YOURSELF!
OH.
NOT YOU AGAIN.
WHAT DO YOU WANT?
TO KNOW YOUR EXACT LOCATION!
FIRE!
CHUCK!
CHUCK!
CHUCK!
CHUCK!

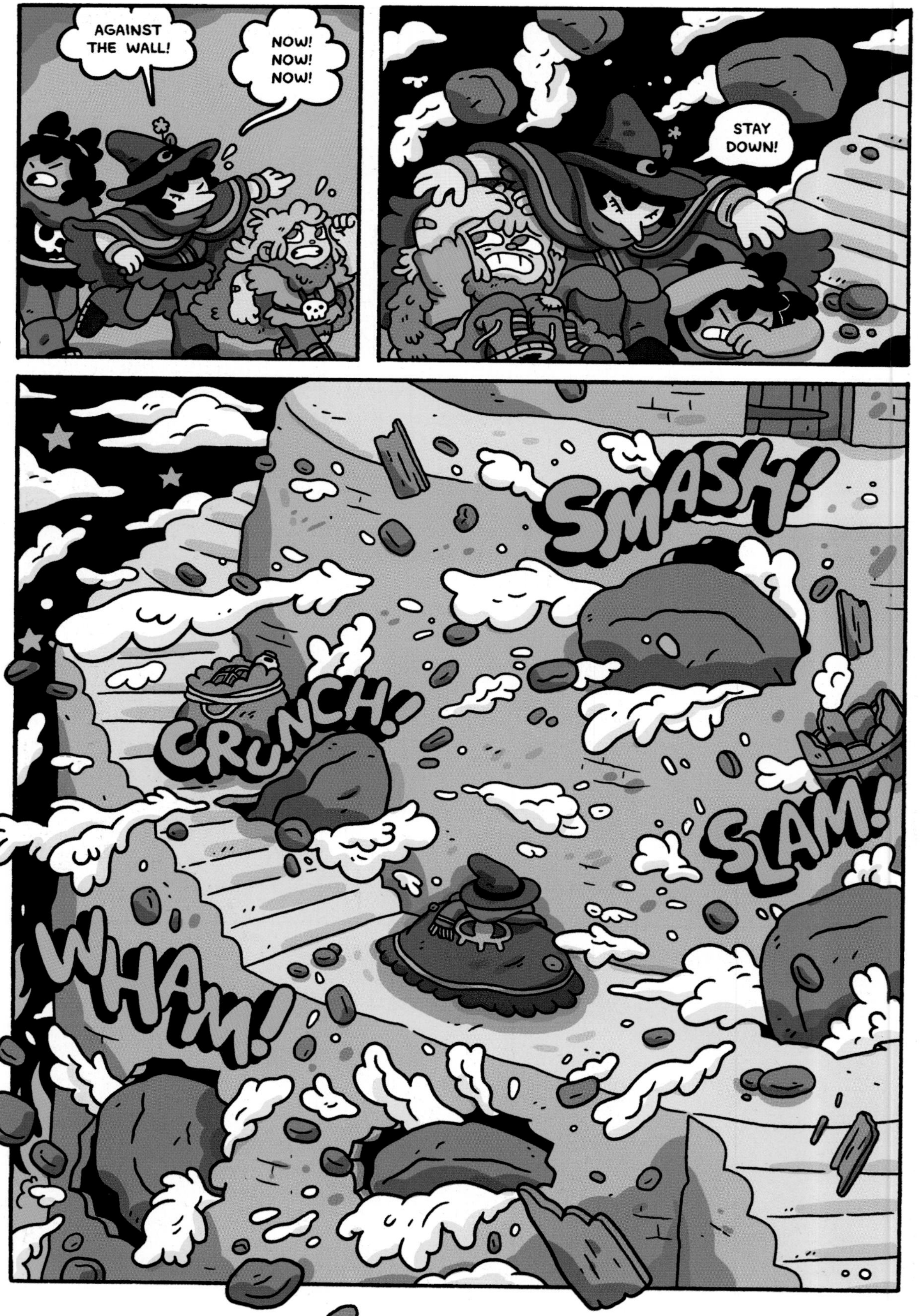
AGAINST THE WALL!
NOW! NOW! NOW!
STAY DOWN!
SMASH!
CRUNCH!
SLAM!
WHAM!

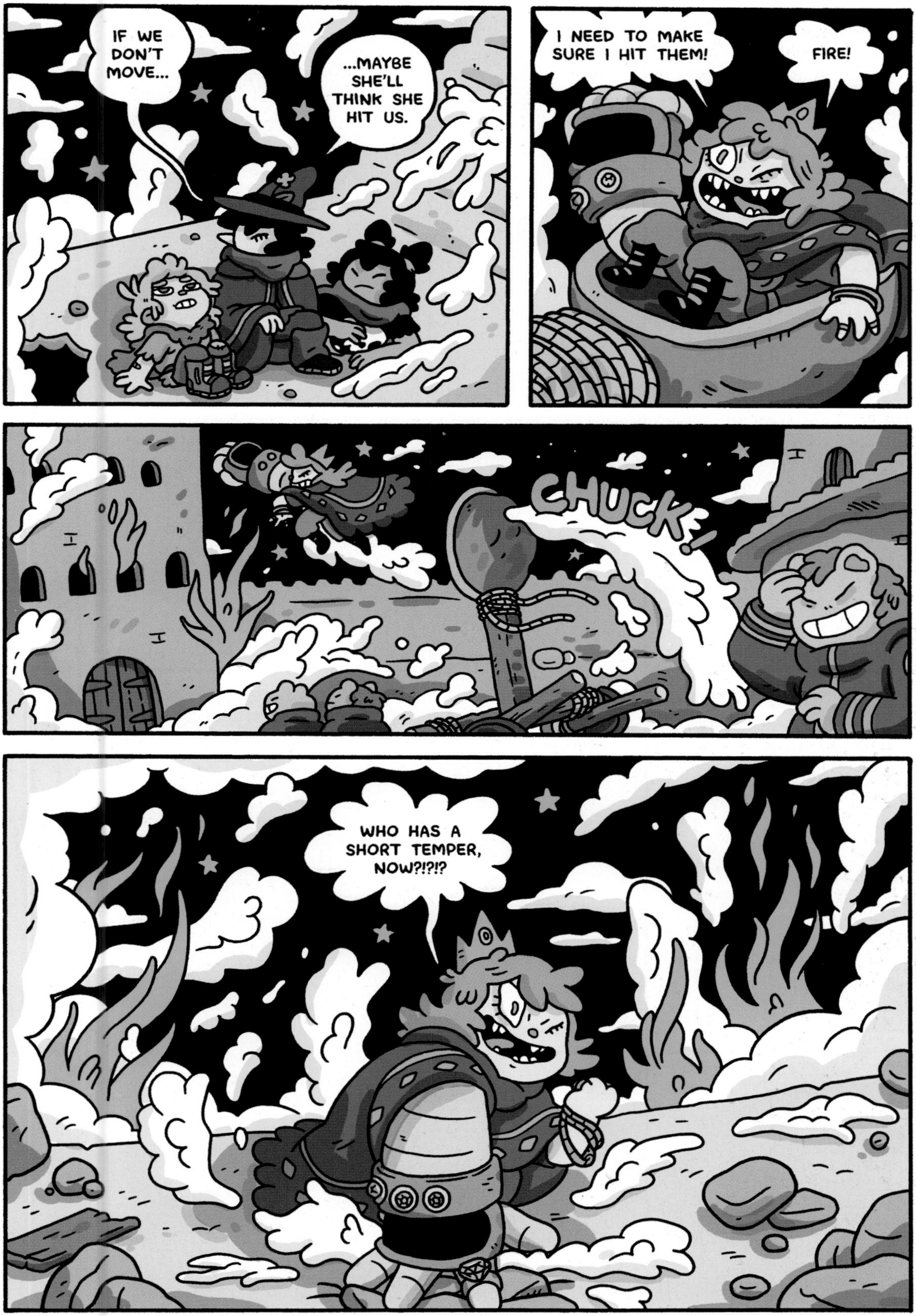
IF WE DON'T MOVE...
...MAYBE SHE'LL THINK SHE HIT US.
I NEED TO MAKE SURE I HIT THEM!
FIRE!
CHUCK!
WHO HAS A SHORT TEMPER, NOW?!?!?

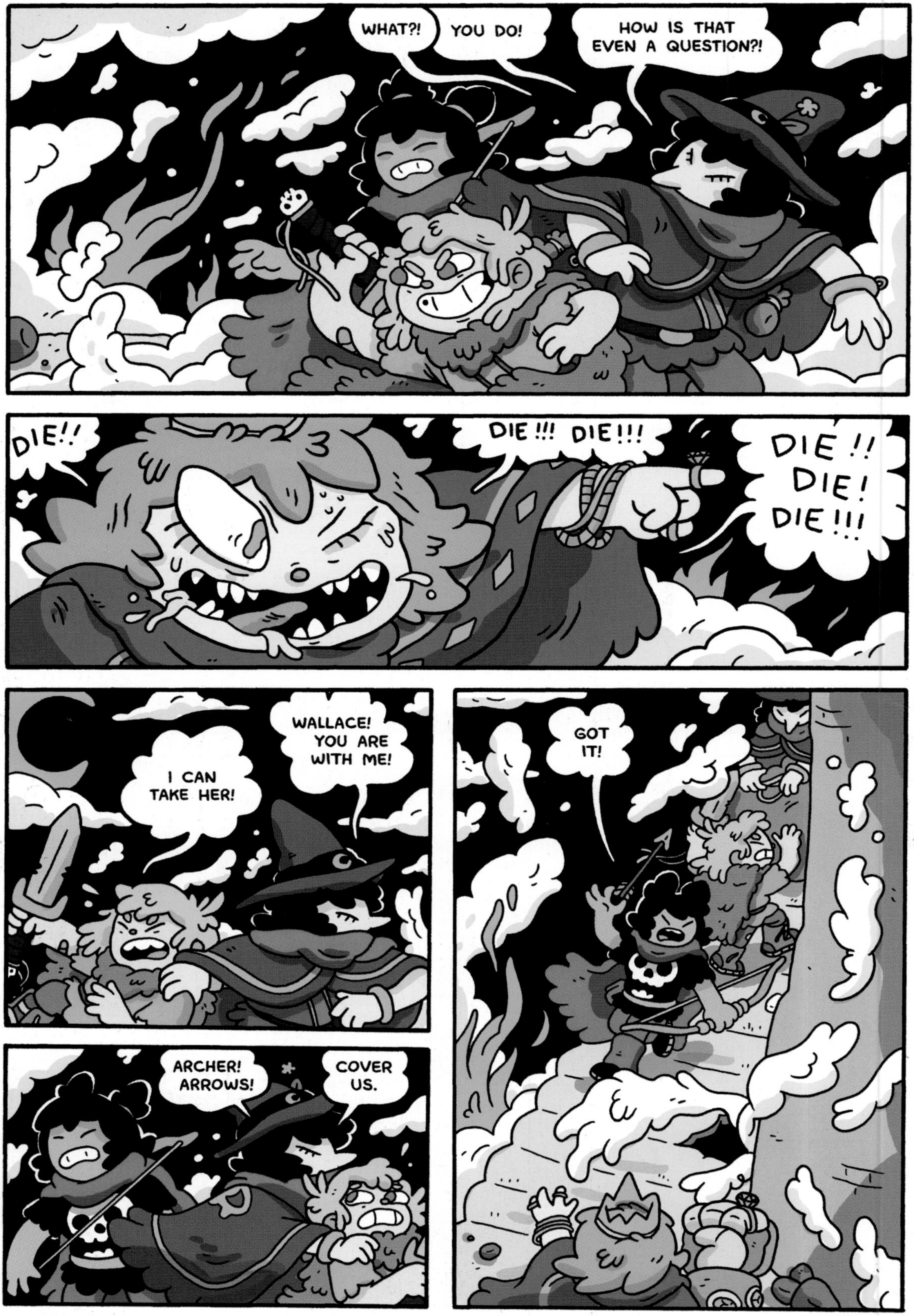

WHAT?!
YOU DO!
HOW IS THAT EVEN A QUESTION?!
DIE!!
DIE!!! DIE!!!
DIE!! DIE! DIE!!!
I CAN TAKE HER!
WALLACE! YOU ARE WITH ME!
ARCHER! ARROWS!
COVER US.
GOT IT!

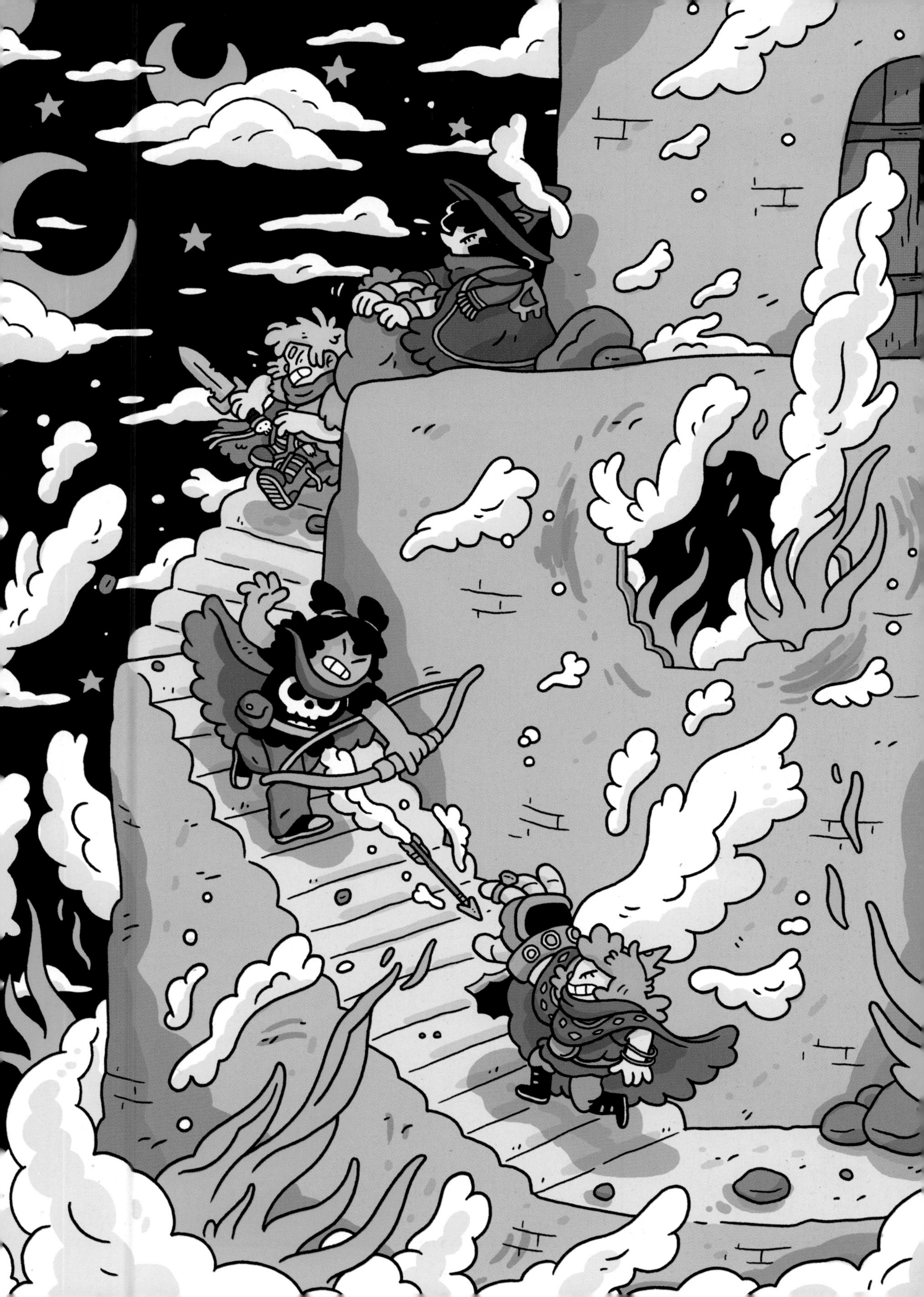

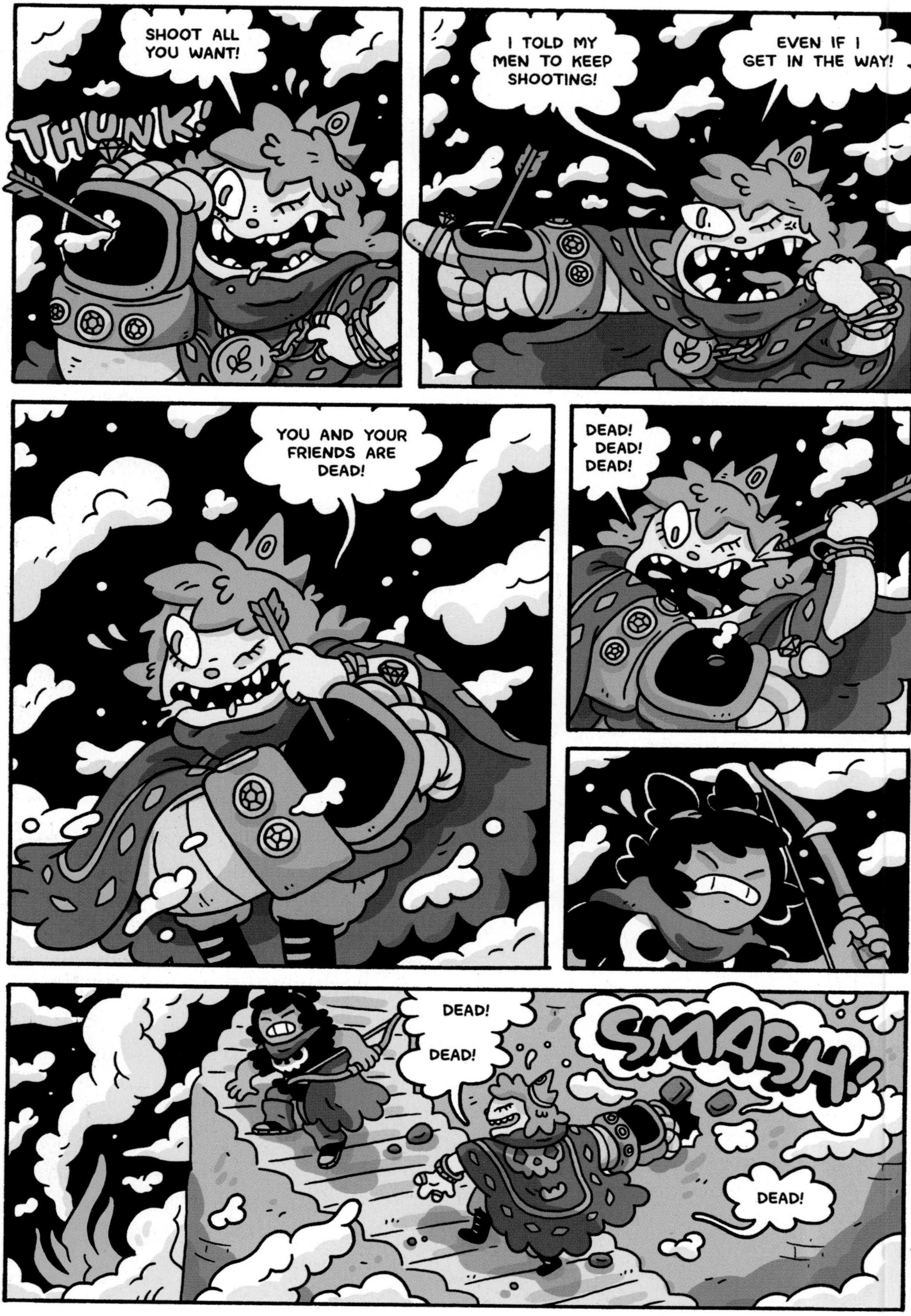
SHOOT ALL YOU WANT!
THUNK!
I TOLD MY MEN TO KEEP SHOOTING!
EVEN IF I GET IN THE WAY!
YOU AND YOUR FRIENDS ARE DEAD!
DEAD! DEAD! DEAD!
DEAD!
DEAD!
SMASH!
DEAD!

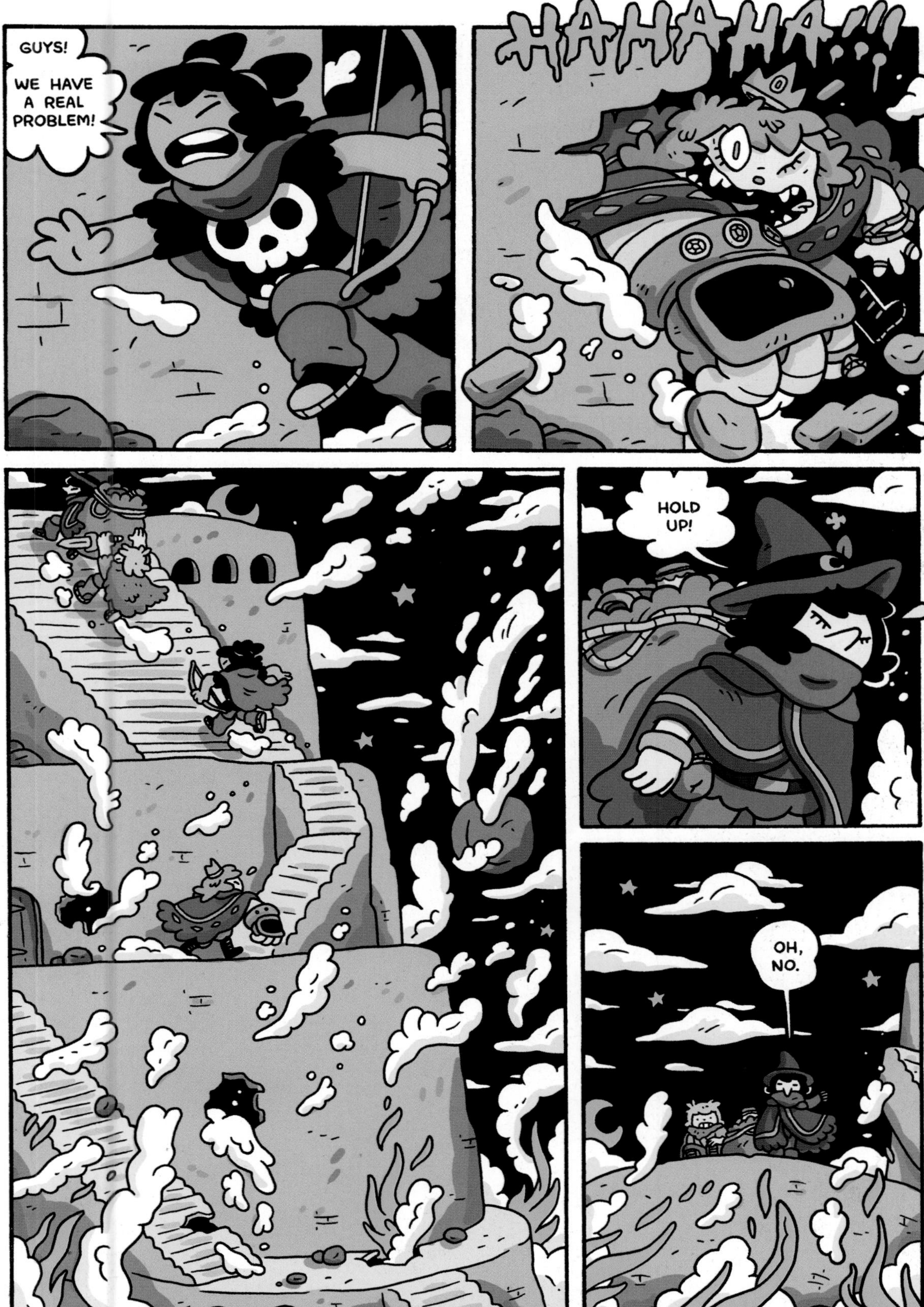
GUYS!
WE HAVE A REAL PROBLEM!
HAHAHA!!!
HOLD UP!
OH, NO.

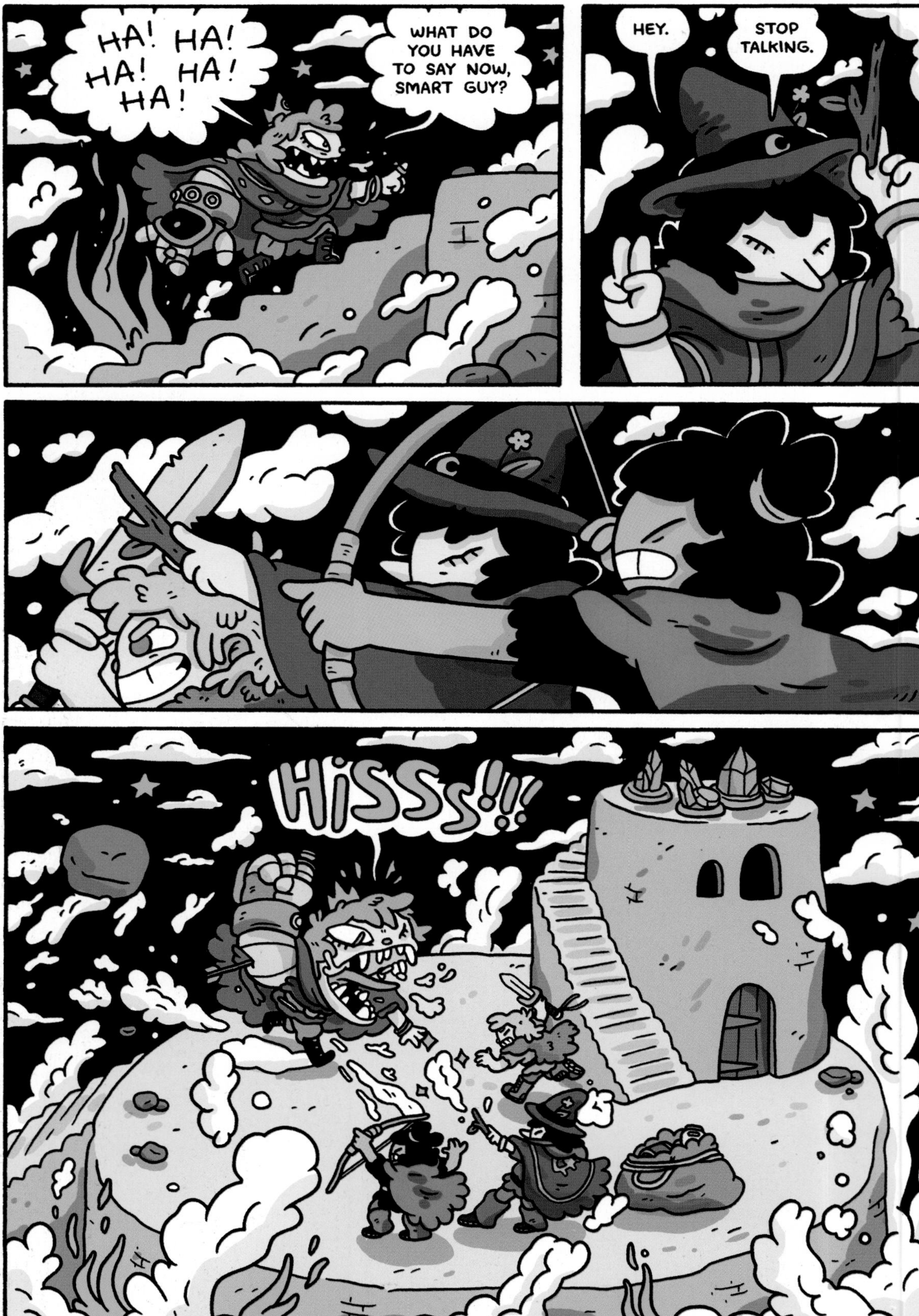
HA! HA! HA! HA! HA!
WHAT DO YOU HAVE TO SAY NOW, SMART GUY?
HEY.
STOP TALKING.
HISSS!!!

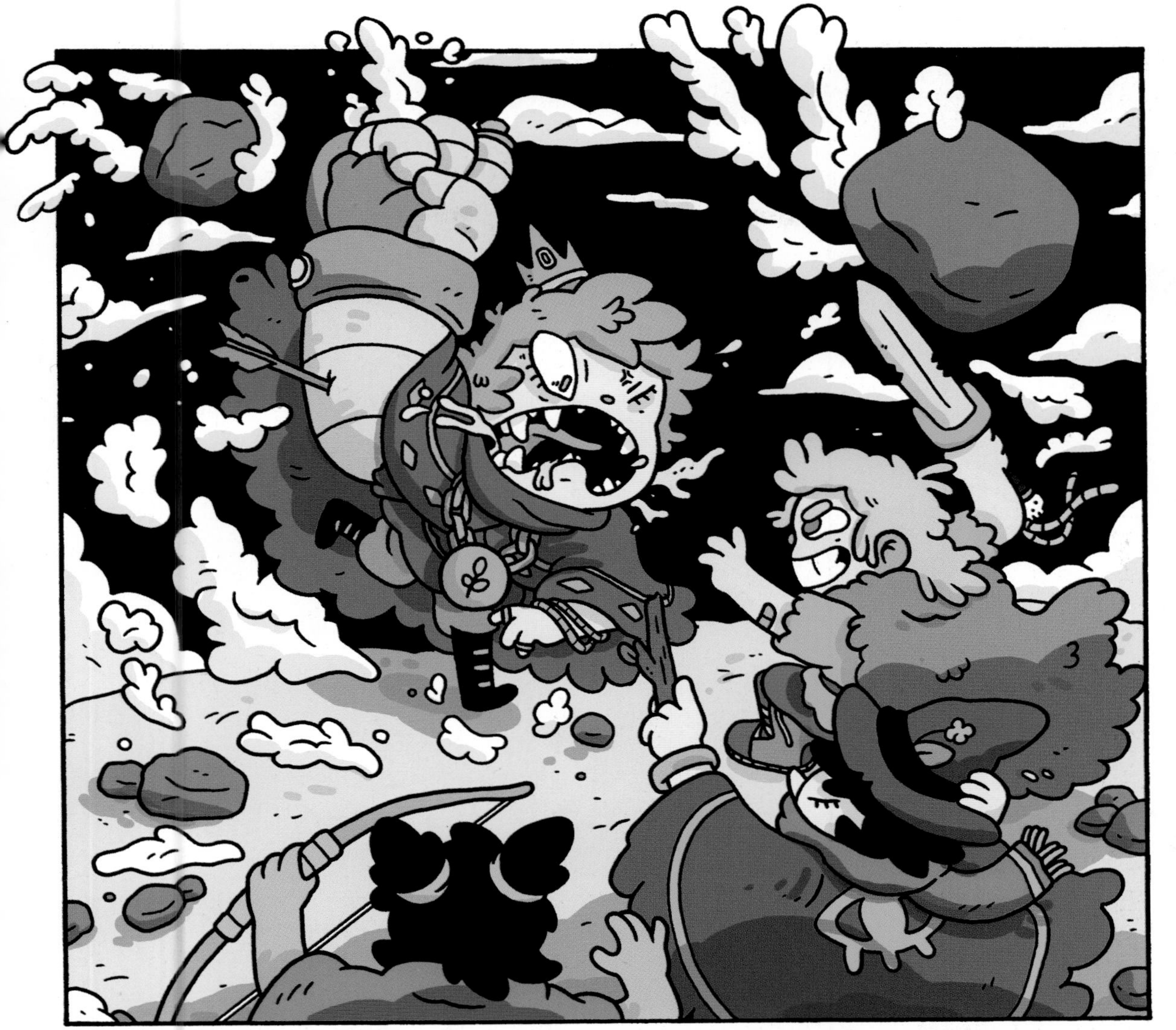

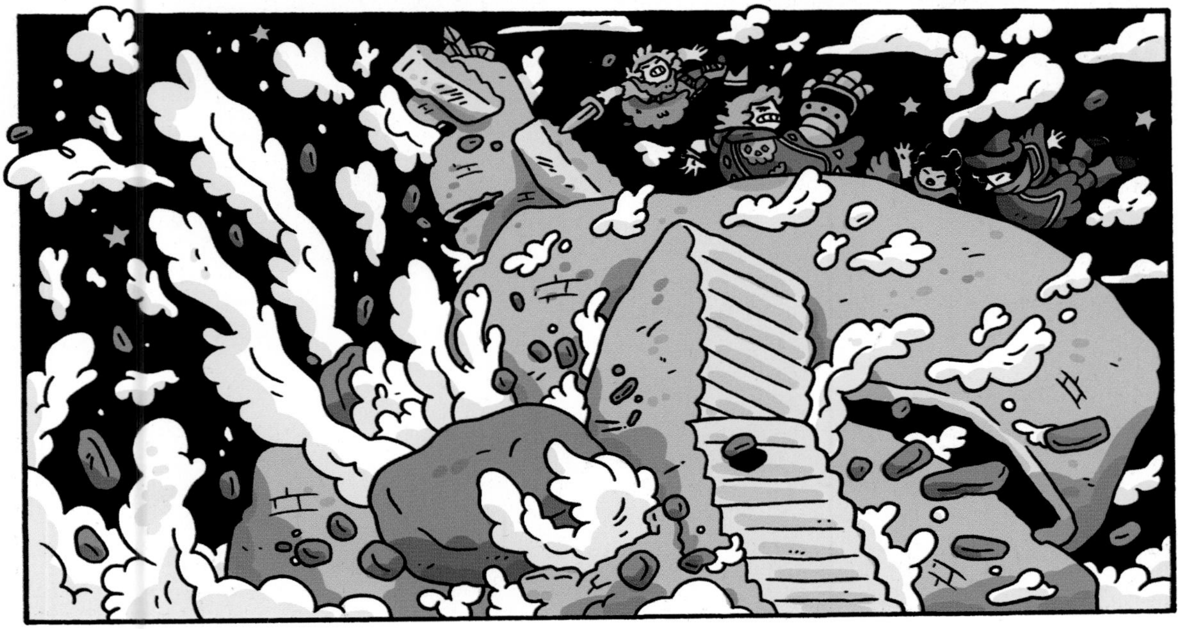

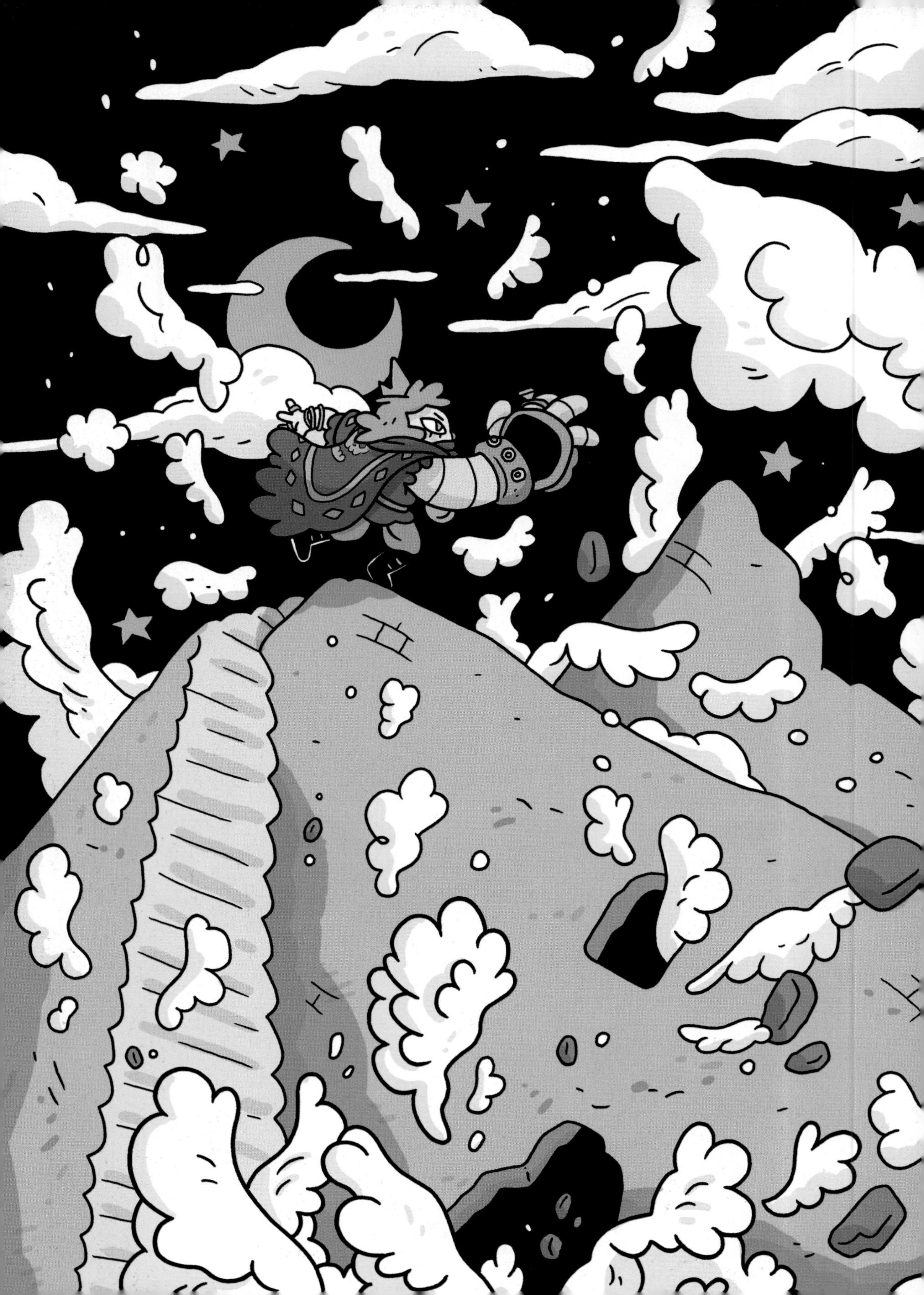

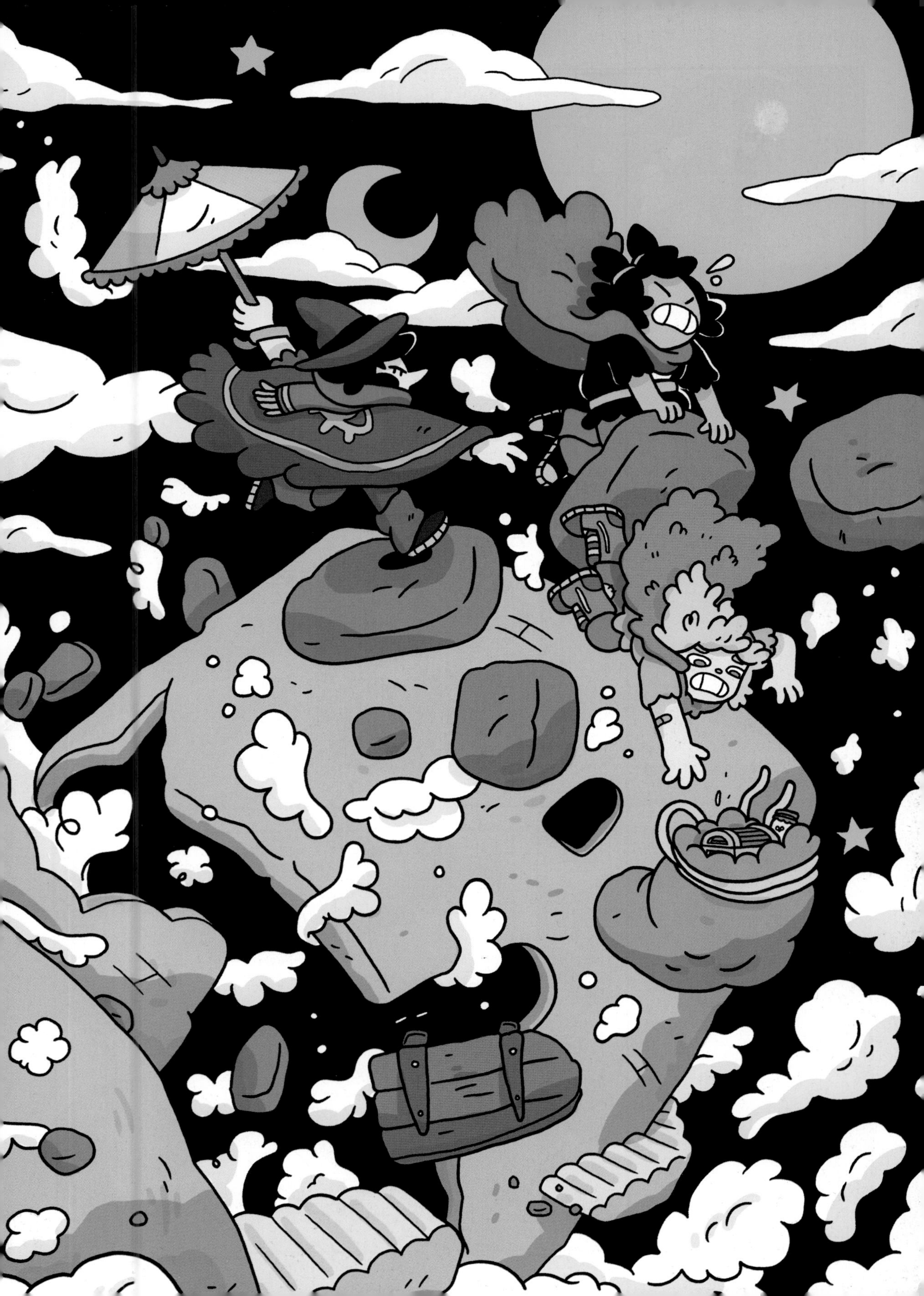

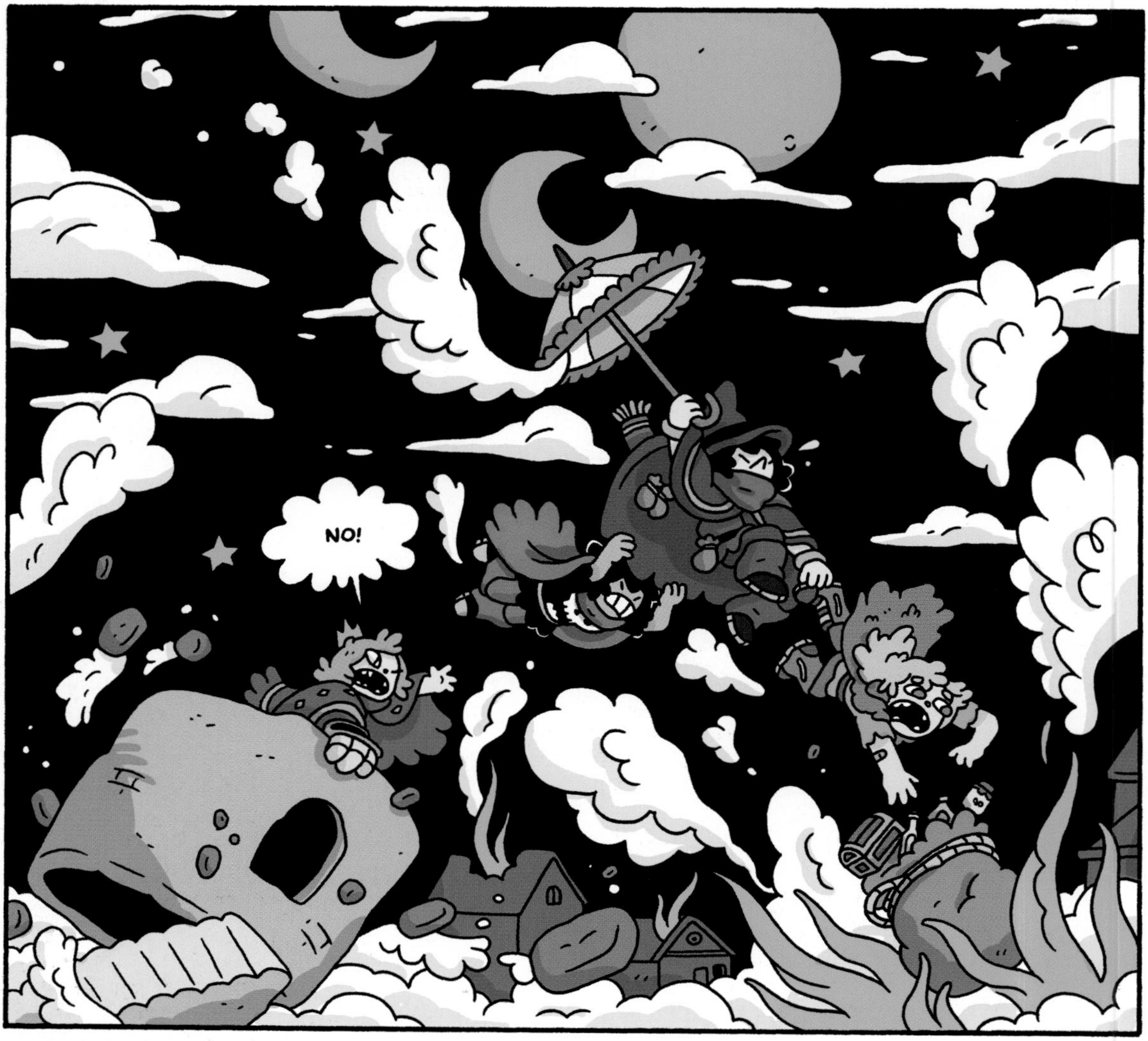
NO!

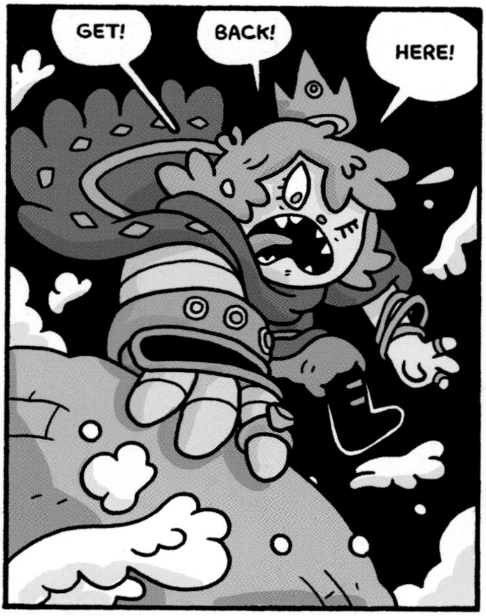
GET!
BACK!
HERE!

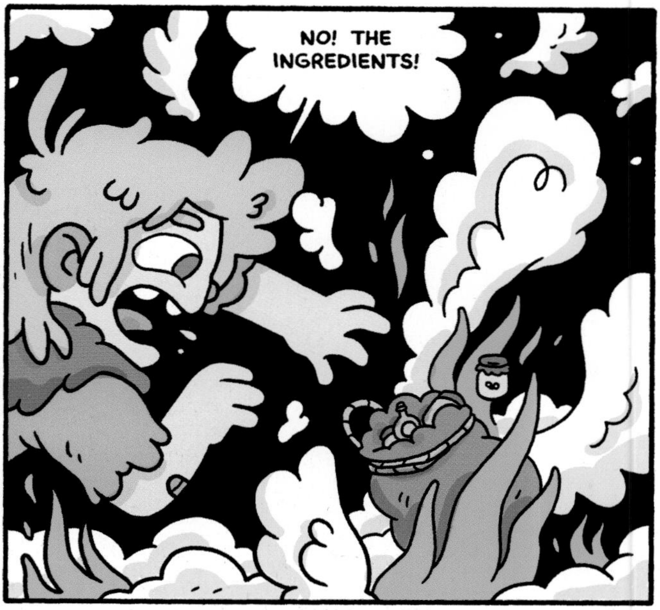
NO! THE INGREDIENTS!

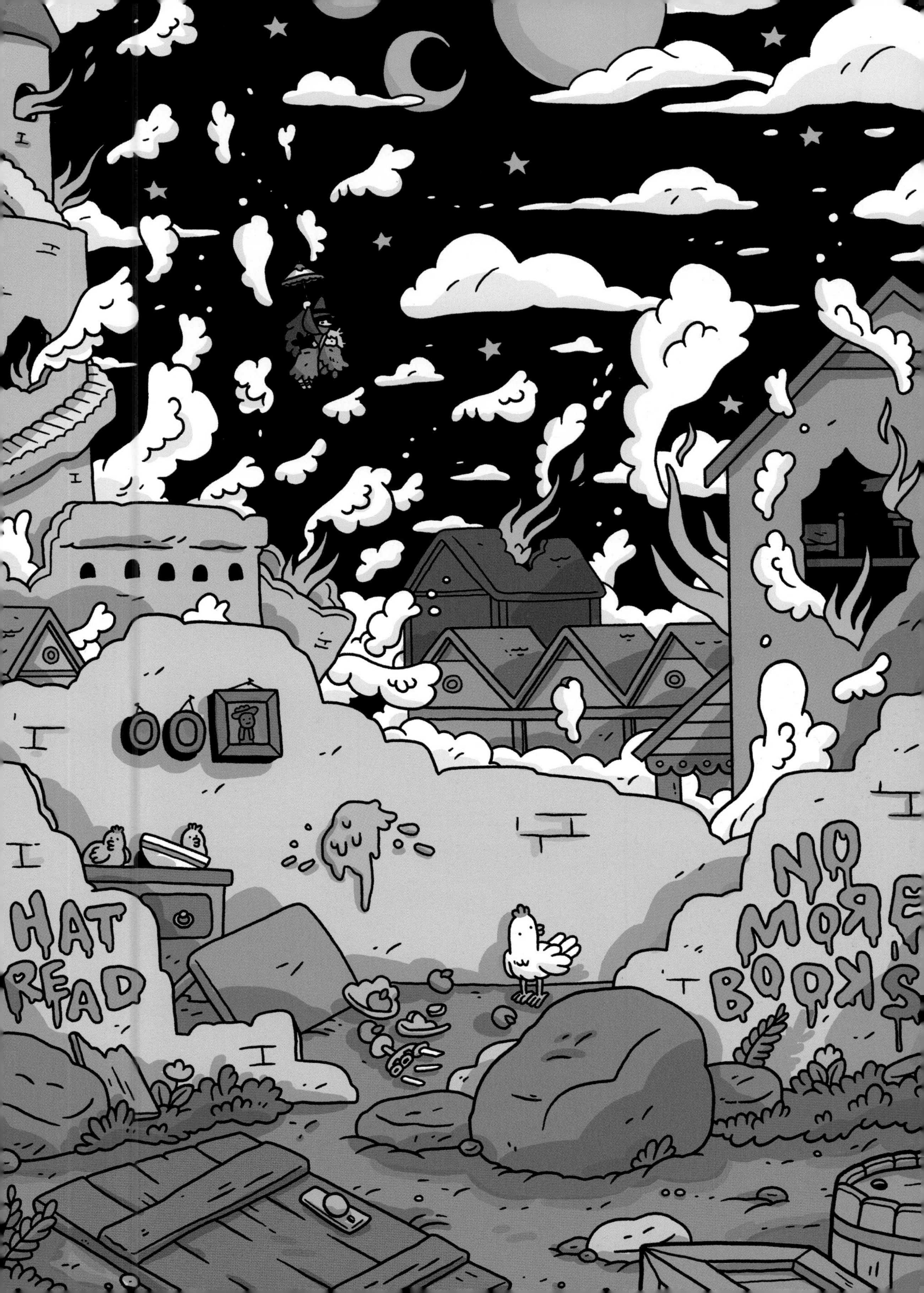
HAT
READ
NO
MORE
BOOKS

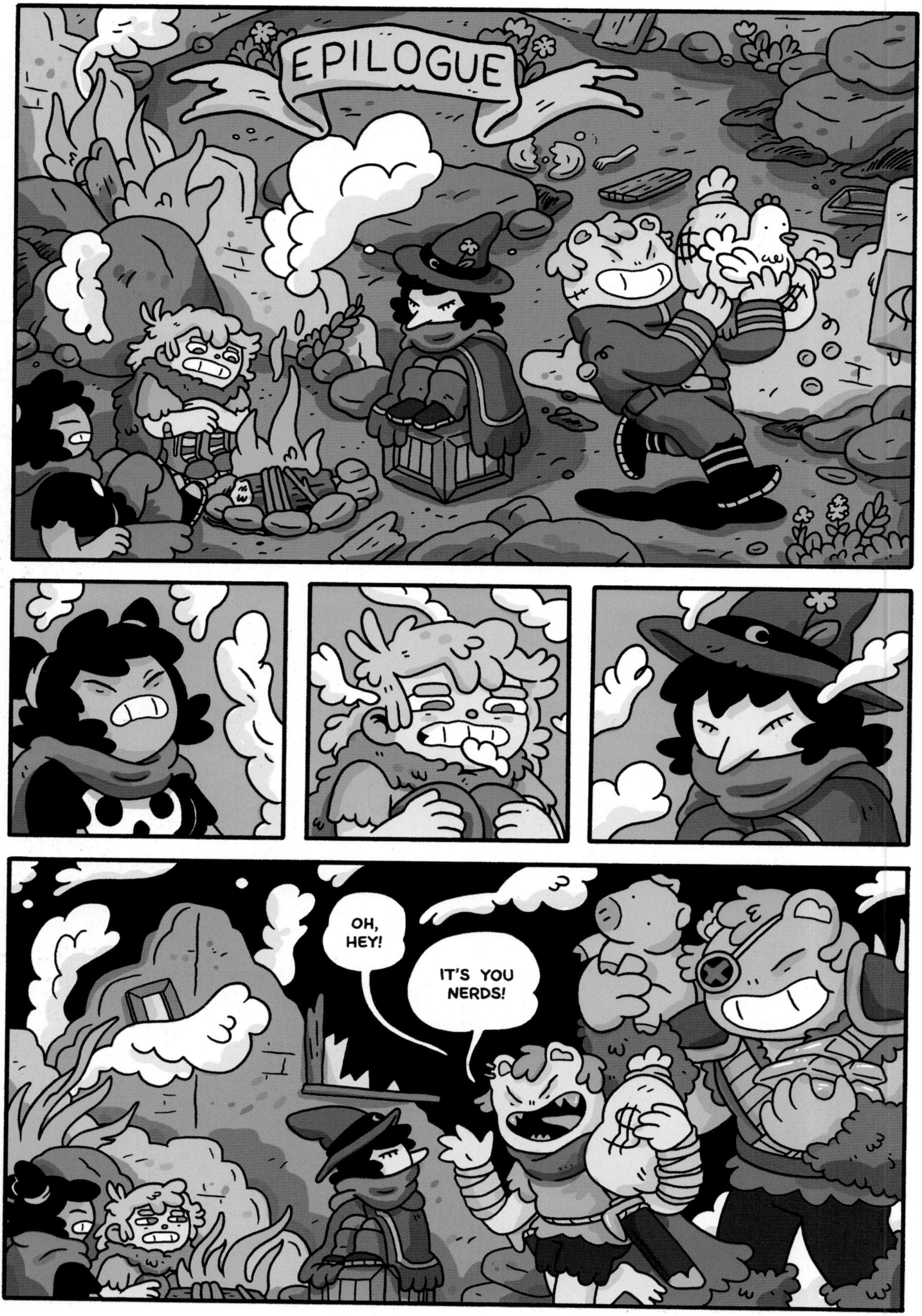
EPILOGUE
OH, HEY!
IT'S YOU NERDS!

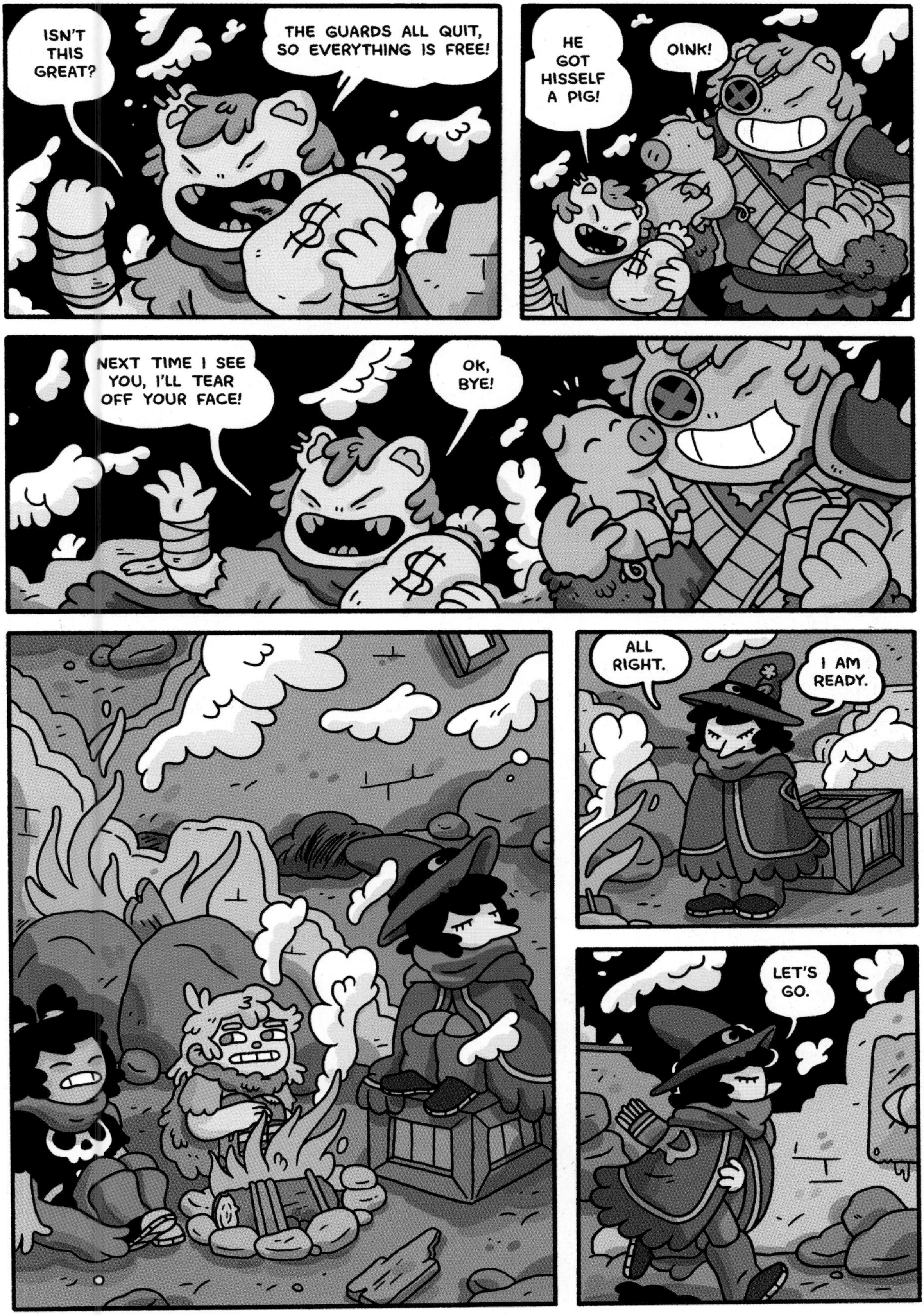
ISN'T THIS GREAT?
THE GUARDS ALL QUIT, SO EVERYTHING IS FREE!
HE GOT HISSELF A PIG!
OINK!
NEXT TIME I SEE YOU, I'LL TEAR OFF YOUR FACE!
OK, BYE!
ALL RIGHT.
I AM READY.
LET'S GO.

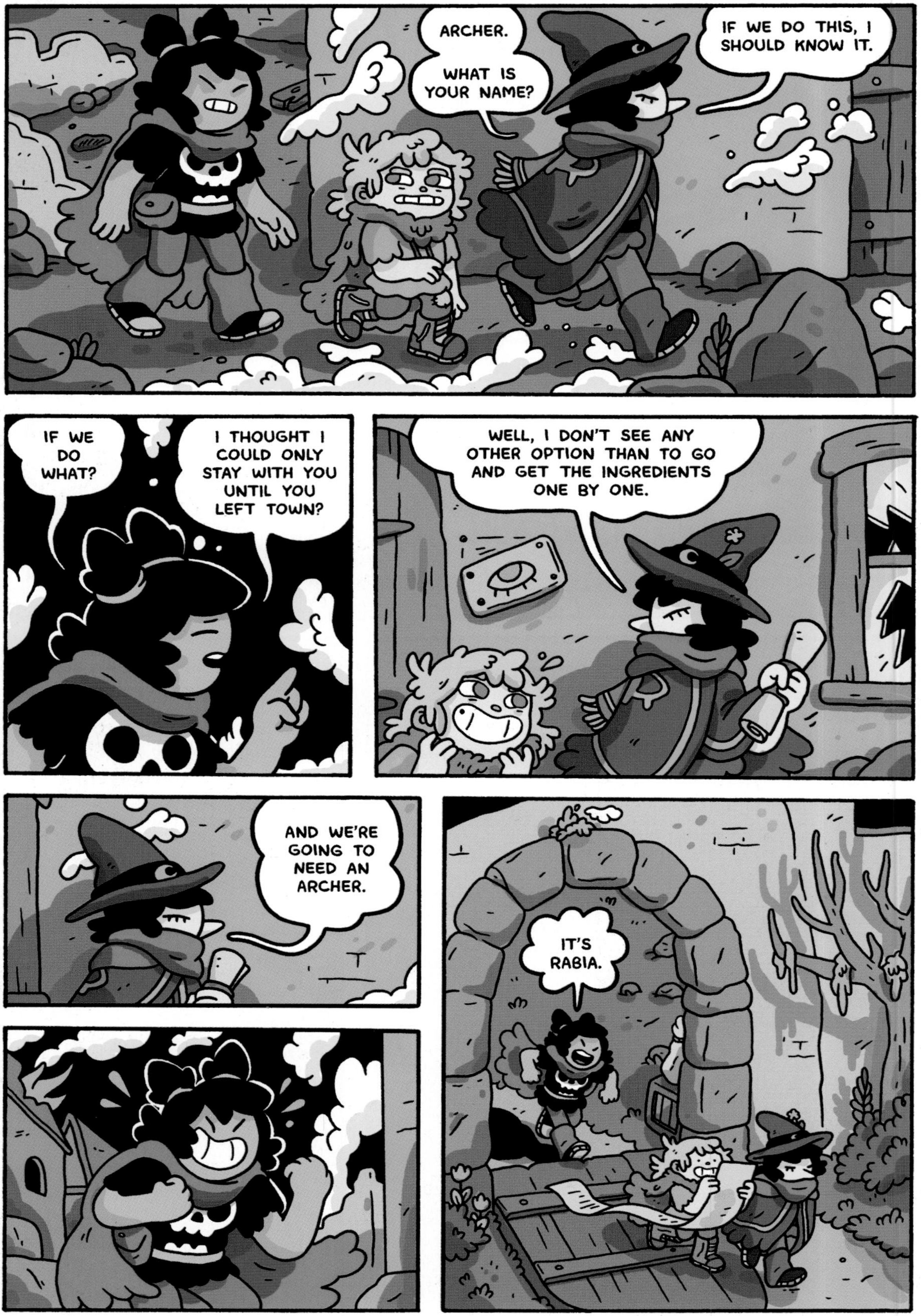
ARCHER.
WHAT IS YOUR NAME?
IF WE DO THIS, I SHOULD KNOW IT.
IF WE DO WHAT?
I THOUGHT I COULD ONLY STAY WITH YOU UNTIL YOU LEFT TOWN?
WELL, I DON'T SEE ANY OTHER OPTION THAN TO GO AND GET THE INGREDIENTS ONE BY ONE.
AND WE'RE GOING TO NEED AN ARCHER.
IT'S RABIA.

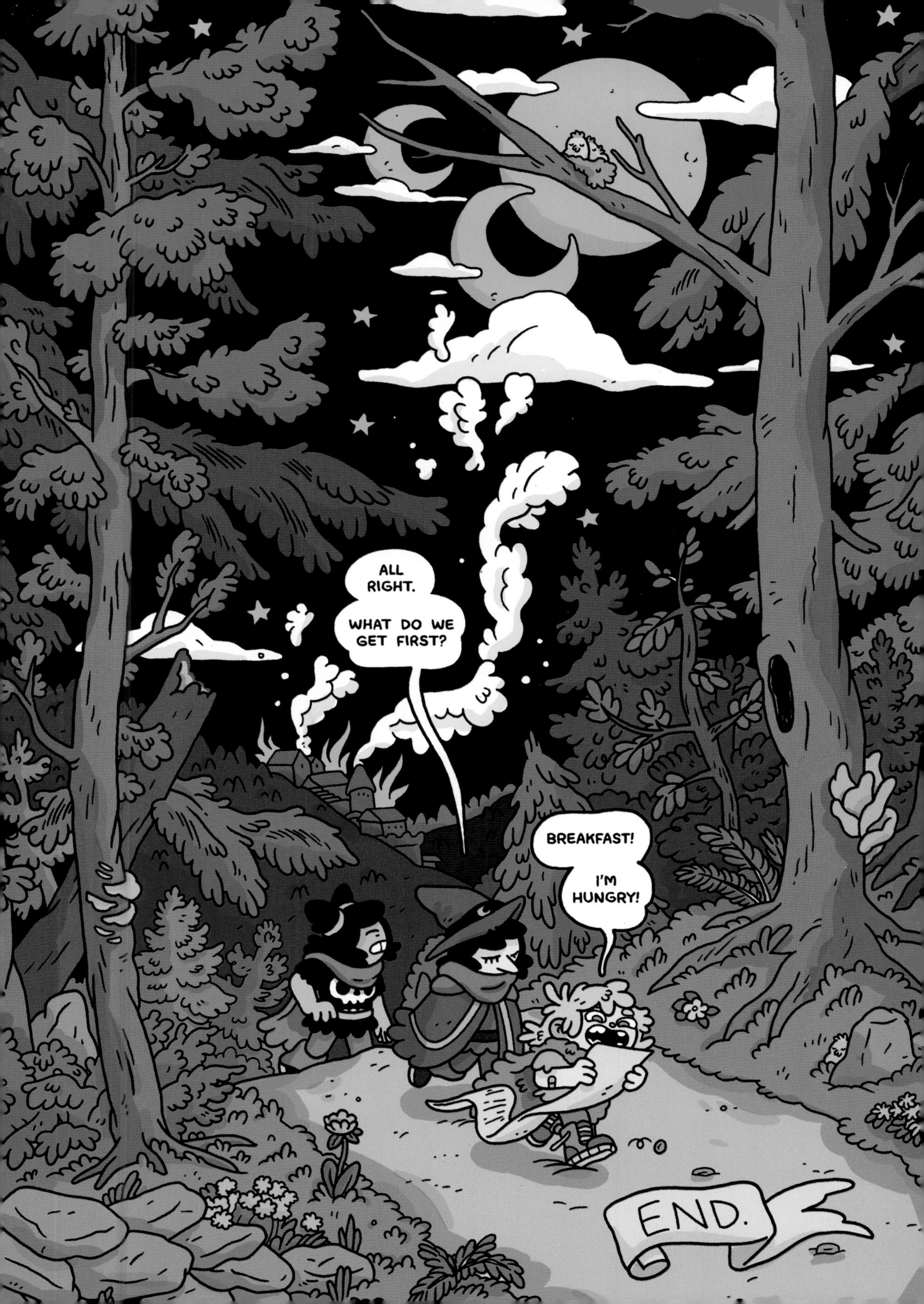
ALL RIGHT.
WHAT DO WE GET FIRST?
BREAKFAST!
I'M HUNGRY!
END.

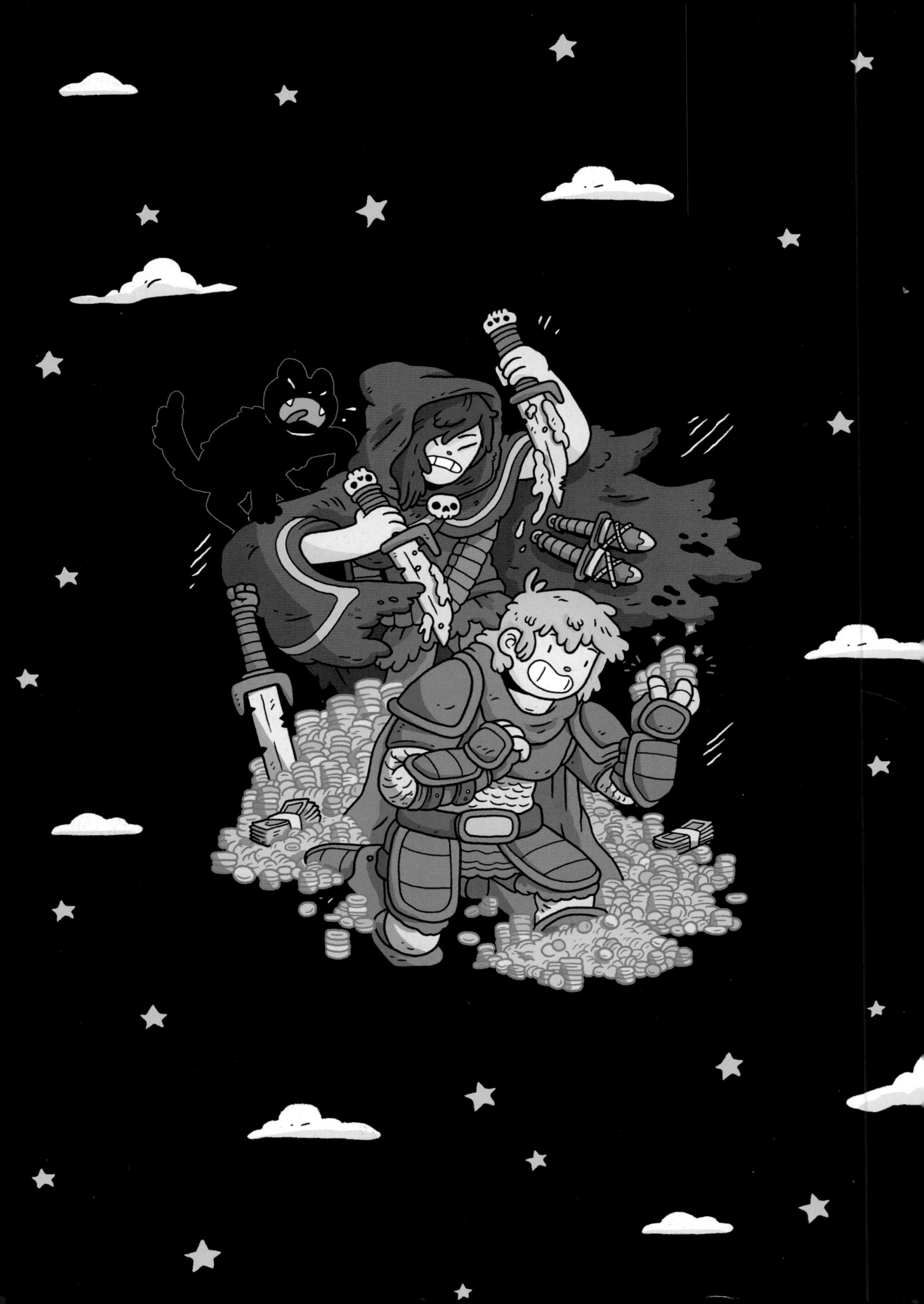

ACKNOWLEDGMENTS

THE AUTHORS WOULD LIKE TO THANK BENJI NATE
AND MIKE LOPEZ, ALONG WITH E AND G. *THE WIZERD*
COULD NOT HAVE BEEN MADE WITHOUT THE SUPPORT
AND PATIENCE OF ANDREA COLVIN, GRACE BORNHOFT,
AND EVERYONE AT ONI PRESS.

MORE FROM ONI PRESS!

SCI-FU
YEHUDI MERCADO

SCI-FU: KICK IT OFF

By Yehudi Mercado

Set in 1980s Brooklyn, Wax is a young mix-master who scratches the perfect beat and accidentally summons a UFO that transports his family, best friend, and current crush to the robot-dominated planet of Discopia. Now Wax and his crew must master the intergalactic musical martial art of Sci-Fu to fight the power and save Earth.

HAPHAVEN

HAPHAVEN

By Norm Harper and Louie Joyce

When ever-superstitious Alex Mills steps on a crack and it actually breaks her mother's back, she must journey through a rainbow to the land where all superstitions draw their power in order to save her mom.

SPACE & BATTLE
LUNCHTIME
VOLUME ONE
LIGHTS, CAMERA, SNACKTION!

SPACE BATTLE LUNCHTIME VOL. 1

By Natalie Riess

Earth baker Peony gets the deal of a lifetime when she agrees to be a contestant on the Universe's hottest reality TV show, *Space Battle Lunchtime!* But that was before she knew that it shoots on location . . . on a spaceship . . . and her alien competitors don't play nice!

FUN FUN FUN
WORLD

FUN FUN FUN WORLD

By Yehudi Mercado

The *Devastorm 5* is an alien warship whose prime directive is to seek out planets to invade and conquer in tribute to the almighty alien queen. The only problem is that the crew is led by Minky, the worst captain in the whole imperium. In a last-ditch effort to be taken more seriously, Minky convinces the crew to conquer Earth once and for all.